During his tenure as the President's Assistant for National Security Affairs and Secretary of State from 1969 through 1976, Henry Kissinger had more impact on the course of American foreign policy than any other official, aside from the president himself. This volume presents—for the first time—an assessment of the interaction between Kissinger's personality and policies from a rigorously analytic perspective. The contributors provide an overview of Kissinger's thought and policies, psychological studies of his personality, quantitatively oriented analyses of his values, and an "operational code" analysis of Kissinger's belief system.

Henry Kissinger

His Personality and Policies

Edited by
Dan Caldwell

Duke Press Policy Studies

Durham, N.C.   1983

Printed in the United States of America
on acid-free paper

Library of Congress Cataloging in Publication Data
  Main entry under title:

  Henry Kissinger, his personality and policies.

  (Duke Press policy studies)
  Bibliography: p.
  Includes index.
    1. Kissinger, Henry, 1923–   —Addresses, essays,
  lectures.   2. United States—Foreign relations—1969–
  1974—Addresses, essays, lectures.   3. United States—
  Foreign relations—1974–1977—Addresses, essays,
  lectures.   I. Caldwell, Dan.   II. Series.
  E840.8.K58H46   1983   327.73′0092′4   83-5710
  ISBN 0-8223-0485-6

2   3   4   5   6   7   8   9

To my parents, John and Hester Caldwell

Contents

Preface

Journalists, historians, and political scientists have devoted more attention to Henry Kissinger than perhaps any other presidential advisor or secretary of state. There are many reasons for this. Kissinger directed the foreign policy of the United States during a time of transition characterized by both competition and conflict. Nixon and Kissinger sought to chart a path from the cold war to "a new international system." Their overtures to the Soviet Union and the People's Republic of China were dramatic moves in the direction of this new system and captured the attention not only of foreign policy specialists but also of people everywhere. Historians and political scientists were interested in the policies that one from their own ranks would develop and implement. Journalists were attracted to the former Harvard professor, an attraction that Kissinger actively cultivated and encouraged.

As a result of the interest in Kissinger and that generated by him, more than forty major articles and twenty books (see bibliography) concerning Kissinger and/or his policies have been published. Why then another book on this subject? Almost all of the previously published articles and books are journalistic accounts and not systematic analyses. In this book, the editor and contributors have sought to provide an analytical assessment, based on relevant academic theories, of Kissinger's personality and policies.

Two of the chapters were previously published, and I would like to express my appreciation to Lloyd de Mause, editor and publisher of the *Journal of Psychohistory*, for permission to publish a revised version of Dana Ward's article "Kissinger: A Psychohistory," which originally appeared in the *History of Childhood Quarterly* (winter 1975), and to Sage Publications for permission to reprint Harvey Starr's article, "The Kissinger Years: Studying Individuals and Foreign Policy," which was originally published in the *International Studies Quarterly* (December 1980).

In the process of preparing this volume, I have incurred a number of debts. I would like to thank James Wilburn, John Nicks, and Clarence Hibbs of Pepperdine University for their support of this project. A semester-long fellowship under the auspices of the Center for International Studies (International Security) at the University of Southern California, directed by Michael Fry, enabled me to complete the manuscript, and I appreciate the hospitality of the members of the center and Dr. Fry while I was at USC. The Center for Foreign Policy Development at Brown University, directed by Mark Garrison, provided support of the final preparation of the manuscript for which I am grateful.

The staff members of Pepperdine University's word processing center, supervised by Helen Kilday, typed several drafts of the entire manuscript and Laine Zachary typed the index. I appreciate their efficient and gracious help. I would also like to thank Richard Rowson and Reynolds Smith of Duke University Press for their encouragement and help from the inception of this project. Finally, I would like to thank the contributors to the book for their hard work and cooperation in producing this volume. It has been a pleasure to work with them.

I have dedicated this book to my parents, John and Hester Caldwell, who have shown me that Shakespeare was right: "The voice of parents is the voice of gods, for to their children they are heaven's lieutenants."

Introduction

During his years as the president's assistant for national security affairs and later as secretary of state, Henry Kissinger was the most important single person, save the president, in determining the course of American foreign policy. Kissinger's influence was at least as great as that of other important presidential advisors, including Colonel Edward House, Harry Hopkins, Dean Acheson, McGeorge Bundy, Walt Rostow, and Dean Rusk. In many respects Kissinger's influence was even more significant than that of previous advisors, given the degree to which Nixon and Kissinger sought to centralize foreign policy decision making in the White House (Destler, 1971–72; Leacacos, 1971–72).

As the Watergate crisis enveloped the Nixon administration, Nixon gave Kissinger greater and greater authority. In September 1973, the President named Kissinger secretary of state, a position he had held on a de facto basis since January 1969. Kissinger retained the position of National Security Council advisor until October 1975. Given the unprecedented resignations of senior officials from the Nixon administration and the eventual fragmentation of the Ford advisory system (Ford, 1980:315–21), Kissinger's continued tenure in office was viewed as essential. After Nixon informed Ford that he was going to resign from office, Ford's first act was to call Kissinger and tell him: "Henry, I need you. The country needs you. I want you to stay. I'll do everything I can to work with you" (Ford, 1980:29). Kissinger's eight-year tenure in office began as influential and significant and grew in importance through the years.

While Kissinger was in office, some of the most far-reaching initiatives in contemporary American foreign policy were made. To what extent were these initiatives taken at the recommendation of Kissinger? Or were they Nixon's ideas which Kissinger dutifully translated into policy? There are indications in Nixon's and Kissinger's memoirs of their relative roles in foreign policy making. For instance, in referring to "shuttle diplomacy" in the Middle East, Kissinger (1982:1124) notes: "I certainly managed the tactics. But no secretary of state, however influential, can make strategy by himself. Only a president could have imposed the complex and tough policy that got us this far and sustained it against a hesitant bureaucracy, vacillating allies, a nervous Soviet Union, and the passionate combatants of the Middle East." One of the interesting questions of the Nixon-Kissinger years concerns the role of each of these men in the making of policy. The systematic analyses of Kissinger's academic and governmental writings contained in the chapters of this book will better enable analysts to determine the genesis of policy during the Nixon and Ford administrations.

In his chapter, Harvey Starr focuses on the first volume of Kissinger's memoirs as an information source concerning Kissinger's personality and policies. Starr reviews previous biographical and psychological studies of Kissinger and compares these analyses with information from the memoirs in three specific areas: Kissinger's views of Nixon the individual and statesman, Kissinger's approach to the bureaucracy, and Kissinger's policy for dealing with the Soviet Union. Starr finds that Kissinger has a clear and consistent world view and that he based his policy prescriptions on this belief system. Starr concludes that there is great continuity between *White House Years* and Kissinger's previous writings and that there is substantial congruence between Kissinger's self-analysis contained in his memoirs and the previous analyses of other scholars.

Robert Tucker (1977:607-08) has pointed out: "There has not been anything approaching a consensus among political scientists that a political leader's personality is a factor of potentially great or even decisive importance in explaining his conduct in the leader-role that he acquires." Despite this lack of consensus, a number of political scientists and psychologists (see, for example, George and George, 1956; Erikson, 1958, 1969) have utilized to good advantage the concept of personality in their studies of political leaders.

There are, in fact, a number of ways that a leader's personality can influence his political behavior. For instance, the selection of politics as a career or the choice and definition of political role are influenced by personality. A number of other aspects of political behavior are also influenced by personality, including: success or failure in the performance of certain role tasks; the ability to attract, hold, and utilize followers; the kind and quality of political associates recruited by the leader; the choice of political goals; and the style and quality of selecting policy alternatives.[1]

In his psychohistorical study of Henry Kissinger, Dana Ward contends that personality is one of many factors that influence political action and that Kissinger's depressive personality influenced his policy choices while in office. Ward presents convincing evidence that, at least in Kissinger's case, there is a strong link between personality and political behavior, particularly concerning U.S. policies toward North Vietnam during the final years of the war.

Instead of focusing on the personality of Kissinger, as Ward does, or focusing on cognitive/psychological factors as Starr does, Albert Eldridge utilizes value analysis in his study of Kissinger's complex world view. This approach, in contrast to others such as operational code or cognitive mapping, enables the researcher to focus on the linkages among various concepts and values. Eldridge finds that harmony and security are the terminal values held by Kissinger and that these values persist from the academic period through the governmental one. There is some shift over time in the rank ordering of Kissinger's instrumental values, but knowledge, flexibility, and authority occupy the most important positions in Kissinger's instrumental value network throughout his academic and governmental careers.

Through his use of value analysis, Eldridge is able to identify Kissinger's values, to map the relationship among these values, and to reach conclusions about his self-concept and world view. Eldridge also addresses the question of whether Kissinger, echoing Oswald Spengler, is pessimistic concerning the future or whether there is some hope for solving the world's problems.

Stephen Walker focuses on Kissinger's extensive academic writings in order to reveal the most significant components of Kissinger's approach to world politics.

Walker finds that Kissinger's academic works reflect his personal philosophy of history and his political philosophy which strongly influenced the policies that Kissinger advocated while in office. Walker reviews Kissinger's thinking about the Soviet Union and the Arab-Israeli conflict and analyzes the degree to which Nixon's and Kissinger's thinking diverged in these two cases. Walker concludes that Kissinger shaped the main components of U.S. foreign policy to conform to the contours of his cognitive map and that his influence on policy outcomes increased during his time in office.

Dan Caldwell describes the major elements of both the grand design and the grand strategy for achieving a new international system that Nixon and Kissinger sought to implement. The objective of this system was to create a moderate international system supported by the United States, the Soviet Union, and the People's Republic of China and at the same time to stop the spread of communism. The means for achieving this tripolar configuration of power included a number of elements, among them the acceptance of strategic nuclear parity, the maintenance of strong collective security arrangements with the members of NATO and Japan, and the maintenance of U.S. foreign policy commitments with reduced public and Congressional support. It was in this last area, Caldwell concludes, that the Nixon-Kissinger policy vision floundered and ultimately failed.

The significance of Henry Kissinger's influence on American foreign policy in the 1970s is indisputable; a major question, however, concerns the magnitude of his impact. Were the policy initiatives of the 1970s the work of Nixon, Ford, or Kissinger? To what extent did Kissinger's academic thinking affect his policy choices? What was the impact of Kissinger's personality on policy making? More broadly, what were the relationships among values, beliefs, attitudes, and action? What were the principal components of the Nixon-Ford-Kissinger foreign policy? These are the important questions addressed by the contributors to this volume.

Henry Kissinger

1. The Kissinger Years: Studying Individuals and Foreign Policy

Harvey Starr

A vast literature has been produced on Henry Kissinger, the man and policy maker.[1] To this has been added two massive volumes of memoirs by Kissinger himself (1979, 1982). These writings may be seen as relating to a complex of questions concerning the study of individuals in the foreign policy process and how scholars can gain access to such individuals. This review will take a brief look at the question of access. It asks where Kissinger's memoirs fit into the study of individuals, into cognitive and psychological approaches to the analysis of foreign policy, and into other scholarly writings about Kissinger. Do Kissinger's memoirs contribute to systematic theory about foreign policy?

One of the first questions that one must ask when looking at individual, idiosyncratic, or psychological approaches to the study of foreign policy is: Do individuals count? Can and do individuals make a difference? Is there, in Greenstein's words (1969), "actor indispensability" (as opposed to "action indispensability")? Henry Kissinger is clearly one of the major foreign policy phenomena of our time. His background, style of behavior, foreign policy positions, relationships with Presidents Nixon and Ford, and preeminence in American foreign policy for eight years have fascinated the man in the street, journalists, and academics alike. Much of this fascination stems not only from the contrast between Kissinger and Nixon (or the rest of Nixon's advisors), but also from Kissinger's preeminence in Nixonian foreign policy. As suggested by the bureaucratic politics literature, Kissinger's dominance derived both from his personal relations with the president and from his position within the formal policy-making process.

Many observers have pointed out the similarity in foreign policy views of Nixon and Kissinger. In his memoirs Kissinger indicates areas of broad agreement with Nixon regarding the structure of the foreign policy process and notes his approval of Nixon. Describing his November 25, 1968 meeting with Nixon at the Hotel Pierre, Kissinger (1979:11–12) says: "Nixon outlined some of his foreign policy views. I was struck by his perceptiveness and knowledge so at variance with my previous image of him."

Along with a similarity of views came the development of Kissinger's central position within the foreign policy process. Kissinger, as national security assistant, controlled the apparatus of the National Security Council and its staff. He became both the conduit and the screen for the great bulk of information about foreign policy and foreign policy alternatives that moved from the bureaucracy upward to the president. As national security advisor, Kissinger came to chair the five major interagency committees that supervised foreign policy: the Washington Special Actions Group (WSAG) dealing with crises, the Defense Programs Review Committee, the Vietnam Special Studies Group, the Forty Committee dealing with covert intelligence operations, and the Verification Panel dealing with the SALT negotiations.

The many and intense bureaucratic politics battles that occurred in the Nixon administration are vividly described by Kissinger time and time again in *White House Years*. In the period covered (up to 1973, before Kissinger assumed the position of secretary of state), the major battles were waged between Kissinger and the nominal secretary of state, William Rogers. Great attention and resources were devoted by Nixon and Kissinger to end-running (backchanneling) Rogers, the State Department, and the foreign service (see, for example, Kissinger, 1979:28–31). As noted, Kissinger won more than his share of bureaucratic victories not only from his position, but also because of presidential support. The memoirs often make it clear that both Kissinger and Nixon recognized the hierarchy of power and responsibility between the two men (Kissinger, 1979:40–41 or 717). Kissinger succinctly describes their working relationship (1979:805):

> By the end of 1970 I had worked with Nixon for nearly two years; we had talked at length almost every day; we had gone through all crises in closest cooperation. He tended more and more to delegate the tactical management of foreign policy to me. During the first year or so I would submit for Nixon's approval an outline of what I proposed to say to Dobrynin or the North Vietnamese, for instance, before every meeting. He rarely changed it, though he rarely failed to add tough-sounding exhortations. By the end of 1970 Nixon no longer required these memoranda. He would approve the strategy, usually orally; he would almost never intervene in its day-to-day implementation.

It seems that, in the case of Henry Kissinger, individuals did count. Kissinger had the official position, the unofficial clout, and the opportunity to shape and execute policy in an important era of American foreign policy. This individual impact was also popularly recognized. In 1972 Kissinger placed fourth in the Gallup Poll's "Most Admired Man Index," and in 1973 he was first. Never before had a secretary of state or any presidential advisor even been placed on the list. In May 1973, 78 percent of Americans were able to identify Kissinger, a number unmatched except for presidents, presidential candidates, and major sports and entertainment figures (Eldridge, 1976:31).

Given that an individual could count, we can move on to the question: How can we study what differences specific individuals make? Over the years a number of observers have referred to the mysterious Kissinger, a man who was inexplicable, unpredictable, full of surprises, or all of the above (see Dickson, 1978:17). Is Kissinger any more mysterious than other individuals, or are there clues to why he behaved as he did? In his Harvard College senior thesis, "The Meaning of History," Kissinger (1951:127) observed: "Everybody is a product of an age, a nation, and environment. But beyond that, he constitutes what is essentially unapproachable by analysis, the form of the form, the creative essense of history, the moral personality." It is hoped that foreign policy makers are not "essentially unapproachable," though the task of studying them is a difficult one.

The Problem of Access

Let us begin with Brody's (1969:116) famous question: "How can we give a Taylor Manifest Anxiety Scale to Khrushchev during the Hungarian revolt, a Semantic Differential to Chiang Kai-shek while Quemoy is being shelled, or simply interview Kennedy during the Cuban missile crisis?" Obviously, we cannot. The question and answer highlight the problems both of access (see, for example, Holsti et al., 1968) and of the crucial need for ways to get at foreign policy decision makers while in office and afterward (and, perhaps, even before they enter office).

In this instance we have Henry Kissinger, an example of the crucial individual in foreign policy during a dramatic era of world politics and dramatic American foreign policy moves—from the "Nixon Doctrine" through the opening to China, detente, and "shuttle diplomacy." What sources of data and techniques for acquiring and analyzing those data do we have? The study of decision making and decision makers presents the researcher with a number of problems. One of the central problems is access to decision makers—how we go about studying them while they are embedded within the vast and overlapping organizational structure of the government of the modern state. Within the broad cognitive and psychological approach to the study of foreign policy there are a number of techniques which can be used to gain access to the belief systems, personalities, and decision-making processes of individuals, some of which specifically attempt to gain access by the study of how individuals use words and symbols: using secondary sources for traditional biographical analysis and more unconventional (and controversial) psychohistorical approaches, operational code analysis, formal content analysis, and events-data analysis.

A growing literature on cognitive and psychological approaches reviews how these approaches can be used, their strengths and weaknesses, promised payoffs and research costs.[2] These approaches depend upon some basic assumptions which, if accepted, permit scholars to attack the problem of access. One set of assumptions is the view that decision makers are subject to the same psychological processes that affect all humans, and that they, like all humans, can act only in terms of their images of the world. As Holsti and his colleagues (1968:129), among many, have pointed out: "The essential point is that the actor's response will be shaped by his perception of the stimulus and not necessarily by the qualities objectively inherent in it." One view found throughout the cognitive literature is that the decision maker's belief system, personality, values, and so on are in some way related to decisions that are made and actions that are taken.

Where do Kissinger's memoirs fit into all of this? A decision maker's recollection and reconstruction of his time in office is a potentially important source of data about his beliefs, values, attitudes, and the various "whys" behind his decisions and behavior. Memoirs, as an additional source of data, provide one further means of access to the decision maker. The question of the actual utility of memoirs, however, is an open one. What can we gain from any specific set of memoirs? With what confidence can we use and apply the information contained within them (given the base assumption that they will be, to some extent, self-serving)? The remainder of this essay will be devoted to these questions. First we will review some of the sources of information, and the methodologies used to gather that information, which have been used to study Henry Kissinger. Then, several specific substantive topics covered in the memoirs will be contrasted with data, analyses, and conclusions from the earlier research to help appraise the utility of *White House Years* in the continuing study of Henry Kissinger and the Nixon-Kissinger era of American foreign policy.

Psychological Approaches

Biographical studies are a traditional means for attempting to understand the nature of public officials as individuals and their policies. The typical goal is to draw a portrait of the individual through history, chronology, and descriptive detail. Again, typically, data sources involve interviews, material written by the subject (especially private documents such as letters and secret memos), secondary material about the subject and his times, chronologies of historical events including journalistic accounts, and sometimes interviews with the subject.

Several biographies and analyses of Kissinger exist which do all of the above. They are useful in setting forth the *public* record of policy while Kissinger was in office and facts about Kissinger's life before he became a high-level decision maker. Such works attempt to describe more fully who Kissinger is—his background, family data, education, and significant events in his life. For Henry Kissinger we have not only a straightforward account of his life in the biography by Blumenfeld (1974) based on over 400 interviews, but also a highly flattering account by Kalb and Kalb (1974) and a highly critical one by Landau (1972). Note that all three arrived in print after Kissinger's clear public emergence as a major foreign policy figure. Since then, most works on Kissinger have concentrated on his foreign policy style and decisions. Stoessinger's (1976) treatment of Kissinger also contains some biographical material.

The more traditional biographical approach, especially in regard to its picture of the pre-decision-making Kissinger, may also be supplemented by the psychobiographical or psychohistorical approach. In this approach, using approximately the same types of data sources, the analyst employs psychoanalytic techniques to draw additional inferences about the personality, psychological makeup, and style of the subject and to link these influences to the subject's behavior. A lively debate over the utility of armchair analysis from a distance began with the publication of the study by George and George (1956) of Woodrow Wilson and has continued with the publication of each of the new works of Mazlish, who has written about Nixon, Kissinger, and, most recently, Jimmy Carter.[3] Mazlish's work on Kissinger (1976) is the main source for the psychobiographical complement to the biographical approach; it attempts to interpret Kissinger's life, style, scholarly writings, and policies from the perspective of his personality and the early life experiences.[4] A second source is Ward's study contained in this volume.

Biography and psychobiography are methods that can be used to study the preofficial lives of foreign policy decision makers. For some, such as Kissinger, there is an additional and important preofficial data base. Kissinger wrote about the world in his position as a faculty member of the Department of Government at Harvard. Thus, we have not only the broad outlines of Kissinger's personal life, but a mine of scholarly writings about international relations and foreign policy by Kissinger before he entered public office (see the bibliography at the end of this book for a complete listing of Kissinger's publications). Several observers have surveyed and reviewed these writings in order to summarize Kissinger's basic intellectual themes (such as Graubard, 1973) or to trace the philosophical basis for his intellectual positions (Dickson, 1978).

Whether the academic writings reveal clues to a broader belief system or can be used as tools to predict behavior are issues not taken up in the standard discussions of Kissinger's writings. There is, however, a form of content analysis which may be used to perform these tasks. Applications of the "operational code" approach have become more numerous and refined in recent years, mostly through the work of George and Holsti.[5] The operational code was designed explicitly to study an individual's belief system, through a set of ten questions concerning "philosophic" and "instrumental" beliefs. These ten questions have been elaborated into an extensive "coding manual" by Holsti (1977).

The operational code has been utilized simply as a guide to research, as a set of independent variables, or at least as a way to narrow the range of choices that an individual might use—by understanding the belief system with which the individual views the world. It is a methodology designed to gain access to decision makers through the content analysis of a broad set of writings. Following the lead set by Holsti (1962a, 1970) in the study of John Foster Dulles, operational code analysis has been performed on Kissinger's preofficial academic writings (Walker, 1977; Starr, 1979, 1980a). The objective here is the delineation of the belief system that the decision maker held upon taking office. In Kissinger's case, this method has been used to study preofficial writings in order to analyze, explain, compare and predict behavior in office.

Kissinger's words can also be studied by more rigorous and quantitative content analysis techniques. Holsti (1962a, 1962b) demonstrated that "evaluative assertion analysis" was a useful methodology for studying the belief system of a high-level decision maker when he used that technique to analyze John Foster Dulles' perceptions of the Soviet Union. In a partial attempt to replicate Holsti's study, this author has also used evaluative assertion analysis to study Kissinger's images of the Soviet Union and the People's Republic of China. By studying an individual's image of the enemy, research is being focused on what a number of scholars feel is a master belief that plays a central role in the construction of an individual's operational code (see, for example, George, 1969, 1979).

Thus, in addition to analyses of Kissinger's preofficial words, there is also this author's study of all of Kissinger's public statements as a high-level decision maker in regard to his images of the Soviet Union and China. Studies of both Kissinger's general belief system—the image of the enemy—are thus available.[6] The evaluative assertion analysis study is particularly relevant to the memoirs, in which Kissinger spends a great deal of time on relations with the Soviet Union and China. Much of Kissinger's interest in triangular diplomacy (1979:763) is reflected in the author's study where Kissinger's perceptions of the USSR and People's Republic of China are analyzed in terms of the triadic patterns of behavior using events-data. In general, the content analysis provides broad empirical data against which to compare the specific statements Kissinger makes in the memoirs.

Thus, we have works concerned with Kissinger's early life, his academic career, and his period as a foreign policy decision maker. There have been only a few attempts to pull all of these strands together. In addition to the author's work, Stoessinger (1976) comes closest to merging these approaches successfully. There are, as we are well aware, a number of articles and books which analyze American foreign policy during the Kissinger tenure (see Brandon, 1973a; Brown, 1979; Caldwell, 1981; and Hoffmann, 1978), as well as specific policy issue areas or decisions (for example, Shawcross, 1979). The Kissinger industry is indeed a large one. This brief review will not specifically deal with the policy-oriented works, as much of those are covered in Stoessinger, in events-data analyses, and in the chronologies found in biographies. Since most of these works do not make the linkages between perceptions, beliefs and style, on the one hand, and his political behavior, on the other, they will not be central to an essay concerned with access and the assessment of one possible source of that access—Kissinger's memoirs.

Consistency in Kissinger's Thought

There are a number of ways by which one could approach and discuss Kissinger's memoirs. As one reviewer of the memoirs has noted, some reviewers, overwhelmed with the amount of material, have fallen back on preconceptions and previous opinions of the Nixon-Kissinger foreign policy (Watt, 1979:59). Rather than re-argue the morality or success of these policies, this essay will examine the utility of the memoirs as a research tool. Given the author's own set of preconceptions—based on the types of research noted above—the idea was to gauge how well *White House Years* reflects Kissinger's views of international relations, how well it helps us understand what he thought he was trying to do, and why. One way would be to see how closely the memoirs reflect Kissinger's view of the world, a style based on deeply rooted personality traits, and his previous views on such issues as the role and impact of bureaucracies. Recognizing that there may always be changes in beliefs (especially during the years in high office), the search will be for *consistency* between the memoirs and previous research on Kissinger. Within limits, high consistency will provide greater confidence in the memoirs as a data source as a means of access. It is hoped that this treatment of the memoirs will also demonstrate a process by which other memoirs could be appraised.

Consistency can be used to summarize several criteria by which an individual can be judged a good subject for operational code analysis as well as content analysis in general. The issue of Kissinger as a useful subject for operational code analysis has been addressed elsewhere (Starr, 1980a:8–11). First, on subjects such as European diplomatic history, the nature and philosophy of international relations in general, contemporary international problems (for example, nuclear weapons policy and strategy), alliance politics, and American foreign policy, Kissinger's academic writings are broad enough to reveal a belief system for operational code and other analyses. Second, judging by secondary sources, discussions with acquaintances, and the content analysis research noted earlier, these academic writings can be considered honest in that they appear to reflect Kissinger's real beliefs. For instance, in discussing Kissinger's senior honors thesis, "The Meaning of History," Graubard (1973:7) observes: "Much of what he learned at Harvard was incorporated into a thesis that *pretended* to deal with selected philosophies of history since the 18th century; it was in fact, a kind of *personal testament*" (italics added).

Finally, Kissinger's writings reflect an important continuity, in that both as a decision maker and as an academic his philosophy and his political style appear to be essentially the same. Such continuity is an important criterion for using an operational code approach. One Kissinger observer has noted, for instance, that Kissinger "turned scholarship into projective biography" (Mazlish, 1976:151). That is, in his writings on international relations, Kissinger was stating quite clearly what he would do as a policy maker under certain circumstances. As Walker (1977) and others have noted, a distinctive characteristic of Kissinger's writing is the tendency to generalize and to hypothesize lessons and conclusions from the analysis of historical cases. Through these generalizations Kissinger developed, articulated, and outlined his operational code and provided a guide to his future behavior. From this we can identify the continuity in Kissinger's thought as reflected in his academic works. When asked, in 1976, about how Professor Kissinger of Harvard was appraised by Secretary of State Kissinger, he replied: "I have tried—with what success historians will have to judge—to have an overriding concept. It can be found in innumerable, maybe pedantic, speeches I have given over the years" (U.S. Department of State, *Bulletin*, July 26, 1976:131). In 1975, when asked if he had changed his basic conception of international politics over the past twenty years, his reply was consistent (if somewhat facetious): "I think it is possible—at least I leave open the theoretical possibility—that I might have changed my mind on something in my life, but don't press me too hard" (U.S. Department of State, *Bulletin*, July 7, 1975).

Many examples of this continuity can be found in Kissinger's academic works and subsequent statements as a foreign policy maker. One of the basic points about world order which Kissinger (1957a:1) makes in his Ph.D. thesis, published as *A World Restored: Castlereagh, Metternich and the Restoration of Peace, 1812–1822*, is about the nature of peace: "Whenever peace—conceived as the avoidance of war—has been the primary objective of a power or a group of powers, the international system has been at the mercy of the most ruthless member of the international community. Whenever the international order has acknowledged that certain principles could not be compromised even for the sake of peace, stability based on equilibrium of force was at least conceivable." These sentiments were echoed in 1974, at hearings before the Senate Foreign Relations Committee (1974:239): "If peace is pursued to the exclusion of any other goal, other values will be compromised and perhaps lost."

Other sections and passages from *A World Restored* have returned time and again in Kissinger's statements as a decision maker. As Stoessinger (1976) and Walker (1977) have pointed out, Kissinger was virtually quoting from several passages in chapter 8 of his dissertation when he explained the Indochina peace agreement at his news conference of January 24, 1973: "It was always clear that a lasting peace could come about only if neither side sought to achieve everything it wanted; indeed that stability depended on the relative satisfaction and therefore the relative dissatisfaction of all the parties concerned" (Stoessinger, 1976:74). Examples of continuity are not limited to Kissinger's dissertation. In an article in *Foreign Affairs* (1956b:349), he discussed the relationship between Kant and contemporary international politics: "In his whimsical essay *Perpetual Peace* written in 1795, the German philosopher Kant predicted that world peace could be attained in one of two ways: by a moral consensus which he identified with a republican form of government, or by a cycle of wars of ever-increasing violence which would reduce the major powers to impotence."

Kissinger then applies this to the impact of nuclear weapons, and quotes Eisenhower's observation that "there is no alternative to peace." In Kissinger's *first* speech as secretary of state, at the United Nations on September 24, 1973, he said: "Two centuries ago, the philosopher Kant predicted that perpetual peace would come about eventually—either as the creation of man's moral aspirations or as the consequence of physical necessity. What seemed utopian then looms as tomorrow's reality; soon there will be no alternative" (Dickson, 1978:51).

The continuity of both these themes is demonstrated in a single passage from Kissinger's *White House Years* (p. 70). Talking about the era of international politics in which he was soon to become a major participant, Kissinger reflects: "In the late eighteenth century the philosopher Immanuel Kant in his essay *Perpetual Peace*, had written that world peace was inevitable; it would come about either because all nations shared the same sense of justice or because a cycle of wars of ever increasing violence would teach men the futility of conflict. . . . But the root dilemma of our time is that if the quest for peace turns into the *sole* objective of policy, the fear of war becomes a weapon in the hands of the most ruthless."

John Stoessinger, a graduate student with Kissinger at Harvard in the early 1950s and an acquaintance ever since, provides us with a useful summary concerning continuity: "His diplomacy as Secretary of State is deeply rooted in the insights of the young doctoral student at Harvard a quarter century ago. It is, in fact, a virtual transplant from the world of thought into the world of power. . . . We are witness here to a unique experiment in the application of scholarship to statesmanship, of history to statecraft" (Stoessinger, 1976:7, 37).

As one way to further test this consistency, the discussion will now turn to three substantive issue areas that arise in the *White House Years*, and contrast Kissinger's views, ideas and policies in those areas with previous analyses based on the methods discussed above.

The Relationship with Richard Nixon

One aspect of *White House Years* and Kissinger's career has been the issue of Kissinger's relationship to Richard Nixon. Critics have often pointed to Kissinger's duplicity in disparaging Nixon the person and yet working for Nixon the president, and even lauding various aspects of Nixon's foreign policy performance. Explanation of this theme is useful because it permits us to link biographical and operational code findings; to get into some of the most basic concepts in Kissinger's operational code; and to demonstrate that the different perspectives on Nixon are consistent with psychological and intellectual components of Kissinger which have been identified by a number of observers over the years. References in *White House Years* to Nixon as both person and statesman support these earlier analyses.

Biographical and psychobiographical material may be used to help us understand the basis for the key concepts in Kissinger's operational code. All of the major works cited above discuss the impact on Kissinger of his family's experiences in Germany—his father's loss of his job, the various acts of persecution against Jews, the forced flight from his home and native land. Similarly, they all quote Kissinger's conscious denial that those days had any effect upon him (a disclaimer which is refuted in Kissinger, 1979:228–29). Fritz Kraemer best sums up the experience. Kraemer was Kissinger's first patron, an older man of the heroic tradition who helped to guide and direct the young Kissinger. The two met in the army during World War II when the Prussian-born, self-exiled Kraemer appealed to Kissinger as a man of principles and action. Kraemer, as all the biographers and analysts have noted, provided Kissinger with his first sense of self-worth and direction and his first role-model. It is ironic that Kraemer was the catalyst for Kissinger's headlong "Americanization" during his time in the army.

Kraemer is quoted as saying: "What the Nazis do to these people is unspeakable. You can do damage to the soul of a man and never touch his body. For five years, the most formative years (10–15), Henry had to undergo this horror. And the real horror is the breakdown of the world. Imagine what it means when your father, who is your authority, the father you admire, is suddenly transformed into a frightened little mouse" (Blumenfeld, 1974:6). Kraemer notes later that Kissinger had confided to him the psychological nature of the Nazi horror (Blumenfeld, 1974:59).

A general theme in analyses of Kissinger is that this early experience forged his basic philosophic belief that the world is a place where the forces of chaos constantly battle the forces of order (this is especially well developed in Mazlish, Stoessinger, and Ward). Kissinger's passion (some say obsession) for stability, balance, and order is supposedly derived from his firsthand experience with the tragedy of upheaval and the desire to prevent it from recurring. Hoffmann (in Blumenfeld, 1974:68–69) summarizes this argument:

These experiences have to have an effect. But the lessons one derives are not predictable. I think he came out of it with a kind of burning need for order . . . this whole emphasis on structures of peace and world order. People in these experiences have a real memory of chaos, of violence and brutality, like the whole world is collapsing under them. Kissinger's whole search has been to impose a stable world order, a moderate order which would not humiliate anybody. Kissinger, more than most, would probably agree with Goethe's statement that disorder is worse than injustice.

Indeed, Stoessinger (1976:14) reports that under his questioning during their days at Harvard, Kissinger used Goethe's words to choose order over justice.

Hoffmann's observation touches on Kissinger's most central belief; on the establishment of limits and constraint in international relations; on his distinctions between states ("legitimate" and "revolutionary") and between leaders ("statesmen," "prophets," and "conquerors") based on their acceptance of limits; and on diplomatic behavior designed to moderate, limit, and order the international environment. The prophet and conqueror were both revolutionaries. In *A World Restored*, Napoleon the conqueror and Czar Alexander the prophet were revolutionaries "because both strove to identify the organization of Europe with their will" (Kissinger, 1957a:316).

The prophet is also viewed as a revolutionary because of the ideologically timeless aspect of his leadership. The prophet's vision is used as the standard for order, truth, and reality. In contrast, Kissinger saw Castlereagh and Metternich as representing statesmen. Statesmen "live in time"—they recognize the limits and possibilities of the present; they conduct themselves on the basis of the recognition of limits which include the survival of the states in the system. Statesmen employ diplomacy and negotiation to recreate and restore international order. In *A World Restored*, Kissinger (1957a:326) characterizes statesmen as follows: "The test of a statesman, then, is his ability to recognize the real relationship of forces and to make this knowledge serve his ends. . . . His instrument is diplomacy, the art of relating states to each other by agreement rather than the exercise of force, by the representation of a ground of action which reconciles particular aspirations with a general consensus . . . diplomacy depends upon persuasion and not imposition." [7]

In his tendency toward projective biography, Kissinger saw himself as a statesman. In relationship to other operational code questions on chance, optimism, pessimism, and mastery over history, this basic conception of political life and how it should be ordered is crucial. Kissinger believed that individuals could make a difference, especially if they understood the basic nature of international relations, the historical context, and were courageous enough to grasp opportunities as they arose. The important point here is that Kissinger, for all his criticism of Nixon's personal style and personality, also saw Richard Nixon as a *statesman* and applauded his performance as a statesman.

In both *White House Years* and *Years of Upheaval*, Kissinger (1979, 1982) gives Nixon high marks for his courage, purpose, and principle in creating, carrying out, and sticking to his foreign policy principles and decisions. Stoessinger (1976:209) notes: "In Kissinger's hierarchy of values, courage and decisiveness came first." In his chapter in this volume, Ward also observes that Kissinger's modern heroes were statesmen who could act alone in facing and overcoming adversity, and could overcome incredible obstacles. Examples abound. While in Moscow during the 1972 summit, faced with powerful bureaucratic pressures from all sides, Nixon agreed to let Kissinger carry on the SALT discussions on the basis of the unequal number of launch vehicles. This conversation was held while Nixon was having his back treated: "Lying naked on the rubbing table, Nixon made one of the more courageous decisions of his Presidency. . . . Nixon took a heroic position from a decidedly unheroic posture" (Kissinger, 1979:1223). In discussing the lattermost stages of the Indochina agreements, Kissinger similarly observes that "maddening as Nixon's conduct could be in calm times, it verged on the heroic when really critical issues were at stake" (p. 1352). Much of this was due to another strength of the statesman which Kissinger saw in Nixon: "No political leader I have met understood the dynamics of negotiations better than Nixon" (Kissinger, 1979:1422).

Of course, in large measure, Nixon was being praised for holding the correct principles—those that Kissinger believed the statesman should hold, and that Kissinger himself possessed. These beliefs centered on the creation and maintenance of a "stable structure of peace" and world order. For example, Kissinger emphasized throughout his writings and diplomacy the point noted above, that peace at *any* price is an invitation to disaster. In describing a meeting between Nixon and Prime Minister Heath in December 1971 in which they reviewed the world situation, Nixon repeated: "Part of our reason for conducting our Vietnam withdrawal so slowly is to give some message that we are not prepared to pay *any* price for ending a war; we must now ask ourselves what we are willing to pay to avert war. If we are not, we have tough days ahead." Kissinger's response to Nixon's full review of U.S. and Atlantic relationships was: "Nixon's later fate must not obscure the importance of this passage. He [Nixon] was right; he had diagnosed both the American and Atlantic problem correctly" (Kissinger, 1979:956).

Significantly, Kissinger (1979:1475–76) ends the first volume of his memoirs trying to deal with the contradictions between Nixon the individual and Nixon the statesman:

> What extraordinary vehicles destiny selects to accomplish its design. This man, so lonely in his hour of triumph, so ungenerous in some of his motivations, had navigated our nation through one of the most anguishing periods in its history. Not by nature courageous, he had steeled himself to conspicuous acts of rare courage. Not normally outgoing, he had forced himself to rally his people to its challenge. He had striven for a revolution in American foreign policy so that it would overcome the disastrous oscillations between overcommitment and isolation. Despised by the Establishment, ambiguous in his human perceptions, he had yet held fast to a sense of national honor and responsibility.

Nixon the individual held little charm for Kissinger. He was not the typical patron who had figured so conspicuously in Kissinger's personal and professional development. Three men became important patrons in Kissinger's life—Kraemer, William Yandell Elliott (Kissinger's mentor at Harvard), and Nelson Rockefeller. As Mazlish (1976:77) and others have pointed out, Kissinger's patrons fit a basic mold, "Renaissance types, men of seigneurial presence." Not only were these men great gentlemen, but also they were courageous individuals willing to take on the forces of history. Additionally, Rockefeller had been Kissinger's final and "quintessential patron: a renaissance man who was also a Prince" (Mazlish, 1976:128).

Both Ward and Mazlish point out that as the years passed, Kissinger also sought out men whose intellectual positions fit his own. Ward (in this volume) comments that Kissinger "would commit himself to the ideas of Nixon, a man for whom he has no personal respect." Mazlish notes that the relationship between the two was formal and intellectual; that the two men never became friends. Mazlish (1976:212) contends that Kissinger's relationship with Nixon supported Mazlish's propositions that Kissinger had a unique ability to fit with different kinds of men.

What is clear, however, is that Nixon was not of the mold of former patrons. It is obvious from interviews, and from numerous passages in *White House Years*, that Nixon as an individual did not hold Kissinger's esteem. Kissinger uses phrases such as: "this lonely, tortured and insecure man" (1979:1086); a "vulnerable and austere" personality, "eager for acceptance, but incapable of the act of grace" that could have brought him such acceptance (1979:933); "shy" and "ill at ease with strangers" (1979:760). Nixon is often portrayed as petty—as in the case of forbidding any channel of communication with China being opened through Canada due to his thorough dislike for Trudeau (Kissinger, 1979:736); overly concerned with image and public relations (for example 1979:734); and paranoid—pursued by the "same liberal conspiracy that had sought to destroy him ever since the Alger Hiss case" (1979:299).

The interesting aspect of all this is a certain parallel with criticisms that have been made of Kissinger's own personality. Landau (1972) in particular calls attention to Kissinger's paranoia while a faculty member at Harvard. Ward's description of Kissinger as a "dysmutual" or depressive personality mirrors many of the observations that Kissinger makes of Nixon. Mazlish (1976:96–97) presents a clear example of Kissinger's use of projection as a psychological defense mechanism. He discusses Kissinger's dependency on his patrons, yet his total rejection of those who were, in turn, dependent upon him. Landau, Mazlish, and the Kalbs discuss Kissinger's dislike and harsh treatment of graduate students, secretarial help, and his first wife, Ann Fleischer Kissinger. Mazlish (1976:96) observes, "Thus, his dislike of dependency in others mirrored his feelings about himself."

Another argument supporting Kissinger's use of projection in regard to Nixon is evidence that both men could be classified as "active-negatives" in Barber's (1972) classification system. Kissinger graphically describes Nixon's active-negative personality. In a number of references in his memoirs, Kissinger discusses how Nixon would be most withdrawn, unhappy, and mean at points when he should have been the most exultant (for example, in discussing the first inauguration, see Kissinger, 1979:1). Concerning Nixon's ruthless handling of his staff after his landslide victory in 1972, Kissinger (1979:1406–8) observes: "He seemed not at all elated. Rather, he was grim and remote as if the more fateful period of his life lay ahead." Indeed, describing Nixon's first presidential visit to Great Britain in February 1969, with all its pomp, ceremony, and history, Kissinger (1979:93) writes: "It all produced one of the few occasions of nearly spontaneous joy I witnessed in my acquaintance with this withdrawn and elusive man."

The discussion of Kissinger's personality and projection by Mazlish and Ward gives us an understanding of Kissinger that is consistent with his observations of the personal Nixon. A knowledge of Kissinger's writings and operational code brings us an understanding of his concept of the "statesman," the prominent, positive place it holds in his belief system, and his application of the concept to Nixon. His descriptions in *White House Years* of Richard Nixon are neither petty nor inconsistent, but derive from his background and a long-standing intellectual concept.

The Obstacle of the Bureaucracy

In constructing Kissinger's operational code, especially the instrumental beliefs, one encounters an ongoing concern throughout Kissinger's writings with the *constraints* that the statesman faces. As statesmen, both Kissinger and Nixon were confronted by the various international and domestic constraints that Kissinger first described in *A World Restored*, to which he returned time after time in his writings. These constraints are summarized by Kissinger (1957a:326):

> The statesman is inevitably confronted by the inertia of his material, by the fact that other powers are not factors to be manipulated but forces to be reconciled; that the requirements of security differ with the geographic location and the domestic structure of the powers. . . . The acid test of a policy . . . is its ability to obtain domestic support. This has two aspects: the problem of legitimizing a policy within the governmental apparatus, which is a problem of bureaucratic rationality; and that of harmonizing it with the national experience, which is a problem of historical development.

The point here is that in discussing the domestic and international constraints on the statesman and the various shortcomings of both Castlereagh and Metternich, Kissinger made it clear that he believed that certain statesmen, standing at history's fateful moments, could influence history through acts of vision and courage. Such statesmen had, first, to recognize such moments. Second, they had to overcome the constraints of domestic opinion and governmental bureaucracy; and in this the statesman had to take on the role of educator for both the mass and the governmental elites. A leader who thus understands the world (as Kissinger, with his explicit and strongly held concept of world order, would) at a crucial time in history could, through the exercise of will and skillful personal diplomacy, affect history.

Kissinger's view was that the lonely and heroic leader (as reflected in his famous "cowboy" quote to journalist Oriana Fallaci)[8] could be effective only if the statesman was not encumbered by the webs and weight of bureaucracy. This view was in accord both with his academic writings and with his personality and style (see Mazlish, 1976:96, 152, 167). Both Nixon and Kissinger were, to varying degrees, loners, and Kissinger's view of the bureaucracy fit perfectly with Nixon's desire to tame the bureaucratic system and turn it into his own commissar style system. The Kalbs (1974:98) sum up the point, made by many other observers: "In Kissinger, Nixon found an enthusiastic disciple, equally elitist in orientation, equally distrustful of the bureaucracy." All descriptions of "Henry's Wonderful Machine" (to use the Kalbs' phrase) point out the mutual delight of both men in creating a national security system that could be controlled from the White House and that would circumvent and ignore the State Department. Kissinger (1979:14–15) sketches an identical picture in reporting the meeting at which Nixon actually offered him the job of national security advisor: "The President-elect repeated essentially the same arguments he had made two days earlier, emphasizing more strongly his view of the incompetence of the CIA and the untrustworthiness of the State Department. The position of security adviser was therefore crucial to him and his plan to run foreign policy from the White House."

Kissinger's antipathy to bureaucratic constraints on the statesman and diplomacy go back to his discussion of the statesman in *A World Restored* (see Graubard, 1973:50–51, 20–21). The theme of the bureaucracy's quest for safety and conservatism which first appeared in that book reappeared in *Nuclear Weapons and Foreign Policy* and subsequent writings. As Mazlish and Stoessinger, among others, have noted, Kissinger's experiences with both the Kennedy and Johnson administrations only served to reinforce his views on bureaucratic constraints. The best summary of these views is to be found in "Domestic Structure and Foreign Policy" (Kissinger: 1969a) and is repeated and elaborated to varying degrees in "The Policy-maker and the Intellectual" (1959c) and "Bureaucracy and Policy Making: The Effect of Insiders and Outsiders on the Policy Process" (1968a).

A number of observations from "Domestic Structure and Foreign Policy" illustrate the position Kissinger took into government three years later. According to Kissinger (1969a:17–18),

> The vast bureaucratic mechanisms that emerge develop a momentum and a vested interest of their own. . . . There is a trend toward autarky. The purpose of the bureaucracy is to devise a standard operating procedure which can cope effectively with most problems. . . . Bureaucracy becomes an obstacle when what it defines as routine does not address the most significant range of issues or when its prescribed mode of action proves irrelevant to the problem. . . . When this occurs, the bureaucracy absorbs the energies of top executives. . . . Serving the machine becomes a more absorbing occupation than defining its purpose.

These observations are reflected in Kissinger's views of the State Department in *White House Years*. There are numerous references to its inertia, lack of imagination, stagnation, and general obstructionism to the necessarily "innovative," "bold," and "heroic" policies of the true statesman. Kissinger (1979:603) writes of the department's "vacillation" and its inertia and conservatism in regard to opening relations with China (1979:690). The bureaucratic battles between Kissinger and Rogers (as well as with Laird at Defense) most often arose after the State Department found out about the real foreign policy being conducted from the White House. The main aim of Kissinger and Nixon was to keep information on their activities from the department, to keep it from dragging its feet on whatever issue was under consideration (1979:694).[9]

Indeed, the Kissinger-Nixon style followed the blueprint Kissinger set out in "Domestic Structure and Foreign Policy." Kissinger (1969a:22–23) predicted that the executive would be forced into "extra-bureaucratic" mechanisms in order to avoid the problems of the "administrative machine": "Faced with an administrative machine which is both elaborate and fragmented, the executive is forced into essentially lateral means of control. . . . All of this drives the executive in the direction of extra-bureaucratic means of decision. The practice of relying on special emissaries or personal envoys is an example; their status outside the bureaucracy frees them from some of its restraints." Kissinger, in another example of projective biography, became just such a special emissary and relied on lateral means of control. Kissinger (1979:589) comments on Nixon's "penchant for operating through his Assistants rather than his Cabinet" in general, and later notes that in deciding on whom to send to Beijing for the first major meeting, Nixon decided that "undoubtedly of all the potential emissaries I was the most subject to his control" (1979:717).

Not only did Nixon get his special extra-bureaucratic emissary, but he also set up elaborate communications procedures by which to end-run the State Department. Some of the most fascinating material in *White House Years* is found in Kissinger's description of the various "backchannels" developed to conduct foreign relations without using the State Department or without its knowledge. Kissinger (1979:28) notes: "As time went by, the President, or I on his behalf, in order to avoid these endless confrontations, came to deal increasingly with key foreign leaders through channels that directly linked the White House Situation Room to the field without going through the State Department—the so-called backchannels. This process started on the day after Inauguration."

The establishment of the backchannel, how it circumvented the State Department, the dual process of carrying out foreign policy negotiations on public (State Department) and private tracks—all came to play a central role in the Nixon-Kissinger foreign policy. The effort was enormous. The purpose was a foreign policy of statesmen unconstrained by the bureaucratic politics, leaks, and the time-consuming nature of working through the State Department. Kissinger (1979:30) sums up the results of this effort:

In May 1971 the Secretary of State did not know of the negotiations in the White House-Kremlin channels that led to the breakthrough in the SALT talks until seventy-two hours before there was a formal announcement. In July 1971 Rogers was told of my secret trip to China only after I was on the way. In April 1972, the President gave Rogers such a convoluted explanation for my trip to Moscow—which had been arranged secretly and which Rogers opposed when he was told at the last minute—that it complicated negotiations. Such examples could be endlessly multiplied.

Whatever Nixon's motives, Kissinger's style as national security adviser adhered to that of the statesman and his continuous battle against the constraints of the bureaucracy. This style derived from Kissinger's idiosyncratic background and an intellectual belief that went back to his dissertation. This belief reemerged in Kissinger the policy maker and is repeated almost verbatim in his memoirs. Kissinger (1979:39) recalls that when he was appointed national security assistant: "My major concern was that a large bureaucracy, however organized, tends to stifle creativity. . . . In the modern state bureaucracies become so large that too often more time is spent on running them than in defining their purposes. . . . It seemed to me no accident that most great statesmen had been locked in permanent struggle with experts in their foreign offices."

Dealing with the Soviet Union

Observers of the Kissinger era foreign policy, those who have analyzed his pre-official writing as well as his speeches as policy maker, have commented that American policy was centered on the Soviet Union (Caldwell, 1981; Hoffmann, 1978). All other policy issues were considered only as they impinged on this central relationship. Partial support for this assertion has come from the author's study of Kissinger's perceptions of the Soviet Union and China, as well as from their triadic interactions. For example, in terms of a Soviet-Chinese comparison, the saliency of the Soviet Union in all of Kissinger's public statements from 1969 to 1976 is clear. Whether one looks at numbers of documents, numbers of evaluative assertions, or percentage of documents, the Soviet Union is by far the more salient attitude object: over four times as many evaluative assertions and more than double the percentage of documents in which one or both of the communist powers are discussed concern the Soviet Union.

Why is this the case in terms particular to Henry Kissinger? The stable world order that is the core of Kissinger's belief system requires that the major opponent in the system be central to one's policy. This is particularly true if that power, along with one's own power, has the military capability to destroy the world. The Soviet-American capability for mass destruction is a common theme in many of Kissinger's public statements while in office.[10] In addition, both Mazlish and Ward comment on Kissinger's fascination with "opponent." Mazlish (1976:44–46) discusses how Kissinger's early experiences promoted a style of interaction which led him to identify with and to be very effective in dealing with opponents.

As discussed in Starr (1980a), Kissinger's instrumental beliefs revolve around the central theme of negotiations as the tool of the statesman and the statesman's use of force and diplomacy. The tools chosen and the strategy for their use depend upon whether the opponent is a legitimate or a revolutionary state. Ideas that appeared in "The Meaning of History" jelled in A World Restored into conceptions of the legitimate state and the revolutionary state which have been significant in Kissinger's analyses ever since. The legitimate state used diplomacy for achieving limited objectives; it accepted the international context as legitimate and agreed to negotiate its differences within the rules and constraints of that context. The revolutionary state, like the revolutionary statesman, was ideological in its pursuit of unlimited objectives and thus did not accept as axiomatic the survival of other states.

The design that Kissinger constructed for a stable international order and which he details in *White House Years* was initially developed in 1968 while he wrote foreign policy papers for Rockefeller. It was based on Kissinger's conviction that the Soviet Union and the People's Republic of China were no longer revolutionary states (Stoessinger, 1976:43). Hoffmann (1978) asserts that Kissinger came to the conclusion that the USSR and PRC were no longer revolutionary states through his analysis of their perceived needs and self-interest. The change in weapons technology and the mutual balance of terror, as well as the Sino-Soviet split, brought about the primacy of prudence over ideology, Kissinger concluded (Hoffmann, 1978:44–45).

Hoffmann's assertion can be supported by the following sequence. The USSR was clearly identified as revolutionary by Kissinger in *Nuclear Weapons and Foreign Policy* (1957b). The changeover began in *The Necessity for Choice* (1961a), in which Kissinger developed a number of ideas on arms control. He saw the Soviet Union as willing to enter into arms control agreements through its self-interest in survival. The changeover becomes more explicit in *The Troubled Partnership* (1965a), in which he speaks of both the necessity of nuclear survival and the Sino-Soviet split. The final step comes in early 1968 during Rockefeller's unsuccessful bid for the Republican presidential nomination. Graubard chronicles Rockefeller's public statements (based on Kissinger's policy papers) calling for new "understandings being reached with the Soviet Union and Communist China" (see Graubard, 1973:243, 248, 252, 253).

Thus, the Soviet Union was the central and salient foreign policy object, and it could be dealt with as a legitimate state. As opposed to Dulles' closed or frozen image of the opponent (see Holsti, 1962b), a similar evaluative assertion analysis of Kissinger's perceptions of the Soviet Union reveals an open and flexible image.[11] Kissinger rejected the classic psychological image of the enemy as an omniscient and omnipotent actor, who left nothing to chance and who pursued a coherent "grand strategy" (see Gladstone, 1959). Indeed, in his memoirs Kissinger (1979: 161–62) describes an analysis of Soviet policy sent to Nixon: "It began by rejecting the proposition that Soviet policy necessarily followed a master plan." The document went on: "It is always tempting to arrange diverse Soviet moves into a grand design. The more esoteric brands of Kremlinology often purport to see each and every move as part of a carefully orchestrated score in which events inexorably move to the grand finale. Experience has shown that this has rarely if ever been the case."

Given all this, how was the Soviet Union to be fit into a stable structure of peace? Kissinger's views have always taken two tracks (the dual policy he was to follow as a policy maker): (1) increasing the economic, political, and cultural ties of interdependence, to give any state a major stake in the system, and thus to impose costs on it should it break the rules of the system; and (2) utilizing a balance of power process, based on the costs that countervailing power would impose on states that broke the rules of the system. Again, during his time in office Kissinger often spoke of entangling the Soviet Union within the webs of economic and political relations that existed in the system:

> We have an historic obligation to mankind to engage the Soviet Union in settlements of concrete problems and to push back the shadow of nuclear catastrophe. . . . And we have begun to construct a network of cooperative agreements in a variety of functional areas—economic, scientific, medical, environmental and others—which promise concrete benefits if political conditions permit. . . . It has been our belief that, with patience, a pattern of restraints and a network of vested interests can develop which will give coexistence a more hopeful dimension and make both sides conscious of what they would stand to lose by reverting to the politics of pressure, confrontation and crisis (U.S. Department of State, *Bulletin*, April 5, 1976).

This logic formed the basis for the Kissinger-Nixon ideas of "linkage," where limits (central to Kissinger's operational code) were imposed by self-restraint. This restraint came from understanding that costs would be imposed in other areas for lack of restraint "because in an interdependent world the actions of a major power are inevitably related and have consequences beyond the issue or region immediately concerned" (Kissinger, 1979:129). Restraint would not come from simply demonstrating one's good will. In an article on the Cuban missile crisis, Kissinger (1962a) questioned what sorts of lessons the Soviets learned from U.S. behavior at Suez, in Lebanon, and at the Bay of Pigs. Kissinger's view was Kennanesque in the assumption that unilateral acts of goodwill (in the mold of Osgood's GRIT [Gradual and Reciprocated Initiatives in Tension-reduction] process) would not be enough. Soviet behavior could best be influenced by demonstrating that costs would be imposed. These would come from the loss of cooperative arrangements, or the possibility of the use of military force. Walker (1977) presents an excellent analysis of Kissinger's instrumental beliefs concerning the use and interplay of negotiations and force. While his analysis focuses mostly on the Indochinese negotiations, it is also relevant to this dual-track policy toward the Soviet Union. In his memoirs, Kissinger (1979:818) presents a strategy similar to the one Walker has extracted from preofficial writings: "In dealing with the Soviets a point is inevitably reached where it is important to make clear brutally that the limits of flexibility have been reached, that the time has come either to settle or to end the negotiation. This is a more complex matter than simply getting 'tough'."

To Kissinger, "getting tough" was simply part of a larger process of positive incentives and negative costs which one used to help an opponent see his own interest in restraint, and to impose restraint if necessary. He makes this clear in a 1976 speech (U.S. Department of State, *Bulletin*, April 5, 1976):

> We therefore face the necessity for a dual policy; on the one hand, we are determined to prevent Soviet military power from being used for political expansion;

we will firmly discourage and resist adventurist policies. But at the same time, we cannot escalate every political dispute into a central crisis; nor can we rest on identifying foreign policy with crisis management. We have an obligation to work for a more positive future. We must couple opposition to pressure and irresponsibility with concerned efforts to build a positive world.

Thus, Kissinger's policy toward the Soviet Union was one part detente (the use of positive incentives of mutual benefit and increasing webs of interdependence) and one part Kennan (firm response to adventurist, expansionist, and destabilizing behavior). This dual response comes through in numerous discussions of detente in *White House Years*. For example, he notes, "Our strategy of détente always depended on a firm application of psychological and physical restraints and determined resistance to challenges" (1979:1143). Specifically, "All experience teaches that Soviet military moves, which usually begin as tentative, must be resisted early, unequivocally, and in a fashion that gives Soviet leaders a justification for withdrawal" (1979:569). Early in the memoirs, discussing SALT and U.S. defense policy, Kissinger noted, "It was the perennial debate whether Soviet interest in compromise was best elicited by making unilateral American gestures or by presenting the Kremlin with risks and programs they were eager to stop" (1979:535). In a later discussion on the development of Indochina policies in 1972, Kissinger makes clear how Moscow should be treated: "It was essential to react strongly, if necessary violently, in the early stages of Soviet expansion—I advocated this over Cienfuegos, Jordan, India-Pakistan, and was to do so over Angola. In May [1972] I was prepared to risk the Moscow Summit for whatever was necessary to break Hanoi's offensive" (1979:1158).

Kissinger's insistence that this dual path be followed was a major component of his critiques of the Carter administration's foreign policy—first for ignoring the use of stern restraints, and then for jumping to tough measures without continuing positive measures. His critiques include poor timing on Carter's part, an issue crucial to the use of negotiations and force. Timing is especially relevant to the USSR: "Success in negotiations is a matter of timing, and nowhere more so than with Moscow" (Kissinger, 1979:818). Part of the poor timing is a lack of consistency and clear signals.

Interestingly, these critiques reflect criticisms of his own policy toward the Soviet Union.[12] Many observers never understood how both sides of the dual policy could run together. Critics on the right, of a hawkish persuasion, were dubious and mistrusted any cooperative moves toward the Soviet Union, especially those connected with arms control; critics on the left, of the more dovish sort, attacked the continuing use of or threat of the use of force and the periodic tough confrontationary measures of the Nixon administration. Such activities appeared to be merely a throwback to the days of the cold war. And yet, in policy making up through 1973, Kissinger felt that the dual track had been successful—in SALT, in Vietnam, in Central Europe, even in the Middle East and on the subcontinent. The point, once again, is that Kissinger's views on dealing with opponents in the system, the Soviet

Union in particular, had been presented in his earlier scholarly writings, and had a strong basis in previously analyzed idiosyncratic factors.

Conclusion

The first volume of Henry Kissinger's memoirs, *White House Years*, provides us with one source of data on an important era in American foreign policy, on the processes of the Nixon White House, and on Henry Kissinger the policy maker, intellectual, and individual. How useful is this data source to us, with regard to its general accuracy, its consistency with Kissinger's previous thought and with earlier analyses of him, and its reflection of how Kissinger viewed his policy and behavior? The issue areas selected here are representative of a number of substantive and stylistic areas dealt with in the memoirs which are indeed consistent with earlier, biographical, operational code, content analytic, and policy research on Henry Kissinger.

As noted at the outset, many of these previous studies are psychological or cognitive. In many ways this is quite fitting for analysis of Henry Kissinger. While Kissinger insisted that it was foolish to try to understand him using psychological techniques (Mazlish, 1976: 196), he himself has always used them. His army career introduced him to psychological warfare activities, which he appeared to master easily. A Harvard roommate recalls that at one point Kissinger considered becoming a psychiatrist (Mazlish, 1976: 58), and Graubard's (1973: 11) discussion of *A World Restored* continually highlights Kissinger's concern with knowing and understanding how one's opponents perceive an issue and what they believed. Part of Metternich's genius was in his handling of negotiations with Napoleon: "He had to know Napoleon's mind. . . . For Napoleon to have acted other than he did . . . would have meant that he had ceased to be Napoleon" (Graubard, 1973: 22, 27). In the end, Mazlish (1976: 197) terms Kissinger a "psychiatrist *manque*, a psychological historian."

Just as Kissinger searched for the clues to the personality and world view of the leaders with whom he would be dealing, he had a clear and consistent world view or belief system of his own, and he acted on it. This link between belief system and behavior has been made by Walker (1977) in regard to Kissinger's Indochina policies. Walker has provided an excellent analysis of Kissinger's positions and strategies on the basis of an operational code analysis, especially Kissinger's instrumental values on the use of force and negotiation. This Schelling-like analysis clearly indicated that Kissinger's decision-making behavior followed the outlines set forth in his academic writings. Walker's analyses are reconfirmed in a number of places in the memoirs (see Kissinger, 1979: 308, 436, 478, 498, 1315–6, 1328, 1457). The point is that Kissinger had a well-defined belief system, based on personal and intellectual factors, and he acted on it. His memoirs indicated that he also framed his retrospective in terms of that belief system. He both recalled and described his behavior as policy maker in a manner consistent with his personality and belief system.

Kissinger *is* understandable. He held a coherent and plausible view of the world concerned with certain values and not with others; concerned with order, limits, and restraint; and concerned with a psychological perspective on how one forged agreements with opponents. These views had been set out in detail before he entered office. While in office, he pursued the goals of the statesman with the tools of the statesman. This review is not intended to be a judgment on how accurate that view of the world was or ultimately how successful it was. Such judgments will be left to the policy analysis commentaries that were excluded at the beginning of this chapter. The point is that Kissinger's view is an intellectually respectable and coherent view, and it appears from a variety of analyses that he attempted to follow it.

Acknowledgment

"The Kissinger Years: Studying Individuals and Foreign Policy," by Harvey Starr, is reprinted from *International Studies Quarterly*, vol. 24 (December 1980), pp. 465–96, © 1980 International Studies Association, with permission of the publisher.

2. Kissinger: A Psychohistory

Dana Ward

> Nixon, he is not fit to be President.
>
> Henry Kissinger

Just before Richard Nixon was elected president, the Institute for Defense Analysis prepared a study of the bureaucracies responsible for national security policy in the hope that the incoming president, whoever he would be, might be better prepared to deal with the demands of formulating foreign policy. The study concluded: "Neither practitioners nor students of national security policy should over-emphasize the importance of the procedures of decision making. In the last analysis, the force of personality tends to over-ride procedures" (Clark and Legere, 1969:8). While political scientists have been slow to respond to such admonitions, the argument that personality plays an important, and occasionally decisive, role in the decision-making process has gradually found acceptance in recent years. In this essay the impact of Henry Kissinger's personality on the foreign-policy-making process during Nixon's first administration will be examined.[1]

At the outset it should be emphasized that personality is by no means the *only* determinant of policy outcomes. An explanation of political life from a solely individual, psychological point of view is as sterile as one which ignores personality altogether. Political action is the process by which individuals turn upon their history to transform their lives. There are givens in the world, forces, structures, and belief systems, that require specific responses. But the style of response, the personality factor, is as crucial as the imperative to respond. Political style, then, becomes a critical issue in studies which follow a psychohistorical approach, a method of study which takes into consideration both personal and collective motivation. While the emphasis here is clearly on personality, it should not be forgotten that the proper balance between personality and politics cannot be achieved unless the psychological analysis offered here is seen in light of the political analyses of other writers.

In this essay I hope to show how various conflicts in Kissinger's psychological makeup contributed to the style with which Kissinger practiced politics and then to suggest how that style foreclosed alternative solutions to the problems facing American diplomacy during the period under study. As will be demonstrated below, there are a number of basic tensions in Kissinger's psyche which influence the manner in which he perceives the world and consequently the actions which he recommends and undertakes. While on a personal, inner level Kissinger tends to have an undervalued sense of self which gives rise to depression, timidness, and lack of confidence, he presents a public figure of arrogance, strong will, and competence. Kissinger has a tendency to use theoretical abstractions as a means of keeping people away, yet he exhibits a countervailing, excessive need for love and praise. Accompanying this tendency toward abstraction is a lack of concern for human considerations in his intellectual formulations. Most importantly, for our purposes, there seems to be a tension between the avoidance of, and compulsive confrontation with, risks. This tendency leads Kissinger to place himself in situations where he can publicly test his will and consequently prove his inherent goodness and worth. An attempt also will be made to assess the role that Kissinger's attachment to historical and contemporary individuals has played in his attempt to resolve the inner tensions mentioned above. Finally, I will try to demonstrate that these various tendencies coalesce into a configuration of behavior typical of the depressive, or dysmutual, personality (Wolman, 1972), and that the patterns of behavior attendant upon such an organization of personality have combined to affect specific policy decisions such as the invasion of Cambodia, the mining of Haiphong, the secret peace negotiations, the peace settlement, and our relations with our allies.

The Early Days in Germany

Fürth, the town in which Alfred Heinz Kissinger was born early in the morning on May 27, 1923, was a south German industrial city with a population at the time of about 64,000. Fürth was a natural settling place for many Jews who were not allowed to live in nearby Nuremburg. The city had a century-old reputation for religious toleration, and one of the families attracted to Fürth was that of the Kissingers. But the Kissingers were not to enjoy the fruits of religious toleration. While Fürth's reputation perhaps forestalled the effects of Hitler's rise to power, in the end Fürth, too, would bear the scar of Hitler's terror. Through either emigration or extermination "of Fürth's pre-1933 population of 3,000 Jews, only 70 were on hand to attend the first post-war religious services" (*Chicago Daily News*, May 2, 1974).

Obviously, life for Jews in Fürth was not easy. With the passage of the Nuremburg laws in 1935, the somewhat stable middle-class lives that, even through the depression, many were able to maintain were permanently disrupted. And among those families that suffered humiliation, privation, and death at the hands of the Nazis were the Kissingers. Included among those who were killed by the Nazis were thirteen relatives in Kissinger's family (Kissinger, 1982:203).

Louis Kissinger was the head of the Kissinger household. In 1922, at the age of thirty-five, he married Paula Stern, then twenty-one and his former student, who came from a middle-class Jewish family. A year later their first of two sons was born. The birth certificate listed the child's name as Alfred Heinz, but until fifteen years later when he changed his name to Henry, the Alfred was dropped and he would be called Heinz. Another year passed and in 1924 the second last of the Kissinger children was born and named Walter Bernhard. Louis Kissinger, "a gentle, soft-hearted teacher in a girls' high school" (Collier, 1971:104), was himself a son of a village school teacher. The home that he maintained for his wife and two children can be best described as middle class. The Kissingers lived in a five-room flat containing many books and a piano, and they were well enough off to be able to maintain a servant. Louis Kissinger was a deeply religious man, and the children were brought up accordingly. The elder Kissinger was a respected man in his community. In Germany, the position of *Studienrat* which he held at the Mädchen Lyceum was of much greater social standing than the equivalent status of a high school teacher in the United States. A boarder who lived with the Kissingers in the early thirties has recalled: "Mr. Kissinger is a very serious, conscientious individual. Uppermost in his mind was providing for his family. And I think he felt he couldn't take too many chances" (author's interview with Jack Heiman, August 28, 1974; hereafter cited as "Heiman interview"). To be deprived of his teaching position then would have had a devastating effect upon him and his family. That, however, was precisely what occurred in 1935 when Nuremberg laws forbade any Jew from holding a government position. Louis Kissinger lost his job and with it the economic security his family had enjoyed until then.[2]

But economic security was not all that the Kissingers were to suffer. In addition to the strictures on holding government jobs, the Nuremberg laws also required that Jewish children leave public schools to attend special, all-Jewish institutions. Thus Heinz was forced to attend the special school. Heinz was not a particularly bright student while in Germany—at least according to the usual indicators such as grades (Beloff, 1969). But in light of his brilliant performance in more favorable circumstances after he left Germany, it is likely that Heinz's grades suffered as a result of the adverse conditions during this period.

One could hardly blame young Heinz if his mind were not on his studies. He would have had to be aware of the fragility of his father's status and his father's anxiety undoubtedly would have been transmitted to the children. But if somehow the situation at home escaped Heinz's attention, he became painfully aware of what it meant to be Jewish when he was on the streets of Fürth. "Jewish children, when they ventured onto the streets or playground would be cornered and beaten up by Hitler Youth. Among the children getting this bloody lesson in politics was Heinz Kissinger" (Shaw, 1972). In his later years Kissinger would comment: "My life in Fürth passed without leaving any lasting impressions. I can't remember any interesting or amusing incidents." But the lessons of the street did leave a lasting, although hardly amusing, impression. One of the incidents that he does remember is that: "The other children would beat us up" (*Time*, February 14, 1971). This was a painful reminder that he was not like the others. In his later life, while there were numerous other factors, his treatment at the hands of other children would be one contribution to Kissinger's anxiety about being left out and disliked.

Aside from a few references to soccer and to the beatings suffered on the streets of Fürth, Henry Kissinger has been uniformly reluctant to attribute any significance to his early life, or for that matter, even to talk about it. While a member of the White House staff, Kissinger sloughed off reporters' questions about his life in Germany by saying that his life in Fürth "left no lasting impressions," or "that part of my childhood is not a key to anything" (Collier, 1971: 105). Even more strongly: "I was not consciously unhappy. I was not so acutely aware of what was going on. For children those things are not that serious. It is fashionable now to explain everything psychoanalytically, but let me tell you, the political persecutions of my childhood are not what control my life" (Collier, 1971 : 105).

If not to children, then to whom are "those things" serious? Kissinger was fifteen years old when he left Germany, an age when he simply could not have been unaware of what was happening around him. By 1938 Jews were being murdered on the streets, and that year marks the beginning of Hitler's systematic roundup of Jews. It would seem that Kissinger's poor memory is a sustained effort to decrease the value and importance of his early life. This period in Germany was the "bad time"—it only served, in Kissinger's view, as a restraint, as an obstacle to overcome, and once overcome, to be forgotten.

Jack Heiman, a child three years older than Henry, lived for five years in the Kissinger household as a boarder, yet his memory of that period is somewhat less hazy: "The whole community was aware of what was coming. And maybe being so close to Nuremberg where they had the Party Congresses we got an earlier warning" (Heiman interview). Living in the same household, the young boarder received a very different, almost opposite, impression; rather than being unaware, the Jewish community in Fürth seems to have received an earlier warning of the coming chaos.

Kissinger has devoted much of his life to trying to understand how such disruptions as Hitler's persecution of Jews and expansionary provocations arise, and how best to avert the pain and suffering attendant upon such disruptions, yet he refuses to make the connection that his own experience as an object of such chaos was important for his later pursuits. Throughout Kissinger's work is the theme of the opposition between the forces of chaos and the forces of order (Ward, 1973). Kissinger's concerns for balance and chaos are not unrelated, but rather they form two sides of an almost arithmetic law in Kissinger's psycho-logic. Kissinger has been described by close friends as possessing a "morbid preoccupation" with the contemplation of chaos. Thus it would appear that Kissinger's denial of the importance of his early years is somehow overdetermined; rather than those years being unimportant as he would have us believe, they are the rock upon which his personality and life have been built.

In an article which attempted to describe the social origins of the depressive personality, Howard Rome has pointed to the tendency for such individuals to view the world as one in which chaos is the predominant characteristic. He says: "It is a world in which man's views of the universe—if he has any—offer little hope and less consolation, in which his view of his fellowmen is jaundiced and malign. It is a world whose predominant characteristic is chaos" (Rome, 1974). Kissinger is certainly not without his views of the universe. As will be shown in the latter discussion of his intellectual work and in the discussion of his identity, Rome's description of the ideology of the depressive personality is consistent with Kissinger's view of the world and himself. We must assume that the conditions of Kissinger's early life in Germany are the social root of what will be shown to be a depressive personality. But the social origins of the depressive personality are only half of the equation. To fully understand the development it is imperative that we look to early childhood family relations.

The depressive personality is a diagnostic category for a broad, but specific range of behavior. It is not intended as a pigeonhole, but simply as a conceptual tool for trying to understand the dynamics of an individual's interaction with the world. The analysis of numerous case studies has revealed that the depressive personality is the consequence of a particular kind of family politics. The basic family alignment is characterized by ambivalent parents and a favored sibling. The father is often uninvolved with the children, and the mother may feel resentment toward her husband, may never really have wanted to be a mother, or feels that the child is both a burden and an obstacle precluding her escape from marriage. Lack of involvement or absence from the family on the part of the parents leads to a sense of abandonment on the part of the child; he feels alone. This feeling is reinforced if there is a sibling who receives the attention of the parents. The sense that the child derives from the parents' behavior is that one is not automatically loved and accepted, nor is one automatically good. Acceptance and goodness are earned, and love is the reward. The corollary is that the child feels basically worthless and bad.

It is this sense of worthlessness and the inability to elicit love which is the root feeling of the depressive personality. The predominant feelings experienced by the child are weakness, inferiority, and a lack of self-esteem. There is a tendency to withdraw from others, and an inability to form meaningful relationships for fear that the other will discover one's worthlessness.

The behaviors which result from the familial politics and existential experience of the self are many. Wolman (1972:244) points out: "The dysmutual tries to overcome his low self-esteem in many ways, one of which is through extreme ambition. Some dysmutuals, in milder stages of the disorder, rather than escape into manic moods, try to compensate for feelings of inferiority by excessive work, long working hours and an over-all drive for supremacy." In addition, "Dysmutuals are *insatiable* in love, sex, friendship, glory, status or possessions" (1972:233). They tend also to be tactless, alienating their friends. "They are perpetually depressed and always on the defensive. Pleasant and friendly moods are like rays of sunshine that break through the clouds" (1972:234). There is in addition a tendency to be vulnerable to criticism. Finally, the dysmutual "repeats the pattern of his childhood, forever trying to induce women to love him" (1972:238).

It should be emphasized that the depressive personality can range from well integrated to psychotic depression. The purpose of classification is not to determine how neurotic an individual might be. The category simply represents an overall pattern of behavior, world view, and values which are consistent regardless of the degree of personality integration. By matching the hypothesized behavior with the actual behavior we are able to assess the validity, or falsity, of the hypothesis. From there we can begin to understand the dynamic tensions and the reasons behind actions. To what degree then do the characteristics described above fit the family pattern in the Kissinger household?

Most people who knew the family and have commented upon it thought the Kissinger household was a harmonious one. Both parents were respected by the children and there seems to have been little conflict between the parents. Just as uniformly, the impression has been that Mrs. Kissinger was the dominant influence in the family. Jack Heiman, the man who as a child came to live with the Kissingers, has said: "While Louis was the authority figure in Fürth, his wife dominated the family with her charm, a quality that became more significant later, in exile. He was the boss, but she was a strong woman, a very intelligent, aggressive woman" (Heiman interview). Interviews that I had with Kissinger's friends have also borne out this impression. It is felt that the power behind the paternal throne lay with Mrs. Kissinger. As we will see below, it is Mrs. Kissinger who is the model for action and who in the early years in New York was the economic and social backbone of the family.

Louis Kissinger, in fact, was little involved with the children. And it may be this lack of involvement which was the most predominant characteristic of the father's role in the family. Even much later this attitude is reflected with respect to Henry's rise to power: "Louis Kissinger . . . had been a bit diffident about his eldest son's success, because it entailed so much travel on the Sabbath, a Washington Heights rabbi said. But with the Nobel Prize, Louis' joy was complete. 'Henry had made good to the nth degree' " (*New York Post*, 1974). This comment coming from a man close to Louis Kissinger may very well reflect the ambivalent atmosphere in which Henry grew up—one in which he was expected to make good in order to be loved. Indeed, one suspects that making good was by no means enough, given his father's "diffident" attitude even after so much success.

Every indication is that for the most part the children were the mother's responsibility. Louis Kissinger's most immediate involvement was as a disburser of familial justice, although Mrs. Kissinger herself was not the least bit hesitant to assume that role. As the boarder in the family recalls: "From a disciplinary point of view, if she didn't like anything she didn't need Mr. Kissinger. If Walter or Henry did something wrong she took matters in her own hands and didn't burden her husband with the everyday events. She is a very resolute, energetic woman. A strong-willed woman" (Heiman interview).

The first pattern of behavior which emerges that may shed light on the significant events in Henry's early development is the difference between him and his brother Wally. His father recalls: "Henry was always the thinker. He was more inhibited than Wally. Wally was more the doer, more the extrovert" (Shearer, 1971). Jack Heiman also recalled when I asked about the differences between the two boys: "Like night and day. Now remember, it was a long time ago, but Walter was the more out-going . . . Henry was withdrawn, studious and a dreamer. . . . I would say Henry takes after his father and Walter after his mother" (Heiman interview).

The differences between Walter and Henry are an interesting comparison. All who knew the family in Germany recall that Henry was even then a loner, withdrawn and timid. Walter on the other hand seems to have impressed others with his ingenuity and his outgoing, aggressive manner. Surprise is often expressed by those who knew the family in the early years that it was Henry and not Walter who has emerged upon the public scene. But what is important is that there is a sharp contrast in personality between the two boys which would lead one to ask what is the source of that difference. Indeed it is not unusual for an active and expressive child to draw more attention than one who is withdrawn, thus reinforcing established patterns. But what was the initial source of the differentiation in personalities?

The difference between the two boys probably lies much earlier in their development. Unfortunately, there is no direct evidence. We can only postulate that with the arrival of a second child, Henry experienced a sense of loss as a result of his mother's need to devote attention to the newborn child. While it is highly doubtful that there was any frank rejection of Henry, the arrival of the new sibling could have led to a sense of neglect, followed by a withdrawal into the self and a sense of self-depreciation. Of course, without any direct source of verification this is simply speculation, but speculation which would begin to explain the earliest experiences which led to basic patterns of behavior in Henry's later years.

Frequently a child who is accustomed to the attentions of his mother interprets the diminished attention that comes with a new sibling as rejection. This sense of rejection is at the core of the depressive personality and its result is a withdrawal into the self. If this is what occurred in Kissinger's case it would begin to explain the differences between himself and Walter. And Kissinger's experience vis-à-vis his brother would be marked by a sense of unsuccessful competition which would reinforce the tendency to withdraw.

In the families of severely disturbed depressive personalities the familial relations are usually characterized by "a hostile mother, a disinterested or hostile father, and siblings favored by the mother" (Wolman, 1972:231). But it is important to note that "parental rejection need not be associated with pathological hostility; an infant may feel rejected whenever his mother is sick, hospitalized, or unable to take care of him, when she is pregnant with another child, or when she works outside her home" (Wolman, 1972:230–31).

To what extent then do Kissinger's parents fit this pattern which can lead to depressive anxiety? The evidence is somewhat sparse, but there is some nevertheless which would indicate that Kissinger felt a sense of rejection and ambivalence from his mother, disinterest from his father, and lived with siblings who were more favored. On this last point we have more substantial evidence upon which to base our judgment.

In 1930, when Henry was seven, Jack Heiman came to live with the Kissingers. Jack was ten at the time, and because there was no Jewish school in his village he came to Fürth to attend the Isrealitisch Realschule where Henry was also going to school. Jack boarded with the Kissingers and moved into the boys' room. Later Heiman became a handicrafts dealer in Chicago and he recalls of his life then: "When I think of it today . . . they treated me like a third son. In fact they leaned over backward to be less strict with me. They never hit me, and they weren't bashful with Henry and Walter. They really got it. We were all in the same bedroom at night sometimes too noisy and rambunctious while Mr. Kissinger was grading papers.

He'd come in and hit them—but not me, even though I was equally guilty" (*New York Post*, 1974).

Here Henry was faced with the entrance of a "third" son who is obviously given preferential treatment. To make matters worse, it appears that Jack became closer friends with Walter than with Henry. "I was closer to Walter even though he was the younger." Thus it would be understandable if Henry got the feeling that he was low man on the totem pole.

Jack's amnesty from corporal punishment was not the only special treatment afforded him by the Kissingers. "I remember that during the time I was there, every afternoon she [Mrs. Kissinger] spent her time tutoring me. She didn't have to but she did. And the boys didn't need it. I was the dummy. They treated me like a third son." Heiman insists that the boys felt no resentment over the fact that their mother devoted her afternoons to him and not to Walter or Henry. But the attention given Jack could hardly have gone unnoticed.[3]

One form of behavior that may have been a means of overcoming this specific situation, but most certainly the general milieu, was what seems to have been a highly competitive relationship between Jack and Henry. Jack recalls: "Henry always had a strong desire to win. Behind the house there was a little yard, and every free moment we went down and tried to play against one another. Henry was a very determined individual." Henry was determined to win against the competition for his mother's attention, perhaps thereby to win her love.

Mrs. Kissinger was described variously by Heiman as "very strong and astute," "very intelligent," "aggressive," "energetic," "resolute," and "strong willed." She was active in her community and "in addition to being a housewife had other intellectual interests." The one characteristic which is particularly important is that "she just wasn't satisfied with housework." It was this dissatisfaction that precipitated Jack's tutoring as a means by which she could exercise her mind and perform a useful function. At the same time however her dissatisfaction must have been communicated to the children. How would they interpret this communication? Were they the cause of her dissatisfaction?

There is one further comment by Heiman which might provide some insight into the atmosphere of the Kissinger household. In this case Heiman is speaking generally, and not in specific reference to the Kissinger household: "This kind of upbringing breeds bashfulness and insecurity. You don't have the opportunity to be on your own. Parents do not impose their will on kids as much now as then, and I think we matured later because of this." The children obeyed the family laws and tried to live up to their parents' expectations, but these were hard tasks and great expectations. It is a situation in which there was little one could do to change the situation. Thus we have the essential elements for the development of the depressive personality: an ambivalent attitude on the part of the parents, depreciation of self-esteem, and a sense of powerlessness.

Of course, none of these feelings were in any way so extreme as to border on the pathological. All I am trying to establish is whether there is any evidence for a familial base upon which the social repression experienced by Kissinger could build an edifice whose most prominent characteristic would be depressive anxiety and the patterns of behavior characteristic of such a personality. Such a supposition is consistent with Kissinger's later personality patterns; all I can show here is that it is not inconsistent with what can be reconstructed of his childhood experience.

It is likely that it was with respect to religion that the greatest paternal expectations were placed upon the children. Until Henry went into the army he would be an extremely religious youth: "He put on tfillin phylacteries for morning prayers and went to synagogue regularly" (*New York Post*, 1974). It also seems that Henry's rebellion against his father was in this crucial area.

Louis's decline as the central figure in the family is the predominant change in the family relations, a change upon which many have commented. The man essential to Kissinger's own personal transformation, Fritz Kraemer, has said (*New York Post*, 1974): "You can do damage to the soul of a man and never touch his body. For five years, the most formative years [10–15], Henry had to undergo this horror. And the real horror is the breakdown of the world. Imagine what it means when your father, who was your authority, the father you admire . . . is suddenly transformed into a frightened little mouse."

When the Kissingers left Germany, Louis' role in the family was even further undermined. "Louis Kissinger, a former teacher over 50 then and fated to end his working life as a bookkeeper, had to accept his changed status meekly" (Heiman interview). We will discuss this process further below, but what happened in Kissinger's relation to his father was to set Henry on a search for strong individuals who would not accept things so meekly. The immediate form this process took was to renounce the role expectation that was most important to his father. "As his father's shadow diminished, Henry slipped out from beneath it, beginning his long rebellion against orthodox Jewishness" (Heiman interview). This was Henry's way of saying, "I will not accept things as they are."

What would the timid and withdrawn youth of Fürth do with the resentment and hostility that he must have felt as a consequence of his familial and social experience? What would he do with the rage he must have felt over his treatment as a Jew? "In the 30's in the streets of Fürth, he was powerless" (Shaw, 1972). He could do nothing and his father could do nothing. About the only viable alternative for the young Heinz would have been to turn his rage inward and withdraw further into his protective shell. This would seem to be the path he followed, and his turning inward would have consequences in the formation of his self-image.

Kissinger was to learn many lessons in Fürth that he would carry with him the rest of his life. He was to discover what it meant to be powerless, to be out of control of one's life, to see his heroes standing helpless, overtaken by events. As Kissinger moved out into the world, he would confront situations that would stir memories, perhaps unconscious, of the time spent in Fürth. As he faced those situations he would often respond as he had learned to respond in the past. And, as he began to form his world view in more explicit terms, he would bring his past with him to be incorporated into his vision. At times, the responses that were adequate for the past would carry him through the present difficulty. But just as often the old ghosts would come back to haunt him—the insecurities, the fear of not being accepted—and his response, both for himself and, as special assistant to the president, for the nation, would confound his difficulties. It was in Fürth that Kissinger experienced the tragedy which he feels has given him an understanding of the world different from other Americans who, having "never suffered disaster, find it difficult to comprehend a policy conducted with a premonition of catastrophe" (Kissinger, 1957a:83).

The Search for a Hero

When Heinz became Henry in New York, it would be some time before he was comfortable with his new identity—the symbol of which was his name change. The move to New York would not substantially change his condition. His father still would find making a living extremely difficult, his mother would become the family's primary financial support, and, most of all, Henry would still be different from the majority. As in Fürth, there would be other refugees who shared his differentness, but to the majority he was still unacceptable, and this feeling would continue to activate his earlier depressive anxieties.

The most immediate symbol of his differentness was his accent. "I was terribly self-conscious about it [his accent]," he says, "I finally lost my self-consciousness over it, I'd say about 1957 or so" (Collier, 1971:105). The date to which he attributes his loss of self-consciousness is by no means arbitrary. It was in 1957 that Kissinger was to be finally accepted. This was the year that the public recognized Kissinger's worth, for his book *Nuclear Weapons and Foreign Policy* was published and stayed on the best seller lists for fourteen weeks. However, his acceptance was not total, particularly in the intellectual world. (Landau, 1972:75–77). And Kissinger's fear that he would not be accepted stayed with him. It is still one reason that until the last year of the first Nixon administration he did not allow his heavily accented voice to be recorded in most news conferences.

Kissinger's former chief of staff, Alexander Haig, has remarked that Kissinger "is not always sure he'll be accepted. He doesn't really believe anybody likes him" (Kraft, 1971). It is this trait that is the most prevalent vestige of his life in Fürth and the early days in New York. His uncertainty is what led some of his colleagues at Harvard to characterize him as a "damp-handed" professor. And it was this uncertainty about his self that led Kissinger to turn inward and retreat into the seeming safety of his inner world. If he never confronted other people, then the world he had maintained within himself would not be disrupted.

Kissinger never really gave anyone the chance to reject him. After he left Germany, he placed himself in a sort of exile that was not simply political. As before, the manner with which he dealt with the threatening environment of New York "was to go deep in his shell. From 1939–43 when he was going to George Washington High School in New York, Kissinger seems to have made no friends—hence the survival of the German accent" (Kraft, 1971). Thus his fear of being unacceptable inadvertently insured that the mark of his difference would not leave him. Perhaps on one level Kissinger was afraid of being swallowed up by the majority. In that case his retreat might be an attempt to maintain what few vestiges of his self he still retained.

As was mentioned, when the Kissinger family left Germany for New York, young Henry's position in the world was not fundamentally changed. True, there was no longer an imminent fear of death, but Kissinger was still the outsider, still in his own mind unacceptable because of his differentness. For the youth, such a cultural position can be just as threatening to the psyche as the political persecutions in Germany were to the person. So in a strict sense, Kissinger was right in saying that the political persecutions of his youth were not what control his life. But the implication that there are no answers to Kissinger's adult life to be found in his youth is utterly wrong. Many of the cultural obstacles to social acceptance that Kissinger found in Germany he would also find in America.

His years in New York passed without any great crisis or turning point. During his days at George Washington High School he worked after school in a shaving brush company squeezing acid out of the brush bristles. After awhile he was promoted to delivery boy. For the most part Henry remained uninvolved with others and withdrawn.

Accompanying Kissinger's tendency to withdraw into himself was a tendency to avoid confrontation with others. He recalls that "if he was walking down the street in New York and saw a group of boys approaching the other way, he would cross to the opposite sidewalk" (Kraft, 1971). This may have been an appropriate response given his experience in Fürth, but nowhere do we have evidence of Kissinger testing his courage and walking through the crowd. Nowhere do we see his willingness to "contemplate the abyss . . . as a challenge to be overcome—or to perish in the process," a position which he later advocated.

This tendency to retreat in the face of confrontation, however, is a trait that on an intellectual level Kissinger dislikes strenuously. Behind his severest criticisms of historical figures (and one of the major criticisms of the Kennedy administration) lay his abhorrence of a "wait and see" attitude or of a policy that avoided confrontation. For example, in *The Necessity for Choice*, Kissinger (1961a:8) argues: "History for Communism is an incentive for action, a guarantee of the meaningfulness of sacrifice. The West, on the other hand, has a tendency to use evolutionary theory as a bromide. Waiting for history to do its work for it, it stands in danger of being engulfed by the currents of our time." Failing to act in the face of the historical imperative is the major sin in Kissinger's international catechism.

Like many of Kissinger's likes and dislikes, this particular idiosyncrasy also has its roots in Fürth. While Kissinger's father was a respected man in his community, he was not a forceful man. He was the "gentle and soft-hearted" man whom Kissinger has described as "a man of great goodness in a world where goodness had no meaning" (Kraft, 1971). In other words, his father was a man whose qualities were irrelevant in the real world. "His father was stripped of his post and humiliated . . . he had been broken in spirit" (Kraft, 1971). "In Manhattan, of course, his erudition was irrelevant and he had to fall back on drearily unskilled clerical work" (Beloff, 1969). Louis Kissinger was not a man who would, or could, stand up against the wave of history. Rather, he would wait things out, wait to see what would happen. Like many other intellectuals "he waited hopefully for Germany to come back to its senses" (Beloff, 1969). Finally he was convinced that waiting was not the answer, but it was not through great deliberation that he came to this conclusion. It was forced upon him by his wife. It was Mrs. Kissinger who was responsible for getting the family out of Germany in 1938. She was the model of action. She made arrangements with relatives in England, took English lessons, and the family escaped from Germany.

Kissinger's mother, like many other refugee women, must have possessed a strong sense of self, for she adapted very well to her new role in America. She was not used to menial labor and in New York where the only work she could get was as a cook, she would have needed a strong sense of self to accept the change in status. The change was generally a difficult thing to handle for most of the German-Jewish refugee families who came to America, particularly for the men. It was difficult for men in the family to carry on as they had been able to do in Germany. This was the case in the Kissinger family. And "the change in status is something which the children [Henry and Wally] were conscious of" (author's interview with an old friend of Kissinger's, December 16, 1972). Although Louis Kissinger had been less of a forceful figure in the family than his wife while they were in Germany, he was still the primary provider and deserving of the children's respect. But in America even this position was undermined.

Henry Kissinger respected and loved his father, but wished that his father would act, that he would stand up and confront history. Kissinger in the midst of the "bad times" was looking for a hero, and he was disappointed that it was not his father.[4] A longtime personal acquaintance of Kissinger has said: "About the deepest things in one's life one can say nothing. Imagine the horror of life in Nazi Germany, imagine seeing a father whom one has loved and revered being made to give up a job, being humiliated. And all this when one is young and defenseless, and so impressionable" (quoted by Landau, 1972:15). Kissinger eventually found men both in history and among his contemporaries who preached the gospel of action and the necessity of confronting history, and it was to these men that he attached himself. But like his father, these men too would ultimately be irrelevant to their times.

Kissinger's search for a hero gave him a version of understanding that he could use in the days of turbulent uprisings by America's youth in the sixties and seventies. On several occasions he remarked that contemporary youth were looking for heroes. After a march in 1969, when Kissinger consulted with a few of the demonstrators, he commented to a reporter: "I can understand the anguish of the younger generation. They lack models, they have no heroes, they see no great purpose in the world" (*Look*, August 12, 1969). One must wonder if it is not Kissinger's own anguish in Fürth, when he needed a model of action, a hero to look to, and a purpose to live for, that provides the basis of his understanding. And in a more revealing statement, he stated (*Time*, December 22, 1969:23): "I find quite chilling the similarities between the revolutionary romanticism of some of our more radical students today and the young German intellectuals of the 1930's—and I don't mean the Nazi thugs but those idealistic students who were looking for commitment for its own sake. My primary feeling about our students is sadness over the conditions that produced them. They are looking for heroes—not brothers, but for fathers."

It is interesting that what Kissinger would like to see established in American foreign policy is a heroic vision. He would hope to provide the "great purpose in the world," or what he calls the administration's "unifying principle." What he finds distasteful is what he regards as an unheroic policy. For instance, in *Necessity for Choice* (1961a:290), he states:

> There was a time when the West believed that an overwhelming economic superiority guaranteed its triumph over Communism—without ever being able to describe just how. Though this attitude was fatuous, it is no less fatuous to draw so much comfort from the hope that when the Soviet Union equals our economic performance it will become as consumer-oriented and bland as we are. This is hardly a heroic attitude, nor one likely to appeal to a world where millions strive for a new sense of direction.

Just as youth need heroes and heroic visions, so do other nations. In order to solve the problems of the world we must rally round our hero.

It would be some time after coming to America that Kissinger's quest for a hero would be fulfilled, and once fulfilled his ambitions would also be significantly altered. Before he went into the army to his fateful meeting with Fritz Kraemer, Kissinger held the modest ambition of becoming an accountant. While at George Washington High School, Kissinger was a straight-A student and upon graduation he began to study accounting at night sessions at the City College of New York, following his father's adopted profession. But after a short time he was drafted in 1943 and would soon go off to war and the turning point of his life.

The most significant aspect of Kissinger's life in New York was his failure (or success) at not becoming assimilated into American culture. He would always be German. He always maintained a sense of regret at having had to flee from Hitler. "He was not among those refugees from Hitler Germany who could look back on their birthplace only with discomfort and bitterness; he was instead one of those refugees who regretted having to leave their country behind." And, "Kissinger would feel an overwhelming affinity for the greater historical and cultural tradition into which he had been born" (Landau, 1972:16). We are unable to know what the source of this affinity is, but evidence suggests that it was the influence of his family life. In his parent's apartment it was Germany. Since he never established real roots in America until much later, even his experience in New York was German. And when in time he became interested in intellectual pursuits, it was not American writers that he would read, but Europeans. Thus the fundamental pillars of his identity are German, but since he was no longer in Germany, his adjustment to his new environment was forestalled. He would find a means of entering the American world and acquiring some form of American identity through that great leveler and Americanizer, the U.S. Army. The army would place the stamp of America on the young unformed Kissinger.

A New Identity in the Army

In order to understand the significance of Kissinger's army experience, it will help first to look at the task facing him in his adolescence.[5] Adolescence is the period in an individual's life during which he gradually enters the adult world and takes on roles for which life in the family has prepared him. This period begins at about age twelve and can, under special conditions, continue on into the late twenties and early thirties. Emancipation from the family and the establishment of a place in the greater culture are the goals of adolescent development. It is the time when the abstract social order and the subjective, inner, familial world become integrated. All the preparation for adulthood which should take place during the earlier years is called upon as a guide to the individual's entrance into the greater society. "To enter history each generation of youth must find an identity consonant with its own childhood, and consonant with an ideological promise in the perceptible historical process" (Erikson, 1968:257). It is to be hoped there is a continuity between the childhood experience and the ideological and concrete structure of the greater culture. When this continuity is lacking, the normal development of adolescent identity formation is disrupted and in many cases prolonged. And it is just such a discontinuity, Howard Rome (1974) argued, that provides the sociological contribution which, along with the familial foundation, contributes to the depressive personality.

Erikson (1968:156) has described this period of prolonged adolescence in the following manner:

> The libido theory offers no adequate account of a second period of delay, namely, prolonged adolescence. Hence the sexually matured individual is more or less retarded in his psychosexual capacity for intimacy and in the psychosocial readiness for parenthood. This period can be viewed as a psycho-social moratorium during which the young adult through free role experimentation may find a niche in some section of his society, a niche which is firmly defined and yet seems to be uniquely made for him.

Kissinger has shown just the sort of reduced capacity for intimacy of which Erikson speaks above, and which is characteristic of the depressive personality. His inability to make friends, his problems with his first marriage, and his relations with women can be viewed partially as the consequence of the historical disruptions which played upon earlier feelings of disorder and rejection. Kissinger, unsure of who he was, was unable to give to others for fear of having nothing left for himself. Kissinger would not find his secure niche until he moved out of his familial world and found a new structure which would provide the necessary roles and role models with which he could identify and into which he could integrate himself.

The role experimentation of adolescence took on a completely different light in view of his new environment. The turning point came with his entrance into the United States Army. In the army Kissinger was able to become an actor, although in a circumscribed sense, rather than an object of history. While army life required submission to a hierarchical order, it also provided channels for action far beyond the scope Kissinger had experienced previously. This partial transformation from object to agent is particularly crucial, for accompanying it is a change in Kissinger's character. The balancing factors which form the dynamic tension of his personality were developed during this period.

The army performed three functions in this process: first, it provided a stable, structured, environmental order outside the family circle; second, it provided his encounter with Fritz Kraemer, the man who was his first heroic model; and third, it provided Kissinger with a means of retribution, an outlet for action against those who had manipulated his earlier life. As Beloff (1969) puts it: "It seems that the real transformation from the oppressed and teased foreigner Heinz, to the successfully and proudly integrated American Henry, came during his army service in World War II." It was in the army that Kissinger was able to effect a compromise between his conflicting identities. Kissinger gathered his forces and came to terms with himself in an environment where lines of authority were clearly drawn, where roles were explicitly understood, and where he could be reasonably sure of what to expect from day to day. In the army Kissinger could have faith in his environment and the men of authority to whom he could look for guidance.

One of these men would stand up above all and would come to play a role in Kissinger's life from then on. After he had been found to have an exceptionally high IQ, Kissinger was sent to a special training program composed of draftees the army was using as insurance, if they needed special skills later in the war. After six months, the program was dropped because of its "undemocratic" character, and Kissinger was transferred to the 84th Division stationed at Camp Clairborne, Louisiana. It was there that Kissinger met Private Fritz Kraemer, who was a refugee from Prussia where he had been trained as a lawyer and had earned two doctorates. Kramer, according to Landau (1972:18–19), was

> fiery and flamboyant and yet indisputably old-world, a capricious European adventurer. . . . Kraemer was a highly intelligent man, winning and captivating in his brilliance, yet his was an intelligence that could not be duplicated by schooling and academic training alone; it was an intelligence filled with eccentricity and high drama, an intelligence that bemoaned the limitations of impotent scholarly thinking and pulsated with the electricity of Kraemer's own life.

Kraemer had asked the commanding general of the 84th if he might be allowed to address the troops on the reasons the United States was fighting the war against Germany. The gospel Kraemer preached to the recruits was "that it was their duty to engage in combat as well as in intellectual exercise because after all, one needed soldiers as well as thinkers to fight a war" (Landau, 1972). This eccentric European had impressed Kissinger with his speech. Kissinger wrote him a note which read: "Dear Pvt. Kraemer: I heard you speak yesterday. This is how it should be done.

Can I help you somehow? Pvt. Kissinger" (Collier, 1971:107). Kraemer responded to the note asking for a meeting and so began their friendship.

Kraemer took Kissinger under his wing and used his influence to have him assigned as an interpreter in the 84th Division. And as the war progressed and the division moved to Europe, Kraemer would do much to advance the career of the young Kissinger. "When the division took the city of Krefeld, it found the city government had vanished along with the fleeing Nazi troops. Something had to be done to provide for the city's nearly 200,000 people. Kraemer suggested, in his matchlessly persuasive way, that since this young Kissinger spoke German, and had an extraordinary intelligence besides, he should be put in charge of reorganizing Krefeld's government" (Collier, 1971:109). As preview to a later government reorganization, Kissinger proved extremely efficient and capable. Within three days the government was functioning again.

In recognition of his ability, within a year Kissinger would be head of the district of Bergstrasse. "He had complete power to arrest anyone, for anything, lived in a castle, and when he was transferred, the people of Bergstrasse begged to keep him there" (Collier, 1971). In contrast to his last stay in Germany, he had certainly become recognized and valued by others.

After his duty in Bergstrasse, Kissinger, through Kraemer's intervention, was appointed to the faculty of the European Command Intelligence School as a twenty-two-year-old sergeant instructing officers up to the rank of lieutenant colonel. In the end the disparity of rank became too embarrassing and he was discharged from the army and hired for a short time at $10,000 a year. Kissinger had come a long way. From the shy, withdrawn refugee, he had come to be a man of means and influence—however limited these might be.

Kissinger had found the outlet for action against those who had manipulated his earlier life. While the army had provided a structured environment, it had also given him a more meaningful vehicle for resolving his inner confusion. The army had provided Kissinger with the means of his return to Germany as the triumphant liberator. It was in the army that Kissinger could prove his worth to those, including himself, who had doubted it.

The military was well suited to meet Kissinger's needs. As Erikson (1968:184) has said, the army is: "one of the social institutions which undertake to channel as they encourage initiative and to provide atonement as they appease guilt." The army, then, for Kissinger was on one level a means of appeasing his own guilt at blaming his father for not acting against Hitler. By his own role in the occupation, he could give to his father's life some relevance since his father sired a son who was part of the group of men united together against the wave of history. In effect, Kissinger completed the life which his father had left unfinished. Kissinger was able to submit to the authority of an ordered life as a compromise "toward sanctioned ways of action," a compromise which worked as support for him on both sides. Kissinger found in the army the symbols that would serve to consolidate his earlier inner conflicts and channel these into useful and culturally accepted modes of expression.

It was also a means by which he could express inner hostility in a socially accepted manner. Given that repressed hostility is considered to be at the core of the depressive personality, the outlet for aggression provided by the army helped to unblock some of his inner tension, allowing the confident and competent Kissinger to emerge. Here is the source of the transition from the oppressed Heinz to the proud Henry.

Fritz Kraemer's contribution to this consolidation was not simply material advancement. He played a central role in Kissinger's cosmos of symbols. This flamboyant, eccentric German may have seemed a bit odd to the young draftees, but not to Kissinger. In the American desert Kissinger had found a German oasis which would quench his thirst for a link between his old and new worlds. But this oasis was part mirage. Kraemer, like Kissinger's father, was an irrelevant man. He lived in an age that had passed him by. Kraemer, like Kissinger's later patron William Elliot, was a man who longed for the days of aristocracy. He held contempt for the present and its absurd worship of technical achievement and hence lack of appreciation for personal eminence. Thus his attitude was almost purely cynical. Kraemer remarked when speaking of Kissinger: "The medium brilliant can be overawed by their own or somebody else's brilliance. The truly brilliant will understand that brilliancy means nothing" (Landau, 1972:20–21). Without action, brilliance is impotent. Here was a man who saw the world as something to be manipulated. Principles are meaningless unless acted upon and brilliance irrelevant unless used. Thus here was a man who would represent to Kissinger what he would have liked his father to be—a man of action who was willing to stand up against the forces of history. The irony, of course, was that Kraemer too was an outsider, a man who really did not fit his times, and in a sense he too was irrelevant to the world in which he lived. But, most important, Kraemer represented the means by which Kissinger could consolidate his inner chaos, and rather than retreat from the world as he had done in the past, turn upon it and act.

Kraemer's importance in Kissinger's development is best shown by the role he played in the young man's decision to change his occupational goals. It can be assumed that it was the groundwork laid by his teacher-father that led to the ease with which Kraemer, the intellectual, became a father-figure. Kraemer's age, his German origin, and his intellectual background, combined with Kissinger's search for an actor, provided the basis for this identification and opened him to being molded, in some degree, by Kraemer's philosophy. "What Kraemer evoked in Kissinger himself was important in shaping the younger man's future: a profound interest in learning and in the intellectual process, and an almost obsessive desire to grasp the roots of man's historical experience. . . . The constant company of a man like Kraemer accentuated something far more important: the *impulse* to learn" (Landau, 1972: 20). And so rather than becoming an accountant, Kissinger decided to be an intellectual.

What must have been a turning point was an exchange that Kissinger recalled some time later. Soon after Kraemer's speech to the troops, Kissinger recalls: "He told me I had a good political mind. It was a thought that had never occurred to me" (Shaw, 1972). Suddenly somebody of short acquaintance says point blank that he was "unbelievably gifted" (which were the words according to Kraemer) and it was a thought that had never occurred to him. It would not be too farfetched to say that this exchange marked the beginning of the transition from the inward-turning Heinz to the outward-turning Henry. Kissinger had embarked on the road to what would become his adult identity.

Kissinger at Harvard

> The relationship between a woman and a man of my type is unavoid-
> ably very complex. One must be cautious. Oh, how hard it is for me to
> explain these things.
>
> Henry Kissinger in the *New
> Republic*, December 16, 1972

Carrying out his decision to follow an intellectual career, Kissinger won a New York state scholarship and was admitted to Harvard. He left his $10,000-a-year job and went to Harvard in September 1946. Going to Harvard was a major turning point in Kissinger's own expectations. He consciously saw it as a real chance to do something with his life. "It was a raising of expectations and he viewed Harvard as *the* big decision in terms of family, friends, and army experience."[6] Kissinger would go to Harvard thinking of himself as a G.I. Bill man who might not otherwise have been able to go if it were not for the army.

Kissinger entered Harvard then, after having just experienced both the security of an ordered environment and the horror of the European holocaust. For the first time a sense of an integrated self seems to have come to Kissinger, even though there was still much doubt about his past. Yet there was quiet. For the time the turbulence and fear of the preceding years had subsided and calm had taken its place, but a calm that had a mushroom cloud hanging over it. The years spent studying at Harvard were years of reflection, a time when Kissinger was able to try to make sense of what lay behind.

The most significant personal event of Kissinger's undergraduate years was his marriage. After a seven-year courtship, Kissinger married Ann Fleischer on February 6, 1949. He and Ann had met while Henry was working his way through high school at the shaving brush factory. Ann was also of a refugee family and shared the same sort of cultural background, although she was not particularly motivated to excel academically. "The men who knew her as boys invariably describe Ann Fleischer as 'reserved' or even 'introverted'" (*New York Post*, 1974). While they were at Harvard she worked in a furniture store and seemed to enjoy being out of the academic world and doing something different. While Ann has been said to have developed toward a more independent personality since the divorce, at the time she was, as a very close friend described her: "gentle and dependent. She has a slight taste for martyrdom, but she is generous and warm-hearted, giving and fearful. She needs to serve and this need is accompanied by dependence." [7] In other words, Ann, in marked contrast to Kissinger's mother, was hardly the type of person who would dominate a relationship.

Ann did not share Kissinger's intellectual world with him, and if she took an interest in what he was doing it was largely because it was Henry that was doing it. There was a clear boundary between their private life and Kissinger's professional life. This boundary was even maintained to the extent of Kissinger later building a study over his garage which had a separate entrance. "Ann was proud of the study, but one Cambridge friend recalls a day when Kissinger 'invited me up there to see it, and have a drink, and Ann came up to sit with us. He told her to get out—he didn't want her there'" (*New York Post*, 1974).

They led a very traditional life in their domestic arrangements. Ann was loyal and serving and Kissinger expected her to perform her wifely duties. Later on in the marriage when Kissinger was writing a book on nuclear weapons for the Council on Foreign Relations, she was still expected not to interfere with his work. As one commentator described the situation: "He worked with single-minded concentration on it [*Nuclear Weapons and Foreign Policy*]. He lived with his wife in a New York apartment, and when he came home at night he forbade her to talk to him because it would interrupt his train of thought" (Collier, 1971). From what is said about their relationship by friends, Kissinger was hard on her and was not particularly supportive or understanding. He was not at all patient with her and would tell her in no uncertain terms when he was irritated. "Henry didn't think Ann was intelligent and he had a tendency to be cruel to her in public. Knowing that she was sensitive he would deride her and criticize her telling her that what she was talking about was absurd and unimportant" (author's interview with a friend of the Kissingers, December 16, 1972).

The main problem was that Kissinger would have liked her to have been more independent, but at the same time he expected her to maintain a subordinate position in the relationship. Ann herself contributed to the problem in that "she bent excessively and this did not enlarge Henry's respect for her or his patience." The marriage seems to have occurred largely because it was expected; after such a long time the courtship was naturally expected to end in marriage. "Ann certainly expected it for some time and this was the major quality about it. Henry doesn't like to commit himself in many ways. She needed commitment and Henry stood away from it" (author's interview, 1972).

It was the kind of marriage where the man gets involved with his profession and leaves the wife behind. They were basically not compatible and finally they grew apart. The break was not immediate and clear-cut. They would spend weekends together, on the surface because of the children, but also because he too found it hard to let go.

Kissinger's life in Germany and later in New York must have made an important contribution to his characteristic insecurity and mistrust because it was an environment that was unpredictable and out of control. The corollary of the renunciation of relationships with others is the need to be in control. An environment that is out of control can cause an individual to retreat into the boundaries of the self. Kissinger's withdrawal and problems with interpersonal relationships constitute the psychological foundation of the fundamental axiom of his political philosophy: "if it [society] cannot master the environment it will become its victim" (Kissinger, 1961a:303). The characteristics of mistrust and insecurity can still be seen as definitive of his relationships throughout his years at Harvard and even after his student years.

Not a great deal is known about Kissinger's years at Harvard; however, there are several significant sources of data. The first is Kissinger's undergraduate work. Kissinger majored in philosophy as an undergraduate and was particularly interested in Spengler. One of Kissinger's colleagues, Stanley Hoffmann, made the remark that Henry "walked, in a way, with the ghost of Spengler at his side." But his concern with Spengler was not a wholehearted embrace. As Landau (1972:21) points out: "The unending decay and death of successive civilizations that seemed inevitable to Spengler was a notion that the young Kissinger rejected. His experience in Germany had taught him that one must never accept inevitability, and that one must do everything in one's power to wrest balance and order from chaos and destruction." Landau commits a fundamental error in his analysis of Kissinger's philosophy in the above observation. Kissinger did indeed accept the inevitable decline of civilization. What was important to Kissinger was that the change in the system is ordered. Kissinger's acceptance of the inevitable is predicated on the belief that one must do everything possible to slow or contain its progress. But Landau is correct in pointing to the influence of Kissinger's past on his academic pursuits. It can hardly be a coincidence that Spengler, the philosopher of gloom, found a place in the heart and mind of the serious and gloomy Harvard undergraduate. As a youth, Kissinger had witnessed one of western civilization's most agonizing moments. It would only be natural for the young man to seize upon Spengler's concept of decline as one of the factors in his ideological simplification of the universe. In Spengler he found one of the building blocks for the "identity consonant with his own childhood" of which Erikson speaks.

Kissinger wrote his undergraduate thesis on Spengler, Toynbee, and Kant. The quiet, withdrawn Kissinger of Fürth and New York had found enough words by the time he got through his undergraduate work to write a 350-page paper that resulted in the school setting a limit of 150 pages on all undergraduate theses in the future. In his thesis, "The Meaning of History," Kissinger (1951) criticized Kant and Spengler because their philosophies left little room for human action and will. According to Spengler and Kant, civilization was moving toward its predestined end and nothing man could do would stop it. Kissinger's past experience had shown him the necessity for human choice and action. His father's passivity, Kraemer's gospel of action, and Professor William Yandell Elliot's preaching of that gospel kept Kissinger searching for the fit between his past and his future.

Kissinger earned his B.A. in three years, graduating summa cum laude in 1950, and went on to graduate school in the government department. In those days, if one had been a summa as an undergraduate, he was not required to take the oral examinations for higher degrees. So this set Kissinger apart from the other students both in his own perception of himself and in the perception of him by his fellow students. But Kissinger seems to have been able to use this separateness as an integrating factor, a source of the pride he developed for acting alone; while the others were studying for their orals, Kissinger was working with professors on their books. The others looked upon him as something special. He was probably the most talked-about graduate student at the time, although scarcely the best liked. "People saw him as arrogant and argumentative. He was moody, unhappy and sour. It was a cause to remark if Henry was in a good mood. He was very sharp with people, and stubborn" (author's interview, 1972).

A second source of data concerning Kissinger's years at Harvard concerns his relationship with his professors and fellow students. William Yandell Elliot, affectionately and sometimes not so affectionately known as "Wild Bill," was a professor of government at Harvard. He had been an all-American tackle at Vanderbilt and a Rhodes scholar, and had written a book in 1924 describing the forces that would result in fascism in the next ten years. From those pillars of success Elliot never rose much higher. Although he was considered to be one of the powers of the Harvard faculty, he was always more than a little annoying to his students and fellow faculty members. Elliot, who came from a small town in Tennessee, was known for throwing students who disagreed with him out of his office. He was a man who, like Kraemer, held disdain for the common man. As Landau (1972:40–41) has noted, Elliot "had attended Balliol College, Oxford, at a time in the 1920's long after the place had been over-taken by the spirit of Benjamin Jowett, the notion that societies trained their elites—and senior scholars prepared their young disciples—for positions in government and other public service. . . . It was this apparition, this tattered image of a by-gone age that Kissinger latched onto while a Harvard undergraduate, and the experience would be lasting."

There is a marked similarity in the two men who played such an important role in Kissinger's young adulthood. Elliot, like Kraemer, was much older than Kissinger. Both men had a flair and a style which were unmistakable. Their style was, to Kissinger, a mark of confidence backed by a tradition of intellectual order. Both longed for a more aristocratic age and possessed fiery and flamboyant personalities which made them stand out among their seemingly more placid contemporaries. Both attempted and succeeded with varying degrees to put their own personal stamp on Kissinger's thinking. Elliot was looking for a disciple and Kissinger was looking for someone to follow, and it was Elliot who began to build the contacts Kissinger needed as he climbed his ladder of success.

Kissinger looked to older men for his close relationships with but a few notable exceptions. One of the few close friends of his peer group at Harvard was Klaus Epstein, and Kissinger spent a great deal of time together with him discussing history and international politics. Epstein read and criticized every page of Kissinger's thesis on Metternich and it is said that he influenced Kissinger's view of history. Even at this early date Kissinger had begun to be identified by his classmates as the person who was always talking about the balance of power. One of his classmates has commented: "Balance was seen as Henry's thing. He was preoccupied with balance and order" (author's interview, 1972).

In the debates of the time about the Soviet Union, nuclear weapons, and the partition of Europe, Kissinger always took a hard line and had a tendency to couch his arguments in black and white terms. He would often become the center of a discussion at parties but generally it was a discussion between himself and one other person with several others listening in but not participating. Kissinger gravitated toward pontification in such situations. He was much more comfortable in a "discussion that was not personal but dealt rather with political, historical or other academic questions. He was not spontaneous, flexible or playful" (author's interview, 1972). His discussions thus reflected another typical depressive characteristic. His pontification in discussions and also in his writing are like the expressions of depressive neurotics who "are full of tabloid wisdom and express their cliche statements as if they were great and original ideas" (Wolman, 1972:247). Thus Kissinger tended to be heavy-handed in his social discourse and uncomfortable dealing with peers on a personal basis.

Kissinger was one of the few students who got along with both of the poles of power in the government department—Carl Friedrich and Elliot. Most students didn't get along with both men but Kissinger had a good rapport with the two. They were awesome figures in the department and Kissinger "always seemed to like powerful personalities who bring together not only the academic world, but the world of the present and participation in that world" (author's interview, 1972). Kissinger at one point was so close to Friedrich that he was identified as *his* professor. Kissinger was struck by both men but did not seem to be overpowered by them. "He was not a 'little Elliot' or a 'little Friedrich.'" It was Elliot with whom he maintained the most lasting friendship, and Elliot was the most influential of the two in Kissinger's own thinking.

A third source of information concerning Kissinger's development while at Harvard is his graduate work. It was in the two years after he finished his undergraduate work that Kissinger found the philosophical framework that would unite history's progress and man's will. He fell upon Hegel's dialectic of history to fill the gap in his personal philosophy. Hegel's philosophy accepted the progress of history but left the end of its path open to speculation. There was room in the dialectic for heroic human action. Man's will could steer civilization away from one obstacle and another as man careened down the hill of history. History's final destination is left open for great men to exert their will. Hegel's philosophy of the rare individual would fit nicely Elliot's Oxford training. Under Elliot, Kissinger would be trained for the role Hegel postulated.

Kissinger continued to wrestle with the meaning of history and for his master's paper he dropped Kant and substituted Hegel, who took his place beside Spengler and Toynbee in Kissinger's philosophical cabinet. Kissinger got his master's degree in 1952 and under Elliot's tutelage would go on to his Ph.D. degree in 1954 as well as to winning the Sumner Prize for outstanding work on the prevention of war.

Kissinger's doctoral dissertation, later published under the title *A World Restored*, was a study of the Congress of Vienna. Significantly, Kissinger dedicated the book to his Harvard mentor, William Elliot. In the book, Kissinger traced the role of one of Hegel's rare historical individuals who transform an era, Klemens von Metternich. In many respects, *A World Restored* stands as a testament to Kissinger's past and to his philosophy, and serves as his blueprint for future international relations.

The Road to Washington

> The intricate web of destiny in which we, both as individuals and as nations, are called upon to function, has caused most of us to become obsessed with personal and national insecurity.
>
> Howard Rome, "Depressive Illness:
> Its Socio-Psychiatric Implications"

When Kissinger received his Ph.D. it was assumed by most, including Kissinger himself, that he would naturally be offered a teaching job at Harvard.

But although his name was seriously considered and well supported, the decision went against him. Details of the argument are of course academic secrets, but according to one of the members of the faculty at that time, he was not only judged personally a difficult colleague (he had the reputation of being much nicer to his superiors than to his subordinates) but still more important the professors suspected that he was less interested in the university or in teaching and research than in making a career in public service (Beloff, 1969:81).

There was another offer at the same time from the University of Chicago and still another from the University of Pennsylvania. Chicago did not generally make offers that they thought would be turned down. According to one reporter (Beloff, 1969), Kissinger had led the University of Chicago to think that he would accept their offer. Even though Chicago offered him a higher position, when Harvard came up with a part-time teaching position in the Department of Government, he accepted the Cambridge offer. His reason for taking the lesser position was based primarily upon the fact that he would be closer to Washington and to his personal contacts.

During his year as an instructor, Elliot and Kissinger founded and directed the International Seminar, which would later serve Kissinger as a major source of international contacts. Again with Elliot's help, Kissinger founded and edited *Confluence*, a scholarly journal in which policy issues were debated.

Then came Kissinger's biggest break up until then. In the winter of 1954–55 a job as the managing editor of *Foreign Affairs* opened. The editor, Hamilton Fish Armstrong, solicited some of his friends at Harvard to see if they had any young prospects for the job. Arthur Schlesinger, Jr., suggested Kissinger, and Armstrong asked Kissinger to come to New York for an interview. Armstrong didn't give him the job but thought Kissinger might be useful in another capacity. The Council on Foreign Relations had been conducting a study group on the question of nuclear weapons and their effect on foreign policy. Armstrong was associated with the group and suggested that Kissinger apply for a spot as the writer of the study group's findings. Kissinger sent in his credentials, including recommendations from Elliot, Schlesinger, and McGeorge Bundy. He was offered the job and accepted. The study group had been meeting for some time to discuss problems of nuclear strategy and by the time Kissinger joined the group, most of the work had been done. What the group needed was a fresh mind to put its work together into a book. The result was Kissinger's best-selling *Nuclear Weapons and Foreign Policy*.

The book served as the cornerstone of Kissinger's popular reputation in the academic world, and for awhile his reputation went beyond the confines of ivy-covered buildings. The book stayed on the best-seller lists for fourteen weeks. What his personal contacts could not do for him, the popularity of his book could. Indeed, Richard Nixon, then vice president, was photographed with a copy of Kissinger's book. His later academic books would never attain the popularity that *Nuclear Weapons and Foreign Policy* did. But the book, while hailed for its originality, was an editing job more than anything else. Of course, Kissinger put his own stamp on the ideas and contributed a few of his own, but here we have an example of Kissinger's greatest asset—his ability to present and order arguments. Jeane Davis, secretary for the NSC staff under Kissinger, told me that the key to Kissinger's relationship with Nixon was Kissinger's ability to organize and present the options to the president in a clear and coherent manner. Ms. Davis has noted: "Nixon is a lawyer and he is influenced by hard factual material. At certain points the president's instinct might point in one direction, but when he sees the options objectively laid out, he's enough of a lawyer to be influenced" (author's interview, May 10, 1972). Kissinger's ability to synthesize arguments, as demonstrated in *Nuclear Weapons and Foreign Policy*, was a key factor in terms of his ability to influence presidential decisions.

The central thrust of *Nuclear Weapons and Foreign Policy* is a criticism of the defense establishment for not creating a place in its planning operations for anything other than full-scale nuclear war. The book offers an alternative approach in which nuclear weapons could be used in a limited war. Kissinger argues that through diplomacy the U.S. would be able to make its intentions not to engage in full-scale war known to the other side. Presumably this knowledge would insure that the enemy would not respond out of proportion to the threat. Thus there is a great reliance upon persuasion in his formula. He argues that if the opponent is adequately informed, then his response will be appropriate should limited nuclear war "become necessary."

Kissinger came to repudiate in part the position taken in *Nuclear Weapons*. In an article entitled "Limited War: Conventional or Nuclear? A Reappraisal," Kissinger (1960c: 143) stated: "Several developments have caused a shift in my view about the relative emphasis to be given conventional forces as against nuclear forces. These are (1) the disagreement within our military establishment and within the alliance about the nature of limited war; (2) the growth of the Soviet nuclear stockpile and the increased significance of long-range missiles; (3) the impact of arms-control negotiations." As can be seen, the reasons he gives for his change of position are purely tactical. Because the practical obstacles in front of the type of coordination necessary are too great, it would be unadvisable to attempt limited nuclear war. There is no reason to believe that if the problems of control could be overcome that

Kissinger would have been unwilling to use tactical nuclear weapons. For instance, if somehow Kissinger could have gained the assurance of China and the Soviet Union that they would not view the use of nuclear weapons in Vietnam as a threat to their national security then Kissinger would have been perfectly willing to use such weapons. Indeed something approaching this is what occurred in the mining of Haiphong harbor. The possibility that a foreign ship would be sunk in such an action carried with it as many of the fears of confrontation with the big powers as had the use of nuclear weapons in the past.

In 1956 while Kissinger was working with the Council on Foreign Relations and writing *Nuclear Weapons and Foreign Policy*, the Rockefeller Brothers' Fund had organized a series of panels to discuss foreign and domestic policy. Kissinger became the director of these panels and was responsible for writing their reports. "The national security panel report of the Rockefeller Brothers' Fund, billed as 'the answer to Sputnik,' became a public document of enormous prestige and influence; Kissinger was its author" (Landau, 1972:55). The paper followed fairly closely the lines of *Nuclear Weapons*, arguing for a strategy based upon limited war and the use of tactical nuclear weapons (see Kissinger, 1958c).

However, it was not the paper that was the most important product of his association with the fund. It was during this period that Kissinger began to cement his ties to Nelson Rockefeller. Kissinger had met Rockefeller in the early fifties at a military conference in Quantico, Virginia. They continued to keep in contact, but primarily on a business basis. Kissinger was an expert and Rockefeller needed advisors. And as Kissinger's reputation began to grow, Rockefeller would call upon Kissinger more and more as an advisor.

Both Rockefeller and Kissinger shared a concern for the establishment of order and the necessity to stand up against those forces which would disrupt that order. Once again we find Kissinger attaching himself to a man who was a staunch interventionist and who possessed a willingness to be tough. "Kissinger, like his hero Metternich, put his great talents at the service of a rickety and anachronistic order. 'The willingness to engage in nuclear war when necessary' said the Rockefeller report, 'is part of the price of our freedom.' This, the ferocious conventional wisdom of the Pentagon, runs like a leitmotiv throughout his work" (Stone, 1972a:22).

Like that theme, the type of men he associates with also have a certain similarity. "The rungs of Kissinger's ladder to success have a common characteristic. At each major step upward he has been the protege of men who believed in military strength, and, if necessary, war and who were obsessed with the postwar struggle for hegemony between the U.S. and the USSR, and fearful of the revolutionary tide in the poorer countries" (Stone, 1972b:14). In Rockefeller we see a man whose personal style was a toned-down version of Kraemer and Elliot but whose intellectual maxims fall into the same sort of willingness to confront the forces of history. By the time Kissinger began to associate with Rockefeller, his own ideas were fairly well established. He was ready to make a commitment to a man not so much because of the man's character, although this was still important, but because of the congruity between the man's ideas and his own. Twelve years later Kissinger would commit himself to the ideas of Nixon, a man for whom he had little personal respect. Perhaps because of his growing confidence in his own ability and ideas, Kissinger became able and willing to accept the challenge of trying to put his ideas into action even if the man who would make the final decision was not a man whom Kissinger particularly admired.

As a result of his connections, Kissinger was given a job as a consultant to the Kennedy administration, and it was then that he encountered the frustration of trying to do battle against the bureaucracy of the executive branch. He had extremely painful experiences while working for Kennedy. Kissinger's old colleague and friend, McGeorge Bundy, was angered by Kissinger's attempt to circumvent him to see the president directly. Bundy gave Kissinger the choice of becoming a full-time consultant or of going back to Harvard. Kissinger was not yet willing to be stuck at a low level of influence, so he stopped making the trip down to Washington.

There is another version of the Kennedy days which also throws light on Kissinger's personality. According to an article in *Newsweek* (December 22, 1969), " 'It was less Henry's views than his style which hurt him,' recalls a sympathetic colleague who served with him at the time, 'he simply wasn't light-footed enough for the Kennedy Circle.' " A story in *Time* (February 14, 1969) relates that Kissinger pursued influencing policy to the point that Kennedy himself was said to be a bit annoyed with the professor's insistence.

Ultimately, Kissinger would resort to submitting anonymous reports through a friend at the State Department in an attempt to have his views expressed. For the most part, however, Kissinger's association with the Kennedy administration was minimal. All told, Kissinger's service was less than eighteen months. "His departure was expedited after he took his wife, Ann, on a personal tour of India, Pakistan and Israel—identifying himself at each stop as a White House consultant, thus giving the trip an official imprimatur and annoying some Kennedy people" (*New York Post*, 1974). Again, both the self-inflated importance and the anonymous, unsolicited advice are basic behavior patterns of the depressive personality: "distortion of truth to please people to impress them, exaggeration . . . [and] the offering of unsolicited guidance," are the processes of compensation for depressive anxiety. Unfortunately, such characteristics often seem to be part of the necessary qualifications for political office.

Kissinger made several other forays into the executive arena before his assignment as special assistant for national security affairs. Johnson had begun looking for a way out of Vietnam when Kissinger mentioned to Averell Harriman that he had an informal channel to Ho Chi Minh through a French acquaintance. Johnson decided it might be helpful to relay some information on U.S. policy to Ho through Kissinger's informal contact. Kissinger was sent to Paris to open what would later be referred to as "backchannel" negotiations, but the talks seem to have had little effect. At any rate, Kissinger got a taste of the kind of secret negotiations he would carry on during the Nixon years.

A far more important association than his role in the Johnson administration was his role as an advisor to Rockefeller in the 1964 and 1968 campaigns. From the first association back in 1956, Kissinger would continue his relationship with Rockefeller. He maintained his position as head of the Rockefeller Brothers' Fund Special Studies Project, and while he published four more books elaborating and updating the basic principles established in *A World Restored*, he would also enjoy a close association with Rockefeller as he made his bid for power. It was as a result of his work for Rockefeller that Nixon once again became aware of the professor who wrote about nuclear weapons and foreign policy.

Kissinger's Depressive Personality

> Americans like the cowboy who leads the wagon train by riding ahead alone on his horse, the cowboy who rides all alone into the town, the village, with his horse and nothing else. Maybe even without a pistol, since he doesn't shoot. He acts, that's all, by being in the right place at the right time.
>
> Henry Kissinger, in Interview with History by Oriana Fallaci (1977:41)

Thanks to Freud, modern man has a greater appreciation for the seemingly lesser events of an individual's life. Often the most minor occurrences can be tied into a broader totality and can be seen as representative of fundamental aspects of the psychic structure. Slips of the tongue or pen and dreams are among the seemingly insignificant aspects of our lives that Freud brought to the forefront of psychological inquiry. There are two such seemingly minor incidents in Kissinger's relations with his colleagues that shed light on an evaluation of Kissinger's personality. While the two events are neither slips nor dreams, Freud's work should remind us that what seems insignificant is not necessarily meaningless. The first incident is related by Landau (1972:84–85):

> His initial clashes and rivalries in Cambridge were not nearly so tied to animosity as they were to his almost total degree of personal insecurity. One close colleague remembers an occasion on which he and Kissinger attended an academic conference outside Cambridge, but accidently saw little of each other during its course. The colleague returned home to find a long, impassioned note from Kissinger accusing him of failing to nod hello or otherwise offer greetings at certain times during the conference, and exclaiming that unless he could offer Kissinger some explanation for this conduct, their friendship would have come to an end. The colleague responded not with an apology, but with a straight forward explanation of why Kissinger's assertions were uncalled-for and somewhat silly, and Kissinger apologized for the outburst. Such episodes reinforced the feeling that Kissinger's occasional difficulty relating to his colleagues was not that he was personally indecent, . . . but that he was . . . a man who saw himself disliked or persecuted far more often than was the case.

The second encounter is of a similar character. This incident, once again, involves a fellow faculty member. Kissinger was at a conference with another Harvard professor with whom he had planned to have dinner in order to discuss some problems relating to the conference. When the friend suggested that they dine together in a hotel room so they could talk without interruption, Kissinger accused his colleague of not wanting to be seen in public with him (Kraft, 1971). The man pointed out how absurd the accusation was and they went on to have dinner in the room.

Kissinger's central fear in both of these incidents is that of rejection. His perception of both encounters was wholly out of proportion to what was called for by the occasions. It would appear that this anxiety has been a life-long characteristic and is what led to Haig's reference to Kissinger's "uncertainty" about being accepted. Both these incidents are clear evidence of Kissinger's lack of self-esteem. The clinical evidence seems to indicate that in a high percentage of cases these characteristics, fear of rejection and lack of self-esteem, point to a basic insecurity dating from infancy, with a corresponding reinforcement of this insecurity in social relations. The usual result is the constellation of characteristics which make up the depressive personality.

I have tried to show that the basic dynamics of Kissinger's personality generally fit the outlines of the depressive character. While the behavioral and social data are fairly clear, the familial data are less so. Certainly Kissinger's family experience provides the foundation upon which the broader culture placed its stamp. I postulated a feeling of rejection on Kissinger's part as a result of the arrival of his brother Walter. This was followed by the entrance of the "third son" who receives preferential treatment, and is allied with Walter, creating a familial situation of rivalry in which Kissinger perceived himself as the loser. His parents' ambivalence further contributed to the familial basis of his depressive anxiety.

In terms of behavior patterns, Kissinger's withdrawn nature, his lack of involvement with others, his treatment in Fürth and New York, his "moodiness" at Harvard, his treatment of his wife and women in general, his tendency to be solicitous to superiors and hostile to inferiors, his self-enhancing distortions in India, his unsolicited advice to Kennedy—all are further behavioral substantiation of my judgment of his personality as depressive.

Other characteristics not fully elaborated are the frequent humorous references on Kissinger's part to his "megalomania" and what others have described as his self-depreciating humor. Since "megalomania is a defense against feelings of inferiority" (Wolman, 1972:248), his humor would also seem to provide further substantiation of the analysis. Kissinger has also evidenced a tendency to overwork and overeat (once remarking that when he negotiates, he eats, and would probably gain 300 pounds in discussions over the Middle East). These again are characteristics of depressive anxiety. "People who are given to this kind of depression feel defeated, lack self-confidence, blame themselves, feel isolated and forsaken, have a pessimistic outlook on life . . . over-eat or under-eat, and dwell on past events" (Wolman, 1972:225). All of these are characteristic of Kissinger.

Even his success is part of the picture: "The dysmutual depressive tries to overcome his low self-esteem in many ways, one of which is through extreme ambition. Some dysmutuals, in milder stages of the disorder, rather than escape into manic moods, try to compensate for their feelings of inferiority by excessive work, long working hours, and an over-all drive for supremacy" (Wolman, 1972:244). These characteristics are evidenced in Kissinger's behavior in the first Nixon administration when he literally exhausted many aides on the National Security Council with his long and intensive hours.

His emotional threat to resign in June 1974 is again a consequence of his fear of rejection. The typical depressive is "exceedingly sensitive and vulnerable to criticism" (Wolman, 1972:225). His public threat to resign came as a result of the criticism of his role in the taping of his subordinates on the National Security Council staff (Kissinger, 1982:1111–23). This was not the first, only the most dramatic, threat of resignation. Aside from much talk about resignation during the Vietnam period, when Kissinger was on Rockefeller's staff, whenever Kissinger's access was blocked by veteran staff members, his "*habitual* solution was to march into Rocky's office and 'resign'" (*New York Post*, 1974).

An aspect of this constellation of behavior that has had significant ramifications for American foreign policy is the tendency toward personal isolation. As the opening quotation above indicates, Kissinger's "acting alone" has been elevated to the highest significance in his conduct of policy. This is in marked contrast to his fear of being unacceptable, rejected, and alone. What was a private experience and fear of being alone in his youth has been transformed into a value in his intellectual formulations. As in his "cowboy" statement, it is the actor standing alone who is supposedly loved by the Americans, and, as Kissinger argues, the policy maker must be willing to stand alone if his accomplishments are to be of value. Thus it is the ability to stand alone and face the abyss which is the primary value in Kissinger's estimation of a policy maker's greatness. What we must assume was the beginning of Kissinger's reformulation of being alone into a virtue was his relation to Kraemer and later being singled out from among his student contemporaries at Harvard as an exceptional individual. Rather than being isolated as one of the unacceptables, Kissinger was set apart and above the other students at Harvard. He must have experienced some of his being separate and different as being better and in a sense greater than his contemporaries. And this also fits the depressive's compensating feeling that he is unique and superior. It must have been then that the negative aspects of being alone—the separateness, unacceptability, and detachment—were counterbalanced by the attributes and advantages of being singled out. Although being alone, as Kissinger himself states, has always been a part of his style, it has not always carried with it the positive connotations he now attaches to it. One distinctive advantage of being alone, as Kissinger may have discovered in his youthful withdrawal, is that being alone, one cannot easily be rejected.

What Kissinger has done is to transform the anxiety-producing condition of being alone in the everyday world into a positive requisite in the world of statesmanship. What Kissinger saw as Metternich's and Bismarck's most important characteristic has become the significant aspect of his image in the American public. Although not a prince, but a cowboy, Kissinger sees himself as the loner, a hero standing before the irresistible forces of history.

Kissinger was motivated to take up his lonely profession in part by the fact that the solitude of the statesman is seen as noble. First Kissinger experienced the pain of isolation which was then followed by the pleasure of singular achievement at Harvard. He followed upon this theme by writing about the profession of statesmen, characterizing it as a lonely undertaking, and then going on himself to take up the noble occupation.

Consonant with his self-image as the loner, Kissinger is not the type to seek out the advice of others. And if he does attempt to gather opinions from others, as his early reputation in the NSC seems to indicate, it is largely for appearance's sake. This same process was replicated in the conduct of relations between the U.S. and its allies. The complaints in Europe, Japan, Taiwan, and South Vietnam over neglect of superficial consultation were not unlike Kissinger's personal relationships. Remembering that one reason given for not initially granting him a position at Harvard was the judgment that he tended to be solicitous toward his superiors and hostile to his inferiors, we can begin to appreciate the failings of his personal diplomacy. Kissinger's personal experience in office had a major effect upon our national experience. His inability to empathize with others, his compulsion to face risk in order to prove his worth, and his tendency to act alone have in fact become significant components of American public policy.

A World and Self Restored

> The statesman is . . . like one of the heroes in classical drama who has had a vision of the future but who cannot transmit it directly to his fellow men and who cannot validate its "truth".

> Henry Kissinger,
> *A World Restored*

In this part of the essay I will attempt to draw upon the themes developed in the previous section in order to offer some partial explanations of American foreign policy, primarily in the first Nixon administration. I emphasize "partial" because I will look at a limited number of issues, focusing on one dimension—personality. What follows is a look at Kissinger's writings, particularly *A World Restored*, in relation to the style of Kissinger's operation, the handling of the Vietnam peace negotiations, the invasion of Cambodia, and the mining of Haiphong harbor.

In *A World Restored*, we see Kissinger first flexing his intellectual muscle and we can trace the development of his later philosophy from the foundations established there. Indeed it could be argued that there has been no basic change in Kissinger's outlook from then until now. The same principles he culled from his study of Metternich have been systematically applied to the modern world. The China policy, the Pakistan debacle, the "State of the World Reports"—all reflect the principle of balance, which Kissinger first elaborated in *A World Restored*.

In addition to the importance of the book for public policy and for foreign affairs, the book is a personal testament of Kissinger's own life. He does not disguise the true focus of his study. He states: "Napoleon is not exactly equivalent to Hitler or

Castlereagh to Churchill. Whatever relationship exists depends not on a precise correspondence, but on a similarity of the problems confronted. And the conclusions will reflect—just as with any other generalization—the ability to abstract from the uniqueness of individual experience" (Kissinger, 1957a:331). While Kissinger did not intend "the uniqueness of individual experience" to refer to himself, the evidence indicates that the lessons of his youth were incorporated in his understanding of history.

Reading through *A World Restored*, one cannot help but be struck by the parallels between Europe after Napoleon and the world after Hitler. Kissinger makes a conscious attempt throughout the book to lead the reader to make comparisons between the two historical periods. And if the reader failed to see the similarities, the final chapter reveals explicitly the reason for the author's concern for the period. Kissinger went back into history to discover the connections of the past with the present. It is an attempt to place in perspective the chaos from which the world had just escaped and which had touched the personal lives of so many like Kissinger himself. The book is both an ordering into a logical continuum of the forces of history and an attempt to identify the problems which those forces will generate—the problems which must be confronted by an America emerging onto the world stage after World War II. In addition, Kissinger's personal life merges with the task he sees facing the United States. He must resolve the inner chaos and uncertainty of his earlier life in order to achieve a maturity capable of sustaining himself as he assumes his adult role and moves out into the world. *A World Restored* is the testament of a youth's struggle to achieve an identity that the world until then had denied him. The work describes not simply a world restored, but a self restored.

One of the more interesting aspects of *A World Restored* can only be appreciated by looking back from the point of view of Kissinger's own period of statesmanship. It is difficult to know to what extent symbols become models of action or are simply appropriate to developments which precede the attachment. Certainly both are a function of symbolic representation; but whatever the case, much can be learned of predictive value by looking at a political actor's model of action.

The similarity that Kissinger paints between the picture of Metternich and the image of Kissinger as statesman is astounding. A comparison of the two reveals the pervasiveness of the identification. One of the more remarkable aspects of the public Henry Kissinger was his newsworthiness: not just his value as a headliner for the *Washington Post*, but his ability to capture the covers of Hollywood's gossip magazines. Of course, the secrecy in which he enveloped himself was a primary source of intrigue, but much of the news value lay more in his playboy image—an image that somehow fit like a suit two sizes too large. There was something of a contrived air about this image, and it would be impossible to place all the blame on overzealous journalists. Few other public officials had date books like Henry Kissinger. When questioned about his proclivity for dating Hollywood starlets and beautiful models, Kissinger tried to disclaim any personal responsibility. He says that the young ladies were simply attracted to his position and not to his person: "I find the playboy image very amusing" (Shaw, 1972). "I am their celebrity of the hour, the new man in town. I don't kid myself" (*Chicago Sun Times*, October 24, 1971). Aside from the lack of self-value which lies beneath the statement, it is curious that he bothered carrying out the ruse. Indeed, he enjoyed his role, and it proved useful in the past as during the secret Paris negotiations, when he could use his dates as a front. However, it appears more as if Kissinger was living up to an image, an image provided by his role model, Prince Metternich. Kissinger (1957a:8–9) writes of Metternich: "His conversation was brilliant but without ultimate seriousness, equally at home in the salon and in the cabinet, graceful and facile, he was the *beau-idéal* of the eighteenth century. . . . He would have moved through the drawing rooms of the fashionable world with his undeniable charm and grace, subtly and aloofly conducting his diplomacy with the circuitousness which is a symbol of certainty." It is as if the nineteenth century has come alive with the dashing statesman flitting between salon and high level negotiation. Kissinger in Paris is the epitome of Metternichian style. Kissinger, here, has almost written his own history.

In addition, there is a striking parallel to this language in his article on Bismarck which sheds light on the importance of personal style in Kissinger's hero-matrix. Kissinger (1970) writes of Bismarck: "Proud in bearing, self-confident in expression, the speaker represented the *beau-ideal* of the Junkers, the large landholders who had built up Prussia." Kissinger is particularly attracted to those individuals who are rooted in an environment in which they received positive reinforcement on all fronts; it is to men like these that Kissinger looks for models.

In order to balance a fear of inadequacy, Kissinger has turned to symbols of power, action, assuredness, or vitality. Metternich's and Bismarck's styles, along with those of Kraemer and Elliot, all share to some degree a flamboyant assuredness which Kissinger's insecurity kept him from having. He had a certain confidence, but confidence is more an attribute than a fundamental form. Confidence is tacked on, learned as it were, after the establishment of the basic form of security or insecurity. The style of Metternich, Bismarck, Kraemer, and Elliot was an attribute which Kissinger incorporated as a means of identifying with the security which he thought was inherent in their style. It is significant that before his appointment as special assistant for national security affairs "Kissinger's major qualm about Nixon, it appears, was the President-elect's lack of individual assertiveness" (Landau, 1972: 134). Thus it seems that individuals who display an outward confidence and assertiveness are extremely attractive to Kissinger.

Metternich grew up in an age described in *A World Restored*, in which "nobody who lived after the French Revolution would ever know how sweet and gentle life could be. And the certitude of the time of youth never left Metternich" (Kissinger, 1957a:8). It was precisely this "certitude of the time of youth" that Kissinger is lacking and which formed one of the corner stones of his attraction to Metternich. It is most revealing that Kissinger focuses on the tranquility of Metternich's youth as the source of his confidence, for it is this tranquility which Kissinger would most have desired as a substitute for his "bad times." Thus lacking the inner calmness of certainty, Kissinger reacts with a front of arrogance in the hope that his inner chaos will go undiscovered by others and so that he might convince himself in his moments of doubt.[8]

Kissinger has admitted that "living as a Jew under the Nazis, then as a refugee in America, and then as a private in the army isn't exactly an experience that builds confidence" (quoted by Kraft, 1971). Elsewhere he has said of the Harvard period: "I was completely unsure of myself. I had gotten out of the army and I felt like an immigrant again" (*New York Post*, 1974). The first half of his life was marked by extreme uncertainty. Today, however, Kissinger can look back on his life and be satisfied that he overcame the barriers of his youth. Indeed, he can even say that the "bad times" were unimportant. But as a graduate student at Harvard, because of his admitted lack of confidence, he would have needed examples of men who overcame great barriers and survived to make history. Metternich then as one such man is even given a fantasized origin in order to make him better fit Kissinger's need for symbols of identification, symbols which would aid him in his effort to understand his past and to consolidate a sense of self.

If we look at Kissinger's modern heroes, de Gaulle and Zhou Enlai for instance, they are men who also overcame incredible obstacles, men who always faced adversity and won—men who stood alone and passed the test. Kissinger has even written of Nixon's heroic qualities. Nixon too is a man who overcame incredible obstacles and came back to shape history. Kissinger himself acknowledges his preference for such individuals. He has said that "the models he would prefer are those 'to whom it is given not only to maintain perfection of order but to have the strength to contemplate chaos, there to find material for fresh creation'" (quoted by Beloff, 1969).

But the positive identifications are not all that are present in his treatment of Metternich. Those who stood idly by against Napoleon are subjected to extreme criticism. In his discussion of Prussia in 1806, there appears a criticism which would reverberate in his critique of past American foreign policy. Kissinger (1957a:16) remarks: "It is the nature of statesmen conducting a policy of petty advantage to seek in vacillation a substitute for action. A policy which lets itself be influenced by events—which in the formal phrase 'awaits developments'—is likely to seek the remedy against a decision recognized as erroneous in adopting its extreme opposite without considering the intermediary solutions." This is the other side of Kissinger's hero coin; the side which includes his father. Those who vacillate, those who are indecisive, those who do not act in the face of the imperative to act, are apt to be overcome by events which pass them by. At every point where Kissinger confronts inaction he is negatively critical. In his article on Bismarck for instance, he says, "A policy that awaits events is likely to become their prisoner." If we remember Kissinger's reluctance to leave Germany, his father's vacillation, Louis's wait-and-see attitude, followed by the sudden reversal into flight, Kissinger's four years of intransigence in Vietnam is given added meaning.

The Vietnam Test

Throughout Kissinger's writing and speaking there is a tendency to place his truths of statesmanship in the context of a test. In *A World Restored*, for example, among several other such tests, "the test of a statesman, then, is his ability to recognize the real relationship of forces and to make this knowledge serve his ends" (Kissinger, 1957a:325). In reading any of Kissinger's books, one cannot help but notice this grammatical structure. Usually, the "test" is linked to some form of "adequacy," "strength," or "ability." For example, "The test of statesmanship is the adequacy of its evaluation before the event" (Kissinger, 1961a:3). The pervasiveness of this choice of terms in Kissinger's writings and statements would seem to indicate that the root of Kissinger's testing lies in his own doubt about himself and his environment. Taken with what we already know of Kissinger's personality it is reasonable to conclude that "the test of" is a means of dealing with his doubt about his own personal reception by his environment. His tests are tools in organizing the world. By testing for the existence of certain desirable qualities, he knows when to advance and when to retreat, when he is strong and when he is weak.

The significant aspect of this mode of perception is the doubt which is inherently attendant upon such ambiguity. What one needs is the courage to face that doubt, or in Kissinger's terms, contemplate the abyss. Therefore, courage is transformed into the primary value, for courage is needed to confront the uncertainty. Kissinger (1959c) castigates those policy makers and intellectuals who lack this courage: "The corollary of the tentativeness of most views is an incurable inward insecurity. Even very eminent people are reluctant to stand alone and they see in concurrence one of their chief tests of validity." This high evaluation of courage, independent action, and certainty is the consequence of Kissinger's formulation of his own life. Kissinger's past doubts and fears of confrontation have been projected onto others, while being alone is raised to a virtue. But there is, inherent in the view that courage, assertiveness, and certainty are the primary values of a statesman, a perpetuation of uncertainty since one must also always be testing his will.

This, then, is the process by which personal motives are transformed into political action. We generally look simply at the rationalizations or political prescriptions of a political actor. That is, if a political actor believes that even ambiguous threats to American power, such as "communist aggression" in Vietnam, must be met with force, then that formula is usually viewed as the reason for an action taken or the reason for supporting such action. Rarely do we ask ourselves why a certain principle is believed or valued. Let us take a closer look at the private motivation in Kissinger's testing process as manifested in Vietnam.

The most significant and confusing aspect of the manner in which Vietnam was handled in the Nixon administration is twofold: on the one hand is the congruity between the *form* advocated by Kissinger to end the conflict before his appointment as assistant to the president and the actual execution of the negotiations; and on the other hand, the almost absolute disjunction between the actual *substance* of the settlement and Kissinger's preappointment prescriptions.

The essential form of Kissinger's plan for negotiation was his two-track formula whereby the United States and Hanoi would hammer out the military questions, leaving the settlement of the political questions to the Vietnamese themselves. Of course, the major obstacle before the accomplishment of this split was the North's insistence that the political questions be resolved before they even began to talk about the ending of military actions. But Kissinger (1969b) countered in his *Foreign Affairs* article that if the United States got bogged down in negotiating explicit details of the political question, then United States' interests would be squandered. He argued that if the U.S. attempted to negotiate a political settlement, it would have to be on the basis of tacit bargaining rather than a formal agreement. In other words, Kissinger thought that if the war were to be resolved, the major issues would have to be left formally unresolved. Ambiguity was the order of the day. And it was the most curious aspect of the final agreement. On the surface, everything political still remained to be resolved, but in fact the die had already been cast.

Two of the points in question which Kissinger warned the United States to stay away from were central to the final settlement. And it was the fact that these two factors were included that lay behind the North's willingness to settle. As Kissinger (1969b:226–27) warned: "Negotiating a ceasefire may well be tantamount to establishing the preconditions of a political settlement. . . . A tacit de facto ceasefire may prove more attainable than a negotiated one. By the same token, a formal ceasefire is likely to predetermine the ultimate settlement and tend toward partition. Ceasefire is thus not so much a step toward a final settlement as a form of it." The reason for this assessment is that in Vietnam there were really no symmetrical lines of engagement. The enemy could not be driven back to an imaginary front line because there was no front line. The enemy was everywhere. So if a cease-fire were negotiated, the only way to insure the political viability of the South would be to insure the withdrawal of enemy troops. Thus Kissinger's first warning was that enemy troops could not be allowed to remain in the South or the peace would be lost.

The second warning was closely tied to the first. In this instance Kissinger (1969b) argued that the United States could not be a party to negotiating a coalition government. "The issue is whether the United States should be party to an attempt to *impose* a coalition government. We must be clear that our involvement in such an effort may well destroy the existing political structure of South Viet Nam and thus lead to a communist takeover." The reason that a coalition government will lead to a communist takeover is illustrated by one of Kissinger's examples of the difficulties a coalition would bring about: "Communist ministers would be foolhardy in the extreme if they entered Saigon without bringing along sufficient military force for their protection. But the introduction of communist military forces into the chief bastion of governmental strength would change the balance of political forces in South Viet Nam" (Kissinger 1969b).

In retrospect, it appears that Kissinger and Nixon spent six years testing our strength and will, and ended by failing the test. The U.S. steadily increased the level of violence in its test of strength but, unlike a weight lifter, kept adding to the weight even after it had become apparent that the weight could not be lifted. If Vietnam had not been viewed as a test, the United States never would have dragged out the war for so long.

The war was a test on many levels. In one sense it was seen as a test of credibility. As Kissinger (1969b:219) argued:

> However fashionable it is to ridicule the terms credibility or prestige, they are not empty phrases; other nations can gear their actions to ours only if they can count on our steadiness. The collapse of the American effort in Viet Nam would not mollify many critics; most of them would simply add the charge of unreliability to the accusation of bad judgment. Those whose safety or national goals depend on American commitment could only be dismayed. In many parts of the world—the Middle East, Europe, Latin America, even Japan—stability depends on confidence in American promises.

But confidence and trust are of little value when the end result is a worse position than what was started with. If the other countries, which were supposedly looking at Vietnam as a test of the American word, looked at the hard reality, they would have realized that the United States could not guarantee internal security with any sort of effectiveness short of destroying a country in order to save it. Those nations would do better to direct their attention to the ills in their own society that give rise to instability rather than to hope for salvation in the form of American military might.

In general, American conduct in Vietnam was a series of test probes designed to demonstrate purposefulness and strength. The invasion of Cambodia, for example, was a test probe which was designed, among other things, to demonstrate to the Soviet Union and to Hanoi that the United States was willing to stretch the limits of the war to the extent necessary to end the conflict. In Kissinger's words, the Soviets would judge the U.S. according to "the general purposefulness" of U.S. performance in Vietnam. We must demonstrate a willingness to face up to the risks of global diplomacy or the Soviets will be encouraged to step up pressures elsewhere. As Nixon said in his speech announcing the invasion of Cambodia: "It is not our power, but our will and character that is being tested tonight" (*U.S. News and World Report*, May 11, 1970). Presumably, if we were to fail the test, the communists would look upon the United States as a paper tiger.

The dynamics of the invasion of Cambodia were remarkably similar to those underlying the decision to mine Haiphong, which is discussed below. The communists in both situations were conducting successful military operations; the U.S. military evaluation of the possibility for success in both instances was dubious at best; in both instances the reasons given for the moves were not necessarily military, but political and psychological; and in both instances the decisions were made in the face of substantial disagreement within the highest levels of the U.S. national security system.

Kissinger's role in the decision was central. It was Kissinger who spent the entire day alone with Nixon the day before the decision was made. On the day of the decision Nixon and Kissinger compared a set of pluses and minuses each had worked out for the operation. "Nixon glanced at Kissinger's list, Kissinger at Nixon's. The lists were almost identical" (Kalb and Kalb, 1974:161). The only people in the entire NSC system who were in favor of the decision were Nixon, Kissinger, and, predictably, the Joint Chiefs of Staff. For the most part, the "formalized machinery of the NSC was largely bypassed . . . there were frequent direct contacts between White House officials [read Kissinger and members of the JCS], with Secretary Laird feeling at times inadequately informed" (*New York Times*, June 14, 1970). Rogers also opposed the action, and at one point Kissinger had a meeting with five of his brightest aids to get their views; all were opposed (Kraft, 1971). Nixon and Kissinger were truly alone.

The Kalbs (1974:164, 169) tell us that during this period, "Kissinger's innate conservatism surfaced. His old fear of America's going the way of the Weimar Republic . . . obsessed him." Kissinger, as he told a group of editors, felt that "what was at stake here was the problem of authority in this society altogether."

It looks, then, as if we have most of the necessary ingredients to activate Kissinger's most fundamental psychological tensions. Here was a perfect opportunity for a test of "character" (as specifically stated by Nixon). There was the necessity to stand alone against great opposition and there were the unavoidable risks—both domestic and foreign—involved in carrying the war beyond the boundaries of Vietnam proper. That these factors were a part of Kissinger's position is difficult to refute in light of the terms used by Nixon to announce his decision—a decision in which Kissinger was the closest and most influential collaborator, undoubtedly having a hand in the wording of the announcement. The mood of the announcement was reported by the *New Yorker* (May 9, 1970) in much the same manner as described here: "According to the President and members of his Administration, the invasion was intended not simply to do something, but also to *prove* something— something about America's 'character' and 'courage'." Thus the invasion of Cambodia was one of the best examples of the role Kissinger's testing and risk taking played in our Vietnam policy. Had an individual been in Kissinger's place who was not "obsessed" with the prospect of America's decline, who did not view the situation as a crisis of authority, who did not feel compelled to demonstrate his willingness to face the abyss alone, who did not need to prove his strength, then it is likely that a different path would have been followed. The question remains, if Kissinger had said no, would Nixon have gone ahead totally alone?

Cambodia was another example of Kissinger's tendency to rely on no other person's judgment but his own. It would seem that this is a further manifestation of Kissinger's self-righteousness (which has permeated his relationships from the time at Harvard when he was judged a "difficult colleague" to his management of the NSC staff where he was said "to bully and berate those underneath him") in collusion with Nixon's needs. This is further evidence that the all-or-nothing quality in Kissinger's moral and intellectual judgments remains.

But it is particularly at this point that the importance of a psychological understanding of Kissinger is best revealed. Erickson (1950:257) has discussed the characteristics of self-righteousness in these terms:

It is the all-or-nothing quality of the super-ego, this organ of moral tradition, that makes moral man a great potential danger to his own ego—and to that of his fellow man. . . . The resulting self-righteousness can later be most intolerantly turned against others. . . . Moral man's initiative is apt to burst the boundaries of self-restriction, permitting him to do to others in his or in other lands, what he would neither do nor tolerate being done to his own home.

We have discussed the danger to his own ego in the tendency of Kissinger to treat himself with a certain self-contempt. But the tendency to direct this contempt outward, as in his bullying of his subordinates, his wife, and his colleagues, took on a new character once Kissinger became special assistant. It would not seem to be a coincidence that the tactical nuclear weapons advocated for use by Kissinger would take place in underdeveloped countries, nor is it a coincidence that the willingness to engage in limited war is largely restricted to those countries. Likewise, it was Kissinger, who in his wisdom declared that Vietnam simply was not a moral issue (*Look*, August 12, 1969), and who proceeded to orchestrate the violation of the boundaries of Cambodia (Shawcross, 1979). It is the distinction of such "moral men" that morality is posited solely in their person, to be distributed according to their view of what deserves to be considered a moral issue. Rather than bullying subordinates or his wife, he became a principal actor in the bullying of North Vietnam in an attempt to force that country into a settlement on American terms.

Up from the Test

Kissinger views his own performance in terms of uncertainty and as a test, as is shown in his remarks about his own period of statesmanship. He has said: "The great danger of any policy is to project the present into the future. You have to base your bet on a judgment which cannot be proved true. This takes inward strength. It takes someone who is not worried by being alone a while" (*Newsweek*, August 21, 1972). A bet is another form of test. There is the same uncertainty and in effect a bet is simply a test of intuition, or, in the sense implied by Kissinger, of knowledge of the situation. The policy maker does not base his decision, but his bet, on a judgment which cannot be proved.

When there is a bureaucratic structure in which all information is funneled through one channel, and responsibility for decision making is a lonely process, this tendency toward risk taking increases the possibility of losing the bet or failing the test. It is refreshing to have leaders who at least tacitly recognize their fallibility, but it would be best to *avoid* risks rather than to always confront uncertainty.

Kissinger, backed by American firepower, offset his past avoidance of risks, behavior for which he severely castigated others, with a need to place himself in situations where he could demonstrate his courage, strength, adequacy, or ability. His entire philosophy as expounded in *Nuclear Weapons and Foreign Policy* is based on the "willingness to face up to the risks." This is in marked contrast to the young boy who ran to the other side of the street to avoid the risk of an oncoming threat. Unfortunately, his personal tests became meshed with national tests.

There is a second aspect to this sort of behavior. As emphasized in his cowboy statement, and his bet statement, and his statement referring to the lack of courage on the part of intellectuals and policy makers, the political actor is viewed as one who must act *alone*. Kissinger made a revealing comment on the subject when he said: "This amazing, romantic character suits me precisely because to be alone has always been part of my style, or, if you like, my technique" (Fallaci, 1977:41). If we remember Kissinger's lauding Metternich's technique, which was a "symbol of certainty," then it would seem that Kissinger views himself in much the same romanticized manner as he viewed his "*beau-idéals*." But somehow Kissinger decked out in chaps and spurs, riding his horse with a briefcase tucked beneath his arm, is a tragically ridiculous figure.

"Being alone" was the symbol of the Nixon administration. Decisions were not cooperative and consultative decisions, but lonely decisions. Nixon's retreat to Camp David or to Key Biscayne before major decisions had an air of deliberativeness about them. But there is another side to the coin. If one makes decisions alone, there is no one present who can sense or see doubt. No one to turn to and admit uncertainty, no one to see weakness. Neither is there anyone to suggest alternatives. Psychologically, being alone is one means of protection from a world perceived as hostile and is a protection against a self which is experienced as unembodied or dismembered in the presence of others. To what extent is this the motivation behind both Nixon's and Kissinger's retreat into isolation? From what we know of Kissinger's past and his personality, being alone serves as a means of protection against revealing doubt or uncertainty and is felt as a safe and strong condition. Thus a personal, psychological characteristic became a public, governmental method of operation. Decisions became personal tests; national pride was tested in Vietnam and our willingness to stand up and fight was tested in Hanoi.

If we take Kissinger's marked intellectual preference for facing risks and his belief that leaders must stand alone on certain issues against public opinion, we can begin to understand his psychological readiness to escalate the level of violence in Vietnam. The four years of Nixon's first administration exceeded the boundaries of violence set by President Johnson. It was after Nixon's election that the United States moved into Cambodia, mined Haiphong Harbor, bombed Hanoi, and, to an extent not matched in any other period, exported violence in the form of "protective reaction strikes" outside the area of Vietnam proper.

It may well be the loneliness theme which provides for the increased readiness to ignore the human costs of violence. One aspect of the depressive personality that is an important component of this style is the tendency toward withdrawal and lack of involvement or empathy with others. Significantly Kissinger's concerns are largely with the abstract: with women as a diversion, not in their uniqueness; with order and chaos, and not individual lives and individual deaths.

It was largely as a result of the consultative nature of Kennedy's handling of the Cuban missile crisis that a blockade was settled upon rather than the more violent "surgical air strikes" which were Kennedy's first instinctive reactions. The pressure of others who were involved in the actual decision making was one of the reasons why an alternative was settled upon. On Kissinger's "lonely road" there is no opportunity for those who would exercise caution to have their views heard.[9]

There can be little doubt that at the bottom of Kissinger's political actions are his private motivations. Kissinger has searched for an external order that can substitute for his inner chaos. Uncomfortable with ambiguity, he responds with a pervasive moral certainty. Countering internal threats to his being, he projects his anxiety onto appropriate objects in the real world and invests them with an affect that indicates an intensity much greater than might seem appropriate. The displacement is then transformed into an intellectual rationalization in an attempt to tame and strip his fears of their power over him. As a political actor he attempts to transform his intellectual rationalizations into political reality.

Acknowledgment

An earlier version of this essay was published in *History of Childhood Quarterly* 2, 3 (winter 1975). This revised version is printed here with the permission of the journal's publishers, The Institute for Psychohistory.

3. Pondering Intangibles: A Value Analysis of Henry Kissinger

Albert F. Eldridge

> The individual who understands intangibles realizes that no state can give up its visions of legitimacy and no individual his *raison d' être*, not because it is physically but because it is psychologically impossible.
>
> Henry Kissinger, *A World Restored*

Many contemporary anxieties over and criticisms of American foreign policy have arisen as a result of the conceptions of foreign policy and international politics held by former Secretary of State Henry Kissinger.[1] These conceptions, recorded both in office and in his academic writings, concerning what he really means, have fueled widespread interest and produced an impressive body of literature. The task of the present study is not to challenge any previous interpretations of these conceptions, but rather to shed new light on this elusive and important area of inquiry through the useful tool of value analysis.

Previous Interpretations: The Problem of Analysis

Henry Kissinger's conceptual framework of world affairs has eluded previous analysts for several reasons. One is that most commentators who write for popular consumption do not possess the inclination, the intellectual acumen, or the time to engage in a detailed, systematic analysis of his public statements or writings. Indeed, as Nora Beloff (1969) suggests, Kissinger's academic background, intellectual stature, and professional acclaim as a scholar tend to intimidate journalists, few of whom have the stamina to read any of his works in their entirety or to analyze systematically the whole corpus of his scholarly writings. Accordingly, Kissinger's complex framework either has been reduced to a small number of operating principles or has been abandoned in favor of emphasis on his personality. The most popular interpretations have focused on "power" and its use, his notions of and questionable concern for "morality," and his views on and glorification of "diplomacy" (Kraft, 1971; Landau, 1972, Stone, 1972; Kalb and Kalb, 1974), and they have drawn comparisons between his world view and that of such notable statesmen as Metternich, Bismarck, George F. Kennan, and Charles de Gaulle. These analyses do little, however, to lead us to a full understanding of Kissinger's framework. The difficulty, of course, is that the elements of his very complex view identified by most commentators are grounded in their own personal perspectives and predispositions.

The growing number of systematic analyses has also failed to address satisfactorily the problem of complexity. The nature of this failure is methodological and theoretical. That is, these analyses have not recognized that concepts such as power, morality, and diplomacy serve as perceptual lenses for Kissinger, as cognitive organizing devices which bring pertinent aspects of his experience to bear on current situations. Further, they have neglected to show how these concepts, in turn, are interrelated and how the various clusters of interrelated concepts provide him with a framework, a world view.

Such a complex, multidimensional framework serves two purposes: it provides Kissinger with an empirical account of his multiple relationships with his environment, and it furnishes a context in which to evaluate the framework normatively. Multidimensional concepts, however, are very difficult to grapple with empirically and theoretically (Fishbein, 1965). The difficulty is compounded when attempts are made to assess relationships among concepts or to describe belief systems. Examples of such attempts include operational code analysis and cognitive mapping techniques.

Operational code analysis has been used fruitfully to identify an individual's beliefs about important political phenomena by Alexander George and others (George, 1969; Holsti, 1970; Walker, 1977). It has limitations since it does not address inherent relationships among political beliefs that constitute the code or the concurrent normative dimension of values. Consequently, operational code analysis only identifies fragments of an individual's cognitive framework. The research in cognitive mapping conducted by Robert Axelrod (1976), however, has advanced identification of crucial relationships among beliefs and concepts. Yet we continue to lack valuable clues about which values are associated with particular clusters of cognitions, concepts, and beliefs. In this respect studies in concept formation, learning theory, and value acquisition show great promise in delineating relationships between concepts and norms, and the structure of belief systems (Fishbein, 1965; Rhine, 1967; Rokeach, 1972; Bell, 1974).

It is a conventional assumption that concepts shape perceptions—we "think with words and we see the world through them" (Bell, 1974:12). It also is known that concepts have cognitive and evaluative dimensions. Thus, a concept not only has connotational and denotational meaning; it also has a negative, neutral, or positive meaning, which in turn, is related to specific values.[2] This simplified account of the relationship between concepts and values suggests that we can learn what an individual sees in the environment and how he feels about it by analyzing concepts, particularly how they are used and in which contexts. Further, we can fathom the scope and complexity of the belief system and its relation to perception by identifying linkages among various concepts and values.

The Research Task and Methodology

The fundamental assumption underlying this study is that Henry Kissinger's concept of foreign policy reflects a specific, complex, highly integrated value system which influences his behavior. This behavior, in turn, has affected dramatically the direction and substance of American foreign policy. The aim of this study is to establish the multidimensionality of Kissinger's concepts, the relationships among them, and the extent to which they inform his approach to policy decisions. More specifically, there are three research objectives. The first two objectives involve the identification of recurrent values in Kissinger's public statements and writings and the cognitive and evaluative linkages among these preferences. With respect to these objectives, it is important to note that values do not exist independently of each other. Like attitudes, beliefs, and cognitions, they are organized into cognitively and functionally related networks, which can be classified by two methods. One method distinguishes between terminal values, that is, preferable endstates of existence or simply ends, and instrumental values. These reflect an individual's preference for certain modes of conduct in realizing personal and social ends. Rokeach (1972:159) defines an instrumental value in such a way that the value preference cannot be issue- or situationally defined. If it is, then a belief or possibly even a segment of an attitudinal network has been identified, but an instrumental value that is constant in all cases has not been. The other method rank-orders values along a continuum of importance, that is, a center/periphery continuum. Both methods are employed in this study.[3] The third research objective is to identify certain significant relationships between the resulting value system and Kissinger's perception of his role as secretary of state, bearing in mind Rokeach's assertion that the more central the belief and value, the more resistant it is to change (Rokeach, 1972:3). Because neither operational code analysis nor cognitive mapping achieves these objectives, value analysis is employed.

The work of Ralph K. White (1947, 1949, 1951) represents one of the earliest attempts to formulate a systematic technique for conducting value analysis. His methodology subsequently has been applied and refined by others (Eckhardt, 1965, 1967). As a form of quantitative analysis, it focuses on the inherent cognitive and evaluative psychological dimensions of an individual's verbal expressions. As a content analytical technique, it permits systematic analysis of verbal data while not obscuring the underlying emotional dynamics of the subject (White, 1947) or the values inherent in verbal expressions. These merits make value analysis appropriate for the study at hand.

The procedure involves several steps. First, I selected a sample of Henry Kissinger's public foreign policy pronouncements. This sample includes articles from the 1954–60 period and verbatim transcripts of his speeches, interviews, and press conferences from January 1974 to May 1975. This selection is extensive enough to be statistically reliable and to allow comparisons of values between the two important periods of his life, the academic and the governmental. The conceptual themes in these materials were analyzed using an adaptation of White's coding manuals (White, 1951). Coding was based on value preferences which were stated explicitly or implied clearly by the material. Judgments about the meaning or implication of a concept or evaluative theme were guided by White's caveat always to take the total context of a theme or word into account (see the appendix to this chapter for a list of the value categories). By so doing, two pitfalls of content analysis—that the manifest content of statements may be taken at face value and that it is an end in itself rather than a means for understanding the psychological dimension of verbal expression—were avoided. In brief, we are interested in the intangibles of meaning and preference—the meanings and values that Kissinger attempts to communicate in his pronouncements. In value analysis the context, the strength, and the meaning of a statement are very important.

We confronted, then, a daunting task given the great number and complexity of beliefs reflected in Kissinger's statements—where to start coding these beliefs and their inherent values. It is not possible (nor particularly important) to analyze each of them, so those beliefs that seemed to stand for and/or incorporate other beliefs were identified initially. The concept of national security can be used to illustrate this point. It clearly is important, as it permeates Kissinger's statements. Moreover, its meaning varies. National security is a gathering point for and symbol of other beliefs such as deterrence, equilibrium, and order. Each of them is rooted in particular values. For example, equilibrium is evaluated positively and linked to the value of stability. The most inclusive gathering-point belief deals with foreign policy. In this study the gathering-point beliefs dealing with diplomacy and statesmanship, which emerge from two interrelated value systems, and their convergence in Kissinger's perception of stability are emphasized.

This perception of the importance of stability in the international political system runs recurrently through Henry Kissinger's writings. Stephen Graubard (1973:14) observes that Kissinger's early studies of the nineteenth-century European state system were conducted so that its swift, far-reaching upheavals would shed precious light on those of our times. In his later studies of American national security policy, Kissinger focused on two central, related questions: What is the nature of stability? How can stability be achieved in a social order that is undergoing rapid transformation? His answers to these questions mirror certain general beliefs derived from his specific views.

Findings

The analysis of Kissinger's statements over a seven-year period disclosed the presence of thirteen primary values. By definition, these values transcend specific issues and situational contexts and, therefore, indicate his ultimate goals and standards of judgment. The values can be classified into four terminal values: safety, justice, self-regard, harmony; and nine instrumental values: determination, creative self-expression, knowledge, flexibility, risk taking, intelligence, subtlety, timing, and authority. I believe that Kissinger's beliefs about the nature of stability are based primarily on his terminal value system, whereas those about prospects for stability are based on his instrumental value system. Both systems, as well as the separate values that constitute each, are related cognitively and functionally.[4]

The Terminal Value System: Safety and Harmony

A rank ordering of Kissinger's four terminal values reveals that safety is most important, followed in decreasing order of importance by harmony, justice, and self-regard. This section of the paper discusses safety and harmony. White defines safety as "physical security, absence of war, violence, physical aggression, pain, injury or death, and no fear or danger of these things; peace, order." Kissinger's concern for safety is paramount throughout his works, but it is particularly evident in his examination of two international systems. In the "revolutionary" system, Kissinger (1957a) characterizes international political life as "violent," "chaotic," "confrontational," "prone to war," "unorderly," "tense," "insecure," "antagonistic," and "dangerous." Life in a "legitimate" system on the other hand, is described as "orderly," "stable," "competitive," "secure," "prone to reconciliation," "peaceful," and "just." While Kissinger does not believe that competition, aggression, or even violence will not occur in a legitimate order, he does appear to believe that the threat to safety is minimal, and that even if violence is used it will eventually result in, or restore, safety and security. Aggression is viewed by Kissinger as a corrective process within the legitimate social order; it is primarily self-defensive and/or adjustive in nature, and it ultimately insures the goal of security.

The importance of safety in Henry Kissinger's concern with stability can be extrapolated from an interesting question—can absolute safety ever exist in any international order? He observes in the revolutionary order a tendency to seek absolute solutions in foreign policy; there is a quest for safety, which leads ultimately to complete insecurity. Kissinger (1956c:264) states in an essay on the Congress of Vienna: ". . . the foundation of a stable order is the *relative* security—and therefore the *relative* insecurity—of its members." An important characteristic of the legitimate order, however, is its expression of security through equilibrium, that is, a balance or harmony of conflicting claims of safety: ". . . the security of a domestic order resides in the preponderant power of authority, that of an international order in the balance of forces and in its expression, the equilibrium" (Kissinger, 1956c:265).

Prior to pursuing this preference for harmony, a comment about the portrayal of Kissinger as aggressive, as prone to favor force in international politics, is in order. This portrayal should be tempered by understanding his major concern for safety and security. That is, the international environment of the early 1950s was perceived by him as manifesting revolutionary attributes and as a dangerous time that threatened international peace and American national security. This threat could be met by the use of force, including the limited use of nuclear weapons (Kissinger, 1957b). His arguments have been levelled against him to portray him as aggressive. Alternatively, the primacy of safety in his value system does not indicate aggressiveness but, rather, defensiveness; he (and his goals of safety and national security) and the country occupy an ominous, indeed, hostile environment. According to White (1947:451), an individual who is concerned primarily with safety will respond to this environment by defiant aggression. The analogy at the national level is the use of force.[5]

As mentioned, value analysis of Kissinger's statements documents the crucial role played by harmony in his beliefs about stability. This value also is connected to the value of safety and surfaces in his use of other terms such as "commensurability," "proportionality," "equilibrium," and "confluence."

Qualitative analysis of such coded statements uncovers three primary themes that constitute Kissinger's conception of harmony. These are preferences for dependency, mutual accommodation, and restraint. These themes are also central in the writings of conflict strategists such as Thomas Schelling (1963:5) who contends that strategy essentially is "not concerned with the efficient application of force but with the exploitation of potential force." This contention closely parallels Kissinger's concept of the interdependence of force and diplomacy, which according to Kissinger (1956b:352) "are not discrete realms; on the contrary, the ultimate pressures during negotiation have always been the possibility that recourse might be had to force" (Kissinger, 1956b:352). In a criticism of the doctrine of massive retaliation and its slogan, "there is no alternative to peace," Kissinger (1956b:352) asserted, "to the extent that the slogan . . . is taken seriously by the Soviets as a statement of American intentions it will remove a powerful brake on the Soviet probing actions and any incentive for the Soviet Union to make concessions." Accordingly, the exploitation of potential force becomes the instrument of harmony, and once dependency is realized and mutual accommodation becomes a goal of diplomacy, some almost automatic restraint on conflictual actions would ensue. The themes which emerge in this thinking about harmony deserve close scrutiny.

In the company of a number of conflict theorists, Kissinger subscribes to the view that the central issues of international politics lie beyond the realm of unilateral control. When a country is deluded into thinking that it alone has the power to resolve conflict or to provide its own national security, instability results. On this point Kissinger's early writings and Schelling's *The Strategy of Conflict* again complement each other. The resonance is especially apparent in Schelling's (1963:5) statement: "Conflict situations are essentially bargaining situations. They are situations in which the ability of one participant to gain his ends is *dependent* [emphasis added] to an important degree on the choices or decisions that other participants will make." Further, Kissinger (1963b:16), in an argument reminiscent of Schelling's term "the theory of interdependent decision," believes that dependency and opposition exist in international politics. If war is to be avoided or conducted on a limited scale so as to minimize damage to the adversaries, mutual dependencies must be understood by decision makers. If a country's decision makers are to evaluate adequately the consequences of their actions, the identification of mutual dependencies must be set as an important task of diplomacy. The acceptance of this task of diplomacy brings us to the crux of statecraft—the best course of action for any country depends on what it expects other countries to do, and strategy involves influencing the other country's choices by acting on its expectation of how one's behavior is related to his own. In summary, then, an acknowledgment that mutual dependencies exist and are acted upon forms the core of any theory of interdependent decisions. This view is supported substantially by Kissinger's belief statements about harmony.

Those statements by Kissinger which exhibit disapproval of zero-sum strategies are related to mutual accommodation as to another theme of harmony. In his writing on the use of force and diplomacy Kissinger (1956b:361) asks, "is it possible to bring about a climate in which national survival is thought not to be at stake?" And he defines the central task of diplomacy as "to make clear that we do not aim for unconditional surrender, to create a framework in which the question of national survival is not involved in every issue" (Kissinger, 1956b:363). Kissinger contends that an awareness of mutual dependency enhances the probability of countries arriving at mutual accommodations, and he professes a preference for accommodation of disputes throughout his writings. Indeed, a primary criticism levelled against the doctrine of massive retaliation is that it ignores the positive advantages of dependency, that is, the necessity of mutual accommodation; by so doing, a "paralysis of policy" was generated in the United States, thus freeing the Soviet Union from the necessity of accommodation (Kissinger, 1956b:351–53). To continue with the game-theory metaphor, Kissinger appears to suggest that international conflicts are not interpretable always as constant-sum games (only in the revolutionary system is more for one inexorably linked with less for the other), and he suggests further that diplomacy must aim to demonstrate that some outcomes are either more beneficial or more detrimental than others for both adversaries. We will return to mutual accommodation as a theme of harmony in our discussion of the instrumental value of flexibility.

The third element of Kissinger's emphasis on harmony is a preference for restraint in the actions of countries. Kissinger (1956c, 1957a, 1964b) states this preference repeatedly in his writings on the Congress of Vienna; that is, no country can gain security without restraint. The ideas about restraint flow logically from his beliefs about the interrelatedness of an awareness of dependency and the quest for mutual accommodation. Restraint does not obtain in the revolutionary system because neither dependency nor the necessity of mutual accommodation is realized. The absence of restraint is accompanied by a lack of harmony, stability, and, consequently, security.

The data on this value are interesting. The original coding of Kissinger's statements developed no evidence that either aggression or force was a terminal value. That is, although Kissinger's writings frequently discuss conflict and force, no cases explicitly or implicitly reflected a preference for their implementation as an end. Yet a small number of cases did yield situationally circumscribed preference. If we adopt Rokeach's definition, cited above, this preference is not a terminal value.

Standing in stark contrast to these patterns in the original coding are a number of cases in which a preference for harmony is expressed within the context of a theme on the use of force in international politics. Indeed, 42 percent of the value statements about harmony echoed contexts of force and its use, and in one article, "Force and Diplomacy in The Nuclear Age" (Kissinger, 1956b), 73 percent of the preferences for harmony were defined in terms of a strategy of force. This high correspondence between a preference for harmony and the conflict of force poses a dilemma: if force is not a terminal value and Kissinger's statements about force do not seem to indicate an instrumental preference for it, then how can the cognitive relationship between harmony and force be explained? This prompted a reexamination of his value statements.

Figure 3.1
Terminal Value-Belief Network
The Nature of Diplomacy and Statesmanship

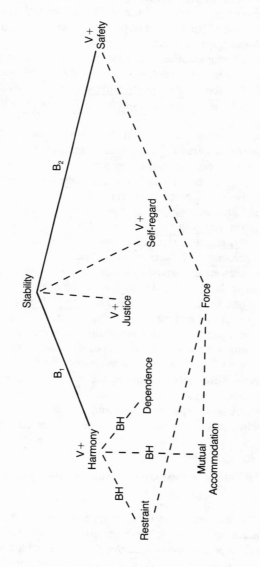

Legend:
V +   Terminal values
B₁, B₂ Primary terminal belief statements linking values, concepts, and other belief statements
------- Secondary terminal belief statements
--BH-- Specific beliefs about the nature of harmony

One particularly appealing explanation based on this reexamination is that the use of force constitutes a fourth theme in Kissinger's conception of harmony. Moreover, there is some evidence to suggest that Kissinger views force as an instrumental element in the achievement of mutual accommodation and restraint. Consequently, an ability to threaten the use of force—to exploit the potentially damaging outcome of war to adversaries—nurtures and reinforces the awareness of dependency and the necessity for mutual accommodation, enhances the incentives for mutual restraint, and thus contributes to, rather than detracts from, system stability. This is similar to his argument (presented above) that rebuts criticisms of him as an aggressor and a warmonger; Kissinger believes that the potential use of force facilitates safety and security.

By way of summary and clarification of the relationships in Henry Kissinger's value/belief network, this network is depicted diagrammatically in figure 3.1. It facilitates identification of his terminal values, the normative dimensions and common cognitive origins of his beliefs, and the relationships among his beliefs as they emanate from cognitively and functionally related values.

The center of the figure is occupied by stability, conceptualized in terms of two terminal values: the primary values of safety and harmony. Kissinger's preference for both values is designated V^+. His beliefs that safety (security) and harmony produce stability are represented by the connecting lines B_1 and B_2. Each of these two primary beliefs can then be employed to generate a series of more specific belief statements about particular issues and situations. Moreover, the data reveal that his preference for harmony reflects preferences for dependency, mutual accommodation, and restraint. Cognitive and functional linkages exist between preferences for the latter two and the potential use of force, which is not an explicit instrumental value, but rather an implicit one that forms part of Kissinger's definition of and preference for the elements of harmony.[6] The interrelatedness of these elements is captured by the connecting lines BH. Similar to the primary values, these statements permit additional, more specific statements as well as analysis and explanation of Kissinger's attitudes about specific issues and situations, but only when a sufficient number of belief statements have been found and placed within the cognitive network.

The Instrumental Values: Knowledge, Flexibility, Intelligence, and Risk Taking

This section of the study seeks to identify specific benefits that are perceived as inherent in specific means by Henry Kissinger, for example, why flexibility, as one of nine instrumental values, is favored as a mechanism by which to attain the terminal value of safety/security. These nine values were rank-ordered by the same technique that was applied to the terminal values. In so doing Kissinger's preferences for knowledge and flexibility tied as most important, intelligence and risk taking tied as second most important, and then determination, authority, creativity, subtlety, and timing followed in decreasing order of importance. These values are framed by two contexts. One involves an international level of analysis; Kissinger (1955b:425) prefers countries to formulate flexible policies: "An all-or-nothing military policy therefore makes for a paralysis of diplomacy." The other is the means for realizing an individual's objectives; Kissinger (1959c:33) favors creative self-expression: "In his desire to be helpful, the intellectual is too frequently compelled to sacrifice what should be his greatest contribution to society: his creativity." Moreover, the same preference can be expressed in both contexts, as flexibility emerges in statements on national diplomacy or preferred personal skills of diplomats and statesmen.

The central importance of knowledge in Kissinger's instrumental value network merits discussion. It is revealed most frequently by terms such as concept, design, framework, or conceptual framework, each of which allows phenomena to be analyzed systematically. Indeed, Kissinger argues that conceptualization aids by "imposing a pattern on events or to impart a sense of direction to his action" (Kissinger, 1959c:31), which is especially beneficial in a chaotic, threatening environment. It is an environment whose potential for instability and uncertainty can be magnified if diplomacy does not manifest a comprehensive grasp of factors and relationships that characterize the international order, an awareness of essential problems in this order, and a definition of the principal issues that challenge statecraft. Briefly, although the uncertainty that is characteristic of diplomacy never can be eliminated totally, this uncertainty can be reduced by frameworks because they impose a pattern on events, impart a sense of direction to actions, and define the issues.

Without these frameworks or conceptual skills, decision makers are inhibited from developing effective policies because they cannot reflect on (1) the motives and values which infuse their actions and decisions, (2) the relationships that exist among these actions and decisions and between them and the whole, and (3) their own ideas of the essential elements of problems and their willingness to trust this personal view (Kissinger, 1959c:30–31). Rather, policy makers are reduced to viewing problems as isolated cases. Attention is limited to the immediate solution of specific problems. The result, as Kissinger (1959c:31) points out, is that policy is fragmented "into a series of *ad hoc* decisions which make it difficult to achieve a sense of direction or even profit from experience." As Kissinger makes abundantly clear in his writings, these practices must be avoided. He displays an enduring preference for the comprehensiveness believed to reside in the frameworks and conceptions as he transforms discussions of specific issues, such as the doctrine of massive retaliation, the defense of Western Europe, and "summitry," into discussion of the conceptual issues that feed these topics.[7]

Kissinger's preference for conceptualization, then, is related to his value of safety/security through its instrumentality in reducing uncertainty. His preference for flexibility, however, is linked to the value of harmony as a means to foster mutual accommodation and restraint. Flexibility, as revealed by qualitative analysis, comprehends an increase of maneuverability in policy making and implementation, a bulwark against dogmatism, and sensitivity to environmental fluidity and relativity. The goal of diplomacy is to maintain "fluidity in the diplomatic situation," and flexibility will enable a country or individual to adjust actions, to reconcile differences, and thus to contribute to stability.

The preference for flexibility is matched by a marked distaste for rigidity which denies harmony, stability, and hence safety. In discussions of the revolutionary system, the defense of "grey areas," massive retaliation, and prevailing modes of American policy making, he stresses that a country must understand clearly its primary objectives—it must know what it wants—and shirk rigidity in the realization of these goals (Kissinger, 1955b:419). As Kissinger (1955a:7) cautions, "Diplomacy presupposes prior agreement on fundamentals which diplomacy can adjust but not create." If it cannot adjust conflicting interests, then mutual accommodation cannot be implemented and a zero-sum situation develops. By leaving no alternative between uneasy armistice and total nuclear war, it "prevents attempts to ameliorate the situation progressively" (Kissinger, 1955b:425).

Within the realm of policy making the chief attribute of flexibility is that it puts a premium on the creation of multiple contingencies in problem solving. Kissinger's proposals for the use of nuclear weapons and his "little war" thesis are examples of his attempts to generate various contingencies for American policy. His thinking about the utility of freedom of action can be found throughout the literature on international politics.

Analogous to his ideas on the value of knowledge and conceptual frameworks, his idea of freedom for the diplomat entails a number of acceptable alternatives or the development of "variations on the same theme," which are manifestations of a "feeling for nuance" or an awareness of the subtle interrelationships that characterize diplomacy (Kissinger, 1956a:40).

As noted, two other values, intelligence and risk taking, tied as second most important in a rank-ordering of the nine instrumental values. Whereas White defines knowledge, one of the terminal values, as "mental content corresponding to 'reality'—both the having of such content and the degree of 'truth' or correspondence with reality, facts, logic, wisdom, understanding; thinking and planning," intelligence is "mental ability, all 'good' intellectual qualities such as memory, logic, objectivity, intention, perspective and reflection." The possible interface between them necessitates a comment on coding since some of Kissinger's statements posed difficulty for categorization. This difficulty is reflected by a relatively low inter-code reliability score of 0.52 (the inter-coder reliability score for all categories is 0.81).[8] We were able to increase inter-coder reliability in the case of knowledge and intelligence by emphasizing the notion that Kissinger appeared to define knowledge in terms of theory and taxonomies (i.e., analytical constructs, while in the case of intelligence he meant specific personal skills. In the case of differentiating between intelligence (i.e., "all 'good' intellectual qualities") and specific intellectual qualities such as subtlety and creative self-expression, we realize that certain of these specific qualities can be subsumed under the general category of intelligence as White defined it.

Kissinger seems to regard individual self-assurance, a sense of self-confidence, and an inward security essential to "profound policy" formulation, as positive effects of intelligence. As it emerges explicitly and repeatedly in his writings on key figures in nineteenth-century European politics or the prevalent policy making mode in the United States, self-assurance is especially highly valued. Kissinger (1959c:31) states: "The situation is compounded by the personal humility that is one of the most attractive American traits. Most Americans are convinced that no one is ever entirely 'right,' or, as the saying goes, that if there is disagreement each party is probably a little in error. . . . But the corollary of the tentativeness of most views is an incurable inward insecurity. Even very eminent people are reluctant to stand alone."

More specifically, the importance of self-assurance lies in the nexus among Kissinger's beliefs about the usefulness of conceptualization, the value of harmony, and inward security: "Effective policy depends not only on the skill of individual moves but even more importantly on their relationship to each other. It requires a sense of proportion; a sense of style provides it with inner discipline" (Kissinger, 1959c:31). This statement exhibits a confluence of the values of harmony and proportion, a preference for conceptualization which stresses relationships among facets of the environment, and a preference for the intangible quality of discipline or self-control.

For the statesman, knowledge and intelligence will furnish self-assurance. In turn, this self-assurance which underlies the assumption that his view of the world is valid, when coupled with possession of a conceptual framework, permits the statesman to transcend the experience of his society and to act upon his intuition or subjective evaluation of issues. By so doing, he can move against conventional wisdom, be creative and innovative in his actions, and meet effectively changing environmental challenges. This courage, manifested in security, is an important motivating force in Kissinger's thinking, and it contributes directly to the realization of goals.

In the absence of self-assurance, then, conceptualization is timorous; the capacity for innovations and spontaneous reaction to a fluid environment is lessened; and the individual lapses into immobility or stagnation, which Kissinger identifies with the status quo (Kissinger, 1956a:54). The individual is reluctant to assume risks in problem solving.

This assumption of risk introduces another of the second most important instrumental values as well as a paradox. That is, the terminal value of safety/security is very important to Kissinger. Hence, his support for risk taking, both explicitly and implicitly through the exercise of self-assurance, would seem to violate these values since risks naturally generate uncertainty, which he seeks to reduce by use of the conceptual framework, and they potentially threaten cherished goals and objectives. Yet Kissinger values both security and risk taking.

White defines risk as "to entertain chance; to act on the basis of conjecture without knowing all the facts; daring, uncertainty—without certitude." For Kissinger risk is instrumental in generating flexibility which builds harmony and stability. If an individual is not willing to entertain risks, if his views of the future are shaped only by experience and fears, then possible opportunities for creative and innovative action are denied: "A statesman who limits his policy to the experience of his people will doom himself to sterility." (Kissinger, 1956a:54). Similarly, in his criticism of committee policy making, Kissinger (1959c:31) mentions that the system "stresses avoidance of risk rather than boldness of conception." Alternatively stated, "energetic," "bold," "creative," or "profound" policy rests on a willingness to accept risks: "While our history may leave us not well enough prepared to deal with tragedy, it can teach us that great achievement does not result from a quest for safety" (Kissinger, 1956a:56); "Our society requires above all to overcome its current lassitude to risk itself on new approaches" (Kissinger, 1959a:35). In lieu of a willingness to accept risks, a country faces a "paralysis of policy," an elusiveness of achievement, and an inability to cope with a revolutionary power in a rapidly fluctuating international order.

Implicit in these perspectives on risk is a propositional chain. Without risk taking there will be stagnation. With stagnation there is a reduction of alternatives. When options are limited, inflexible actions and responses occur, lessening the motive force or pressure for harmony, particularly mutual accommodation and restraint. A lack of harmony inevitably leads to or heightens environmental instability. Without stability and a sense of proportion, there can be no safety or security. This description of Kissinger's belief preference structure in terms of a propositional chain suggests that although force and risk taking may be antithetical to security, the underlying logic of their relationships is similar. Specifically, Kissinger argues that both force and risk taking are valuable because they lead, albeit indirectly, to the realization of several of his goals.

We now may proceed to illustrate Henry Kissinger's instrumental value network. In the center of figure 3.2 is the undifferentiated terminal value network. These values are achieved through the nine instrumental values, which include those that have not been discussed explicitly. The connections among these terminal and instrumental values are depicted by the letters IB and subscripts 1 through 9. Each instrumental value, acting either alone or with other instrumental values, is responsible for generating more specific beliefs about particular issues and situations, for example, massive retaliation, summit conferences. As stated in the presentation of the terminal value system, when a sufficient number of these belief statements have been located on a cognitive map, the potential for analyzing and explaining Kissinger's attitudes and perceptions increases. Because part of this procedure requires an investigation of value change, this task is addressed next.

The Governmental Period: Modifications in Beliefs and Values

This section of this study focuses on differences and similarities in beliefs and values during the academic and governmental periods of Henry Kissinger's life. This later period involves a sample of statements, made by Kissinger from January 1974 to May 1975 of his governmental service, which were coded and value-analyzed as above. If Rokeach (1972) is correct, the centrality of Kissinger's terminal and instrumental values suggests that their direction and substance should re-

Figure 3.2

Instrumental Value-Belief Network

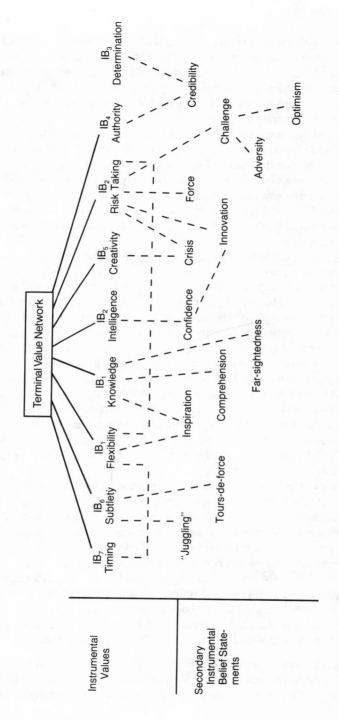

Legend:

IB$_x$ Primary instrumental belief statements linking values, concepts, and other belief statements to terminal values; the subscript indicates the relative importance, from most (IB$_1$) to least (IB$_7$). Some primary instrumental beliefs (i.e. risk taking and determination) do not link directly with the terminal value network. The effect of these values comes through their ability to enhance flexibility, creativity, and authority.

main relatively unchanged over time. This expectation, however, does not deny the possibility of some movement along a center/periphery continuum. Courage, for example, may be a central value at one time but diminish to a peripheral value in a later one. Such movement can be directed by shifts in the rank-order position of a value. A shift from rank position *1* to rank position *3* might indicate that a value is becoming more peripheral.

Application of this analysis to Kissinger's thirteen most important values, the four terminal and nine instrumental values, in his academic period reveals that the significance of the two terminal values of justice and self-regard declines precipitously to rank positions *16* and *21*, respectively, in the governmental period. The other two terminal values, harmony and safety/security, however, do survive into this period. Of these harmony is the most important, with twice the number of linkages between it and other values, except safety/security, than between safety/security and other values, except harmony.

We already have established that Kissinger conceptualizes harmony in terms of the three preferred values of mutual dependency, mutual accommodation and restraint. He argues further that foreign policy objectives, particularly state security and stability, are attainable only if countries and statesmen understand the independent nature of the international order and guide their actions by a design or framework. This theme permeates statements connected with negotiation of a Panama Canal Treaty, testimony on the Trade Reform Act, the United Nations speech of April 15, 1974, answers to questions about detente, and discussions of the oil issue. Indeed, in a press conference held on January 3, 1974, Kissinger responded to a question on American acceptance of the rising price of oil: "You have to understand what the very way you formulate the question demonstrates the nature of the problem. It is not in the power of the U.S. to control the rise of these prices. . . . It is an example *par excellence* of how interdependent the world has become, how impossible purely selfish policies are, and how suicidal for everybody it is to pursue independent courses."

With respect to the importance assigned to the conceptual framework as an analytical construct, statements which involve his preference for harmony in the governmental period also reflect an emphasis on devising a framework for understanding interrelationships. Yet this construction has shifted from an intellectual exercise to the policy process. This shift is indicated by his definition of a framework, which he offered during a press conference (U.S. Department of State, Bureau of Public Affairs, January 10, 1974:15): "There is no precedent in past diplomacy for this particular approach, but there is also no precedent in past diplomacy for this particular problem. What we are talking about is a series of agreements or understandings in a series of related areas." This definition was expanded explicitly and evaluated implicitly in testimony before the Senate Committee on Finance (1974:4):

> Detente is not rooted in agreement on values: it becomes above all necessary because each side recognizes that the other is a potential adversary in a nuclear war. To us, detente is a process of managing relations with a potentially hostile coun-

try in order to preserve peace while maintaining our vital interests. . . . Detente is founded on a frank recognition of basic differences and dangers. Precisely because we are conscious that these differences exist, we have sought to channel our relations with the USSR into a more stable framework—a structure of interrelated and interdependent agreements. Forward movement in our relations must be on a broad front—encompassing a wide range of mutually reinforcing activities—so that groups and individuals in both countries will have a vested interest in the maintenance of peace and the growth of a stable international order.

This statement is interesting not only because it embroiders on Kissinger's definition of a framework, but also because it illustrates the impact of his value system on his perception of a specific policy. That is, Kissinger values harmony and its attributes of mutual dependency, mutual accommodation, and restraint, as well as order, peace, security, stability, and the usefulness of a framework or a structure of interrelated and interdependent agreements to produce these other value objectives. Therefore, he must evaluate detente positively. This logical connection is founded on the facts that detente is possible because neither country claims the universality of its values, that it is necessitated by awareness of mutual dependency, and that its specific policies are part of a larger framework which reflects the "reality of interdependence" in the international order which will "move us from an era of confrontation to a sustained period of peace and international stability." Detente, then, is a mechanism for achieving Kissinger's most important terminal values of safety/security and stability.

Finally, it must be noted that Kissinger's statements continue to mirror a major concern that harmony, now defined primarily as mutual dependency, can be threatened by unrestrained action. The focus of this concern, however, differs between the two periods. In the academic period, he concentrated on the unrestrained action of one country, such as a revolutionary power. In the governmental period it is the unrestrained actions of groups of countries, "unrestricted bilateral competition," "unilateral impositions of order," and "bilateralism" which he condemns because their ensuing policies are corrosive to the positive values of harmony, order, security, and stability. This view is articulated clearly in a speech before the inaugural session of the Conference of Tlatelolco in Mexico City (U.S. Department of State, Bureau of Public Affairs, February 21, 1974:3): "Each nation can try to exploit its particular advantages in resources and skills, and bargain bilaterally for what it needs. . . . But history tells us that this leads to ever more vicious competition . . . and—most fundamental—growing political tensions which unravel the fabric of global stability."

In summary, the importance of the two terminal values of harmony and security persists from the academic to the governmental period, although the emphasis on the former has changed whereas that of the latter has not. The remainder of this section is devoted to variations among the nine instrumental values.

One instrumental value, subtlety, does not survive between the two periods of Kissinger's life, falling to rank position *19*, whereas the other eight do, and three new values, involving preferences for the utility of challenge, credibility, and support, appear. The decreasing rank order of these eleven values is knowledge, flexibility, authority, creativity, determination, risk taking, intelligence, support, challenge, timing, and credibility. Knowledge and flexibility, then, continue to dominate the instrumental network, although, as we shall soon see, Kissinger's view of the utility of knowledge has been modified. Two other interesting differences arise in the rank-ordering of authority and risk taking. Authority moves from rank position *4* to *3*, thereby surpassing determination, risk taking, and intelligence. Risk taking descends from second rank in the academic period to sixth rank in the governmental period, a change which betrays Kissinger's reevaluation of its usefulness compared to other instrumental values such as authority. These shifts of authority and risk taking may be explained by context, for example, Kissinger's struggle with Congress over the Trade Reform Act or the Watergate issue, inducing a reordering of preferences.

Why does authority occupy a central position in Henry Kissinger's instrumental value network? It does because it is intrinsically and functionally valued as linked to other important instrumental values. Moreover, it has been reinforced by his own exercise of governmental authority which flowed from several formal and informal sources. He possessed the constitutionally defined and extended authority of the office of secretary of state. He garnered informal authority from those who shared his goals and perceptions of a design for world order, including, most importantly, Richard Nixon. The compatibility of Nixon's and Kissinger's views strengthened the latter's authority by permitting broad latitude in policy formulation between 1969 and 1972. When the authority of the executive, including both the president and the collective executive, was being challenged during the Watergate investigation and House impeachment proceedings, Kissinger reasoned that these proceedings reduced congressional criticism and increased congressional support of his actions, particularly in the policy-implementing realm and, thus, Congress also embellished his authority. In an interview with James Reston (1974:34) he stated:

> As to support on the Hill, I think one has to distinguish between the very unusual situation that existed before President Nixon's resignation with what could reasonably be expected. Before President Nixon's resignation there was such a sense of horror at the disintegration of authority domestically that everybody had an interest in demonstrating that there was no debate on our foreign policy. There was a desire to preserve one island of authority in this general disintegration.

In the above statement Kissinger refers to an "island of authority" which is clearly his own. Paradoxically, however, he understood that the House proceedings could undermine his own authority and flexibility in the implementation of foreign policy: "So I would think what has happened now, after President Nixon's resignation is the opening of foreign policy to normal partisan debate. Probably in the excitement the pendulum is swinging a bit too far and there are intrusions in day-to-day tactical decisions which Congress really isn't best equipped to handle" (Reston, 1974:1). Later, Kissinger (May 10, 1975) admitted: "We did not foresee that Watergate would sap the Executive authority of the U.S. to such degree that flexibility of Executive action inherently would be circumscribed." This challenge may have been interpreted as one directed more to his ability to implement his concept of world order through selected policies than to this concept. In an interview with Pierre Salinger (U.S. Department of State, Bureau of Public Affairs, April 12, 1975:2) he stated: "So, we face now a problem that, while the design of our policy is intact, the authority to implement it may be impaired; it is a primary responsibility to attempt to restore that through partnership with the Congress and through perhaps getting more of a public consensus." In response to a question that arose during a press conference about his definition of a "crisis of authority," Kissinger declared (U.S. Department of State, Bureau of Public Affairs, January 28, 1975:2): "I am saying that the problem for any society is first whether it is able to recognize the problems it is facing, secondly, whether it is willing to deal with these problems on the basis of long-range decisions. . . . So what is needed is a consensus in the leadership and between the leadership and the parliament that enables the government, or the society, to act with confidence and with some long-range mission."

In this answer Kissinger suggests that part of his authority hinges on an ability to convince others of his assessment of the problems that confront the United States. Moreover, he reiterates explicitly the need for a world view so that problems are identified correctly, a preference for long-range solutions integrated in the policy design, and the importance of confidence and vision; and he implies that a lack of consensus on them and his principles poses a challenge or crisis to his authority.

Kissinger's realization that his authority had diminished may explain several phenomena. One is an increase in his positive evaluations of credibility and support. Another is that his numerous speaking engagements across the country at the time were ammunition in a campaign that was launched to win "more of a public consensus" about policy actions and objectives and by so doing to retrieve some of his authority, especially that based on other people's acceptance of his views of the American interest.

Value Analysis: An Appraisal and Summary

This study began with the assertions that the instrumental and terminal values of Henry Kissinger constitute an important area of scholarly inquiry, and that value analysis is a useful tool for conducting this task. It concludes with an appraisal of this analytical method, a summary of major findings, and some observations on the tone of Kissinger's statements.

In this study of the statements made by Henry Kissinger, the technique of value analysis was not selected in order to substitute a quantitative analysis for a qualitative one. Indeed, as White contends, the technique is not a question of either/or, but rather of both/and. Whereas our quantitative analysis serves to bolster confidence that the impressions conveyed through Kissinger's comments and writings are valid objectively, value analysis, the purpose of which is to describe an individual's motivational dynamics with a maximum of objectivity, presents a more complete picture of that person's beliefs.[9] Moreover, it gives some ideas of the extent to which various beliefs are connected through specific values. Value analysis and content analysis, then, complement each other, but additional research on the integration of the former with the latter, particularly as this research follows the preliminary steps charted by this study in mapping value/belief networks, remains to be done. An application of such research to the views of Henry Kissinger would allow identification of a larger number of general and specific beliefs and their placement within these networks.

Certainly, we should be cheered that value analysis has yielded a precise identification of Kissinger's values, a mapping of cognitive relationships among these values, an understanding of their impact on his actions and thoughts, and consequently some valuable clues about his self-concept and world view. Another consequence of the study is that it sheds light on the tone of Kissinger's statements, both the pessimism which many commentators have detected and the optimism.

That Kissinger's public statements and writings have been interpreted as pessimistic is not surprising, since his perceptions of the world and its problems, which are judged as posing almost insurmountable obstacles to the realization of his goals, *are* pessimistic. He values safety and security, but the world around him is laden with aggression and conflict. He values harmony and stability, but the world is characterized by a lack of accommodation, anxiety, unbridled competition, and tension. He places great faith in the long-term utility of boldness, creativity, and personal knowledge, but society very frequently does not share his faith in these qualities. He firmly believes in his conception of politics, but alternative and opposing conceptualizations confront him. Thus, many of Kissinger's statements as historian and statesman indicate an attempt to grapple with these obstacles—placing them in a specific historical and political context. In some instances he has sought to redefine his environment so that his goals and motives might be achieved even in the face of adverse circumstances. In other instances he has sought to contain, to modify, or to reverse contrary forces and policies. In all instances he had endeavored to instruct others in the wisdom of his views of the world and its problems so that they would come to share these views.

We should not allow ourselves, however, to be blind to the optimism of Henry Kissinger's statements. He affirms the beliefs that people can exert at least a modicum of control over their environment, and that creativity, determination, flexibility, intelligence, and knowledge can direct us a long way towards the development of solutions. Moreover, the faith and hope placed in these values remained unshaken by the challenges of obstacles. An individual can summon certain intangibles of purpose and value—self-assurance, confidence, creativity, vision, a sense of timing—only in the presence of adversity. The importance of these intangibles permeates Kissinger's thinking, the consistency and continuity of which are captured in our comparison of concepts, statements, themes, and word usage in both periods of analysis. Consistency and continuity occurred despite situations which required reevaluation of the importance of intangibles, or which reflected inconsistencies in beliefs and possibly in values and, thus, necessitated a redefinition or reinterpretation of the belief in order to dislodge the inconsistency. For the former, Kissinger's primary beliefs and values resisted change, whereas for the latter his value preference did so. What others regard as dissimilar issues and problems, Kissinger perceives as various facets of his value networks. The intangibles of purpose and value, then, transcend differences of content and issue.

With this man of certainty who lived in uncertain times we have been granted a unique opportunity to enrich our knowledge and understanding of the area of intangibles. It is an area whose fruitful promise merits the further attention of scholars and other observers of politics.

Appendix

Conceptualizations of Value Categories

1. authority
2. safety/security*
3. independence*
4. achievement*
5. recognition
6. self-regard*
7. aggression*
8. creative self-
   expression (creativity)*
9. practicality*
10. knowledge*

11. truthfulness*
12. justice*
13. modesty*
14. strength*
15. determination*
16. intelligence
17. appearance*
18. harmony*
19. flexibility*
20. risk taking
21. subtlety

22. timing
23. challenge
24. credibility
25. support
26. dominance*
27. happiness*
28. obedience*
29. conformity
30. tolerance*

*White's original coding categories (1951)

Illustrative Statements of Value Categories

safety/security: statements dealing with physical security; absence of war, violence, physical aggression, pain, injury or death; and no fear or danger of these things; peace, order; e.g., "The base objective of this organization, the maintenance of our national security, has been the central concern of my life for over two decades as teacher and writer as well as public servant."

creativity: statements dealing with imagination; also "making things" in which at least some element of imagination or originality is involved; e.g., "Profound policy thrives on creativeness."

determination: statements dealing with intensity or tenacity of motivation, especially in the face of difficulty and danger. Will, persistence; bravery and courage; toughness, resolve; e.g.: "We have a moral obligation to persevere. . . . Our willingness to bear vastly reduced but still vital burdens in the area will influence other countries' assessment of our resolve and stamina."

knowledge: statements dealing with mental content corresponding to "reality"—both the having of such content and the degree of "truth" or correspondence with reality; fact, wisdom, understanding; e.g., "It is my duty as secretary of state to define the world as it is."

intelligence: statements dealing with mental ability; all "good" intellectual qualities such as memory, logic, intuition, perspective, reflection; e.g., "Our executives are shaped by a style of life that inhibits reflectiveness."

self-regard: statements dealing with pride, confidence, no feeling of inferiority; also self-respect, inner integrity; e.g.: "Not only can you not announce that you are giving up hope, you must not give up hope. You must believe in what you are doing."

justice: statements dealing with equality; fairness or equal opportunity; fairmindedness or openmindedness; e.g., "No state can doubt its own good faith; it is the vehicle of its social cohesion. . . . The whole domestic effort of a people exhibits an effort to transform force into obligation."

harmony: statements dealing with notions of balance; commensurability and proportionality; to blend opposing forces on relationships; e.g., "Effective policy depends not only on the skill of individual moves but even more importantly on their relationship to each other. It requires a sense of proportion."

flexibility: statements portraying an absence of dogmatism; expressing a willingness to compromise; to adjust; fluidity; e.g.: "It is important to be precise about the deterrent effect of the 'nuclear stalemate': it deters not only aggression, but resistance to it; and it deters not war as such, but all-out war. The side which can present its challenges in less than all-out form may, therefore, be able to use the 'nuclear stalemate'."

risk taking: statements indicating an entertainment of chance; to act on conjecture without all the facts, daring, uncertainty; e.g., "There are intellectuals within the bureaucracy who have avoided the administrative approach but who must share the prevailing confusion because they fail to recognize the inevitable element of conjecture in policy making."

subtlety: statements indicating a preference for discrimination; nuance, finesse; pertaining to an attribute of intelligence and behavior; variation; e.g., "For this reason our policy lacks a feeling for nuance, the ability to come up with variations on the same theme, as the Soviets have done so effectively."

authority: statements dealing with commands; an implication of influence; to be able to enforce compliance; potential power; e.g., "Foreign governments, when they deal with the United States, make a bet in their dealings on the constancy of American policy and on the ability of the United States to carry through on whatever we promise, or fail to promise, or threaten."

timing: statements dealing with a temporal dimension of action; the moment, correctness with respect to time; e.g., "It causes us to overlook the fact that policy exists in time as well as space, that a measure is correct only if it can be carried out at the proper moment."

support: statements dealing with aid; countenance; to substantiate or verify; to maintain, in coordination; e.g., "A statesman who too far outruns the experience of his people will not be able to sell his program at home."

credibility: statements dealing with the worth of a belief; trustworthy, reliable; e.g., "And while we probably might have done nothing anyway, it makes a lot of difference for Hanoi whether it thinks the U.S. probably will not or whether it thinks that we certainly cannot."

challenge: statements dealing with dispute; to contest, or call into question; to test the validity of thoughts and actions; e.g., "Let us act in the spirit of Thucydides that 'the bravest are
surely those who have the clearest vision of what is before them, glory and danger alike,
and yet notwithstanding go out and meet it.'"

4. Cognitive Maps and International Realities: Henry A. Kissinger's Approach to World Politics

Stephen G. Walker

In an age when bureaucracy and technology are important but impersonal tools for managing the nation's complex problems, the belief that human beings are really guiding the nation's destiny has become more important than ever to many Americans.[1] Historically, the president of the United States has been the personal symbol who embodies the average citizen's hopes and fears for the political future. This role in the Nixon and Ford administrations, however, appears to have been shared by Henry Alfred Kissinger, the U.S. secretary of state and president's advisor for national security affairs.[2]

The public magnitude of this role sharing was peculiar to the Nixon presidency, although previous chief executives relied heavily upon trusted and gifted advisors. President Johnson sought counsel from Kissinger's predecessor, Walt Whitman Rostow, regarding foreign policy matters. He also respected the judgments of Robert MacNamara, Dean Rusk, Clark Clifford, and George Ball, but none of them achieved the public preeminence that Kissinger enjoyed. The Kennedy administration included a galaxy of "the best and the brightest" minds from the Ivy League and elsewhere, symbolized by McGeorge Bundy in Rostow's White House spot, plus MacNamara and his "whiz kids" in the Pentagon, and Robert Kennedy in the attorney general's office. Even President Eisenhower had his inside man (Sherman Adams) and his own Agnew (Vice President Nixon). However, none of these presidential lieutenants in the previous three administrations publicly overshadowed their chief executives, who more than held their own as national political symbols.

The emergence of Henry Kissinger as the public personification of the Nixon administration's best feature was at least partly attributable to four circumstances. First, President Nixon was relatively inconspicuous and uncharismatic compared to presidents Eisenhower, Kennedy, and Johnson. Second, Nixon placed enormous emphasis upon foreign policy during his first term, as witnessed by the SALT talks, the visits to Beijing and Moscow, and the continuing effort to terminate the Vietnam War. Third, Kissinger's role as the principal agent for American foreign policy was both genuine and conspicuous; he was consistently recognized as the most important decision maker next to the president himself. Fourth, Kissinger's personality was amenable to popularization and, just as importantly, to humanization. His professional background as a Harvard professor and a specialist in international relations, his reputation as a ladies' man prior to his marriage in 1974, his pleasant and witty public presence, combined to give him an image of professional competence, human foibles, and personal warmth that suggested authenticity and inspired confidence. The communications media quickly identified and magnified these characteristics. During the Watergate trauma and the transition to the Ford administration, Kissinger became a symbol of continuity in an otherwise unsettling period.[3]

The conjunction of these circumstances helps explain how and why Henry Kissinger became a popular phenomenon. More intriguing and important questions remain concerning the nature and degree of Kissinger's influence upon American foreign policy. A comprehensive and definitive treatment of Kissinger's place in history may have to await the opening of American diplomatic archives in the distant future. Nevertheless, the objective of this study is to suggest some preliminary answers to these general questions, based upon readily available evidence from the public record.

Kissinger's Approach to World Politics

The press and the American intelligentsia have tended to equate Henry Kissinger's approach to world politics either with Klemens von Metternich, the Austrian foreign minister who orchestrated the Concert of Europe established at the Congress of Vienna, or with Otto von Bismarck, the Prussian master of the European balance of power between 1862 and 1890 (Brandon, 1973a; Brzezinski, 1972:54–59; Hoffmann, 1972a, 1972b). The first comparison often emphasizes Metternich's balance of power tactics, his concerns for maintaining the status quo in post-Napoleonic Europe, and his conservative views on revolution in making similar, sometimes critical, assessments of Kissinger's management of American foreign policy. Kissinger's academic interest in Metternich and the Congress of Vienna, plus a preoccupation with the Vietnam War by the first Nixon administration, has made such analogies plausible. The justification for the administration's Vietnam policies tended to be "conservative" arguments in the contemporary American intellectual climate, and they reflected a concern for international stability that was genuine. However, a close examination of Kissinger's analysis of Metternich reveals that the parallels between the two men may be overdrawn.

Kissinger criticizes Metternich for making the status quo the legitimizing principle of his foreign policy in the midst of a revolutionary period. The manipulation of balance of power techniques to maintain an equilibrium wedded to the status quo is a futile exercise in an age of revolutionary change, because there is lacking a conception of purpose that can channel revolutionary forces into a constructive direction (Kissinger, 1957a:322). Metternich's agile diplomacy did not solve the fundamental problems of his era, which required the conceptualization of objectives determined independently of diplomatic tactics in order to guide their application: "Metternich had learned the lessons of the eighteenth-century cabinet diplomacy too well. Its skillful sense of proportion was appropriate for a period whose structure was unchallenged and whose components were animated by a consciousness of their safety; but it was sterile in an era of constant flux" (Kissinger, 1957a:323).

The parallels drawn between Kissinger and Bismarck are somewhat similar to those postulated between Kissinger and Metternich. There is an emphasis upon the balance of power approach purportedly common to both men, which substitutes diplomatic manipulation for substantive policy (Brandon, 1973a:35). Again, however, a review of Kissinger's appraisal of Bismarck reveals the analogy and its inferences to be misleading. Kissinger (1970) sees in Bismarck a determination to tackle and solve Prussia's problems, a conception of purpose that Metternich lacks in dealing with Austria's problems. Whereas Metternich used his diplomatic skills simply to delay the impact of the forces unleashed by the industrial, nationalist, and democratic revolutions upon the archaic structure of the Austrian Empire, Bismarck harnessed these forces to unite and modernize the German states under Prussia.[4] Both men understood the historical forces of their age; however, one channeled these forces toward a task of national construction while the other merely tried to deflect their progress. Consequently, Kissinger (1970:348) does not criticize Bismarck's policy for its lack of conception, but he does find it devoid of a legitimizing principle.

> The significance of Bismarck's criticism [of the then fragmented existence of the German states] did not, of course, reside in the fact that it was made . . . but in the manner by which it was justified. Heretofore the attacks on the [then existing] principle of legitimacy had occurred in the name of other principles of presumably greater validity, such as nationalism or liberalism. Bismarck declared the relativity of *all* beliefs; he translated them into forces to be evaluated in terms of the power they could generate.

In his assessment of both Metternich and Bismarck, Kissinger is critical of the mere use of balance of power techniques without an adequate conception of the international milieu in order to guide their application. Such a conception has two essential elements: it must be based upon an accurate empirical assessment of the possibilities inherent in the current historical situation, and it must include a legitimizing principle compatible with the spirit of the contemporary age. Metternich's conception of the international milieu inappropriately applied the monarchical legitimizing principle for the Austrian Empire to the international order. Bismarck based his diplomacy solely upon an estimate of power relationships without a legitimizing principle that would make his policies acceptable at least to the other great powers.[4]

From his analysis of Metternich, Kissinger (1957a:326) has synthesized a profile of the ideal statesman.

> The test of a statesman, then, is his ability to recognize the real relationship of forces and to make this knowledge serve his ends. . . . His instrument is diplomacy, the art of relating states to each other by agreement rather than the exercise of force, by the representation of a ground of action which reconciles particular aspirations with a general consensus. Because diplomacy depends upon persuasion and not imposition, it presupposes a determinate framework, either through an agreement or, theoretically, through an identical interpretation of power relationships, although the latter is in practice the most difficult to attain.

His delineation of the ideal statesman clearly indicates that Kissinger is aware of the pitfalls associated with a diplomacy based primarily upon the expedient manipulation of other nations, a diplomacy either lacking an appropriate legitimizing principle or without a viable conception of historic purpose. Those who make these criticisms of the Kissinger era in American foreign policy need also to explain how a man so obviously sensitive to these weaknesses could pursue such a policy.

One possible avenue of enlightenment is a further examination of his academic writings. They would buttress these criticisms or provide a reinterpretation of Kissinger's foreign policy that is consistent with his canons of statesmanship. Although scattered among several sources, Dr. Kissinger's approach to world politics is unusually well documented and articulated. He wrote many books and articles between 1950 and 1969 (see bibliography) before he became the president's principal foreign policy advisor. An exploration of these sources may reveal important components of Kissinger's approach to world politics and lead to greater insight regarding current American foreign policy.[5]

What kinds of information do these documents contain? They include Kissinger's personal philosophy of history and his political philosophy, which are relatively permanent features of his personality. In addition, Kissinger's writings express his political style by applying these philosophical principles to the analysis of contemporary international issues. Kissinger's scholarly research of European diplomatic history and his more polemical treatises of contemporary international problems share a recurring tendency to generalize and hypothesize lessons and conclusions from the empirical analysis of historical cases. Kissinger has called himself a historian, but he is also a grand political theorist in the classical tradition (Reston, 1974). His scholarship often takes the form of an erudite theoretical essay rather than a historical monograph. As the previous review of Kissinger's evaluation of Metternich and Bismarck implies, he also values such theorizing as a virtue for the policy maker to cultivate. Without a historically rooted, theoretical conception of the world and the national interest, the policy maker cannot really make policy, only react to the policies of other nations (Kissinger, 1957b:431; 1961a:352; 1969a:91–92).

If there is a pattern to the development of Kissinger's academic work, it may be most intelligible in his own efforts to develop a conception of the world and to define the American national interest. His undergraduate honors thesis at Harvard (Kissinger, 1951) is an extensive critique of the philosophies of history formulated by Spengler, Toynbee, and Kant. His doctoral dissertation (Kissinger, 1957a) is a philosophical analysis of the defeat of Napoleon and the emergence of the Concert of Europe. The philosophical beliefs distilled from these two scholarly efforts recur frequently in his later, more famous works, *Nuclear Weapons and Foreign Policy* (1957b), *The Necessity for Choice* (1961a), *The Troubled Partnership* (1965a), and *American Foreign Policy* (1969a). When Henry Kissinger assumed his duties in 1969 as President Nixon's foreign policy advisor, he had already devoted his academic life to activities that cultivated the virtues which he found lacking in his critical analyses of American policy makers.

Although Kissinger's academic research contains a systematic set of premises, the decision to focus initially upon his academic writing rather than upon his performance as a member of the Nixon administration does carry with it certain assumptions. These assumptions must hold in order for the academic sources to enhance the understanding of Kissinger's influence upon American foreign policy.

1. *Continuity*: Kissinger's philosophy and political style did not change after he wrote his books.
2. *Comprehensiveness*: his books cover a range of topics sufficient to reveal important aspects of his approach to world politics.
3. *Honesty*: the judgments in Kissinger's scholarship are not deceptions but instead represent his real opinions and approach.
4. *Fruitfulness*: the understanding of American foreign policy is enhanced by knowing Kissinger's approach to world politics, because he was an influential American decision maker and the decision maker's approach is intrinsically important to know in order to comprehend his foreign policy.

However tenuous some or all of these assumptions may appear, the alternative focus upon Kissinger's governmental performance also creates problems for the researcher. There is the problem of attributability with respect to government documents. To what extent did the president, Secretary Kissinger, or a staffer really formulate "State of the World Reports" to Congress (Nixon, 1970, 1971, 1972, 1973), the public speeches of Nixon and Kissinger, the memoranda and the other documents leaked to the press or formally released for public consumption by the U.S. government? The limited content of the public documents is also problematical. Their content is often topical and sketchy rather than comprehensive, which forces the reader to piece together disparate statements through the *verstehen* procedure. This procedure is very risky when the motivations of the writer are absent either because of the limited scope of the topic or because of national security reasons. These problems with documents are magnified when government behavior rather than rhetoric is the source. In addition, the focus upon either governmental rhetoric or behavior raises the problem of circular reasoning, that is, to infer the components of the decision-making approach from rhetoric and behavior and then to employ that cognitive map to explain the same rhetoric and behavior.

Both the academic and the governmental data sources, therefore, present problems of data reliability and validity. The research strategy for this study is to focus upon Kissinger's cognitive map as it appears in his academic writings.[6] Using these results as a benchmark, the second step is to compare them with the public record of the Nixon and Ford administrations. This sequence of steps initially avoids the reliability and validity problems associated with using only governmental data sources to construct Kissinger's approach to world politics. Simultaneously, from the sequence should emerge comparisons between Kissinger's cognitive map and the conduct of American foreign policy, which test in a preliminary way the validity of the assumptions behind the use of academic sources.

If there is perfect congruity between Kissinger's map and the Nixon administration's foreign policy, this result would support the validity of the academic data source and explain the congruent dimensions of American foreign policy as a consequent. If there is imperfect congruity, then the areas of incongruity may reflect imperfect measurement for either the cognitive map or the foreign policy variables, or indicate aspects of American foreign policy attributable to other exogenous variables. Either of these substantive results would be only a preliminary, tentative conclusion, because of the methodological assumptions behind the profile of Kissinger's cognitive map and the partial reliance upon secondary sources for the analysis of current American foreign policy. However, the results should at least suggest avenues for further research to verify or refute them.

The Contemporary Political Universe

Kissinger (1961a: 171) believes that the challenge to the statesman in the contemporary age is almost totally unprecedented.

> We are living in a period which in retrospect will undoubtedly appear to be one of the great revolutions in history. The self-sufficient nation-state is breaking down. No nation—not even the largest—can survive in isolation or realize its potentialities, material, political, or spiritual on its own. . . . We of the West, who bequeathed the concept of nationalism to others, must summon the initiative and imagination to show the way to a new international order.

Kissinger wrote these words in 1961, in what is probably his most definitive academic treatise of American foreign policy. The revolutionary dimensions of current international relations include the development and proliferation of nuclear weapons, and the emergence of two revolutionary challenges to the present international order in the form of the increasing influence of the communist states and the anti-colonial upheaval in the Third World (Kissinger, 1961a: 1–9).

Eight years later Kissinger's diagnosis of the revolutionary character of today's world remained essentially the same, though couched more abstractly (Kissinger, 1969a: 53):

> The revolutionary character of our age can be summed up in three general statements: (a) the number of participants in the international order has increased and their nature has altered; (b) their technical ability to affect each other has vastly grown; (c) the scope of their purposes has expanded. . . . For the first time foreign policy has become global.

With a change in the participants in the international system comes a period of dislocation, because a challenge to the current notion of legitimacy and a reduction in the influence of some traditional units is likely to accompany the entrance of new states into the system. The current revolution in military technology and the basing of contemporary domestic regimes upon popular support has multiplied the resources available for the conduct of foreign affairs, making the potential for dislocation profound as well as likely (Kissinger, 1969a: 54–55).

As in his earlier analyses of nineteenth-century diplomacy, Kissinger is concerned with the modes of leadership operating in current international politics. He finds three important leadership types: the bureaucratic-pragmatic, the ideological, and the revolutionary-charismatic. The first one, which typifies American leadership, lacks a historically rooted conception of foreign policy and operates within a highly differentiated bureaucracy. It relies upon technological virtuosity and negotiating skill to overcome the constraints upon policy imposed by the absence of a common conception of the future and the rigidities of a bureaucratic framework (Kissinger, 1974:29–34).

The other two types of leadership have a vision that guides their policies. They are variants of the prophetic-revolutionary mode of leadership elaborated earlier in *A World Restored* (1957a). The ideological type, which characterizes Soviet and Chinese leadership, depends upon doctrine for guidance, while the charismatic revolutionary type, common in the Third World, relies upon the personal vision of the individual leader for inspiration. The latter combines vision and flexibility, because of the centralization of power and legitimacy in a single individual, unencumbered by either doctrine or bureaucracy; however, its durability is limited because it is nontransferable and because the tremendous problems of governing a new state make leadership tenure in itself precarious (Kissinger, 1974:34–43).

The ideological type operates in two settings, exemplified by the Soviet Union and China. In a bureaucratized setting, such as the USSR, the leadership operates within two sets of constraints: doctrine and organization. The bureaucratic component weakens revolutionary élan and renders the policy process somewhat more empirical and pragmatic, but the mixture of structural rigidity and ideological residue makes dramatic policy changes unlikely. On the other hand, the first generation of revolutionaries in China operated through the 1970s with a prestige that transcended bureaucratic authority. Consequently, although their ideological fervor is more intense, the Chinese leaders could be more flexible. "If the leadership could change— or if its attitudes are modified—policy could probably be altered much more dramatically in Communist China than in the more institutionalized Communist countries (Kissinger, 1974:34–39).

Kissinger's vision of an international order that is both possible and justifiable within the constraints of the contemporary age has three main themes. The first theme is the renewal and extension of Western political values. He emphasizes the democratic political traditions shared by the United States and the NATO countries. These values should operate as a legitimizing principle for the close coordination of their foreign policies and provide the basis for the emergence of a united Europe, probably including the United States as well. This evolving regional political unit in the North Atlantic area should serve as an exemplar of both democratic politics and the future political unit in world politics. It should be accompanied by a policy which endorses regional organizations among the new nations and encourages the development of democratic values or at least the virtues of justice and self-restraint (Kissinger, 1961a:322).

Kissinger (1961a:298–340) believes that the political framework within which the nations and regions in the Third World develop is extremely important. Social and economic modernization is possible within a variety of political settings, democracy, fascism, and communism, but it is difficult to change the political setting itself once the process is well under way with a strong regime in existence. Therefore, the optimal time for influencing the development of these areas is now. The principal instrument of influence is the demonstration effect. One form of the demonstration effect is the example which the United States sets individually and the North Atlantic nations provide collectively. A second form is the use of economic aid, which should be focused primarily upon one democratically oriented nation per region if it is to be effective. A greater concentration of resources from outside could enable these nations to become local examples for their regions of the attractions of life in a modern, free society.

The second theme is the possibility of coexistence with the communist nations. Kissinger (1961a: 175–210) does not accept the theory of peaceful convergence of Western and communist societies, but he does believe that a power equilibrium and a common fear of nuclear war can provide the empirical and moral basis for coexistence. Arms control agreements can create and maintain a power equilibrium and reduce the probability of nuclear war that both sides share. Agreements with communist nations on other political issues are also possible. However, the test of acceptability should be not the possibility of agreement per se but whether or not the agreement is consistent with our conception of our own purposes. Agreement should not be based upon expectations or perceptions that individual Soviet leaders are more trustworthy, or that Soviet society is undergoing a transformation.

The third theme is the necessity for a new style of leadership to manage American foreign policy. The United States needs to train our ablest people differently for public responsibilities, away from the adversary, legalistic, pragmatic training to a historical, philosophical, humanist education, in which the substantive mastery of political problems is more important than previous executive experience in dealing with other problems in business or law. At the societal level there needs to be a shift in emphasis from materialistic values to the more intangible values in the American heritage, political freedom and the dignity of the individual. These changes are necessary if American foreign policy is to be purposeful and American society is to be an exemplar for the future (Kissinger, 1961a: 352–71).

Cognitive Maps and Foreign Policy

The goal in the following analysis is to establish connections between Kissinger's cognitive map and American foreign policy. The scope of these linkages is logically restricted to decision-making situations with characteristics that permitted Kissinger to exercise his personal influence. Since the style of the former secretary of state was to conduct personally or to dominate all phases of some American foreign policy endeavors, it may be possible to determine the influence of his cognitive map even upon the implementation phase of the foreign policy process.

The conceptualization of foreign policy that will structure the analysis is necessarily somewhat broad and consists of four aspects which are summarized in the following definition: foreign policy is the complex of behaviors (1) and motivations

(2) that constitute a decision maker's response (3) over time to a problem (4). Policies can be differentiated by the definition of the problem which a policy maker selects, the types and sequences of behaviors which characterize the action component of his response, and the identity and scope of the objectives and dispositions which his behavior is intended to satisfy. This conceptualization of foreign policy permits the analysis of a policy's structure, that is, the strategic and tactical mosaic that emerges as the behaviors and motivations that characterize a decision maker's response to a problem are charted over time. If there is a connection between a cognitive map and foreign policy, it should show up as a congruent relationship between the various components of a decision maker's map and the components of his foreign policy. The technique of corroboration is a structural matching exercise, in which the content of the decision maker's cognitive map guides the analysis of his foreign policy activities (Walker, 1977: 133).

As an important member of the Nixon administration, Kissinger was directly concerned with a number of important foreign policy problems, including Soviet-American relations, Sino-American relations, the Arab-Israeli conflict, the Vietnam War, and the Strategic Arms Limitation Talks. In this analysis the focus is upon Soviet-American relations and the Arab-Israeli conflict, in order to determine if American foreign policy behavior is consistent with Kissinger's cognitive map in these two cases.

Soviet-American Relations

When Richard Nixon became president in 1969, he announced the onset of "an era of negotiation" with the nations of the communist bloc. During the remainder of his first term, the Nixon administration produced a number of agreements with the Soviet Union and established contact with the People's Republic of China. Although the opening toward China was more spectacular, the policy of detente toward the Soviet Union yielded more concrete and more controversial results. The specific behaviors that constituted American detente policy are relatively easy to define in a superficial sense. They include the negotiations between the United States and the Soviet Union, which culminated in the series of agreements signed by Nixon and Brezhnev at the Moscow Summit in May 1972. These agreements covered a variety of problems, including economic, cultural, and scientific-technical relations, accompanied by an arms control agreement, a joint communiqué, and a declaration of "Basic Principles" that were supposed to guide future relations between the two superpowers. Taken individually, it is difficult to match a particular behavior in the negotiations process with Kissinger's cognitive map, but considered collectively, the overall pattern of the detente agreements was consistent with several tenets of the secretary's approach to world politics and his conception of the contemporary political universe.

In his academic writings Kissinger consistently describes the contemporary political universe as a revolutionary international order. The dominant characteristic of a revolutionary era is the absence of a generally accepted notion of legitimacy, that is, a general consensus upon the permissible aims and methods of foreign policy.[7] The task of a statesman in a revolutionary era is to shape a generally accepted notion of legitimacy from the available historical material. Negotiations are the means by which a statesman accomplishes this task. If negotiations cannot establish a mutual notion of legitimacy, then they can at least establish a mutual interpretation of power relationships that can limit the aims and methods of foreign policy in the short run (Kissinger, 1957b:4, 141–42, 203). Kissinger's own philosophy contains the principles of self-limitation and tolerance for other philosophical positions; consequently, his transcendent negotiating objective is to communicate this aspect of his foreign policy to other nations and persuade them to base their policies upon a similar sense of limits (Burd, 1975; see also Walker, 1977:139).

Kissinger's conduct of U.S. detente policy appears to match this approach to the selection and implementation of political goals in the international arena. The following three features of American detente policy particularly reflected the influence of Kissinger's cognitive map: (1) the "linkage" strategy that governed the conduct of the SALT negotiations and the timing of the Moscow Summit; (2) the emphasis upon SALT as an integral part of detente; and (3) the Basic Principles issued jointly by the U.S. and USSR at the 1972 Moscow Summit meeting.

In a briefing for reporters several weeks following the inauguration, Kissinger (1979:129) used the term "linkage" specifically: "To take the question of linkage between the political and strategic environment . . . [the president] . . . would like to deal with the problem of peace on the entire front in which peace is challenged and not only on the military one." During their terms in office, Nixon and Kissinger linked progress on one issue to progress on other issues. For instance, they were unwilling to begin the SALT negotiations until the Soviets also agreed to discuss other important issues such as the Middle East, Berlin, and Vietnam (Kissinger, 1979:129–38; Nixon, 1978:346). Kissinger did not insist upon the resolution of these conflicts by negotiation in order for the SALT talks to begin, but he did want an indication that the Soviet attitude was serious regarding the negotiation of an agreement on mutually satisfactory terms.

Kissinger's definition of linkage was consistent with his belief that negotiations should be conducted under conditions where each side recognizes that mutually satisfactory terms are necessary for agreement. The function of negotiations is to adjust competing claims and not to impose one side's will upon the other (Walker, 1977: 410). Some officials in the Nixon administration, however, opposed the linkage concept.

For example, Secretary of State William Rogers favored opening the SALT negotiations immediately and did not want to link SALT to other foreign policy issues (Kissinger, 1979:136). Secretary of Defense Melvin Laird opposed the position of parity and favored superiority as the American strategic objective for the SALT talks (Kalb and Kalb, 1974:111). In the subsequent bureaucratic infighting, Kissinger's views ultimately prevailed. Linkage evolved into detente, as the two superpowers made progress toward a SALT agreement and exchanged views on Vietnam, Berlin, and the Middle East between 1969 and early 1972. Kissinger did not succeed in resolving the conflicts between Soviet and American client states in Southeast Asia and the Middle East through Moscow channels, but progress in the negotiations between Washington and Moscow concerning nuclear weapons and the success of the talks over Berlin led to the scheduling of the summit meeting between Nixon and Brezhnev for May 1972. In spite of the American decision to bomb Hanoi and to mine Haiphong and other North Vietnamese ports on May 8, the Moscow Summit began on schedule on May 22.

The rationale for the SALT agreement and the other agreements dealing with the environment, space, health, and economic relations, which were announced at the Moscow Summit, is consistent with the linkage concept. The links, however, were publicly stated to be between the policy areas covered by the various agreements rather than with the Vietnam or Middle East problems. At a press conference to brief members of Congress on the Strategic Arms Limitation agreements, Kissinger expressed the following rationale, which is consistent with his cognitive map (U.S. Department of State, *Bulletin*, July 10, 1972:47–48):

> For the first time, two great powers, deeply divided by their divergent values, philosophies, and social systems, have agreed to restrain the very armaments on which their national survival depends. No decision of this magnitude could have been taken unless it had been part of a larger decision to place relations on a new foundation of restraint, cooperation, and steadily evolving confidence. A spectrum of agreements on joint efforts with regard to the environment, space, health, and promising negotiations on economic relations provides a prospect for avoiding the failure of the Washington Naval Treaty and the Kellogg-Briand Pact outlawing war, which collapsed in part for lack of an adequate political foundation.

The "larger decision to place relations on a new foundation of restraint, cooperation, and steadily evolving confidence" was articulated in the Basic Principles signed by the two superpowers at the Moscow Summit. Together with the SALT agreements, the Basic Principles accomplished, in Kissinger's view, what he has called the basic tasks of a statesman in a revolutionary era, the achievement of a general consensus upon the permissible aims and methods of foreign policy and a mutual interpretation of power relationships.

Among the provisions in the Basic Principles were the following points committing the U.S. and the Soviet Union to:

1. prevent the development of situations capable of causing a dangerous exacerbation of their relations;
2. do their utmost to avoid military confrontations;
3. recognize that efforts to obtain unilateral advantage at the expense of the other, directly or indirectly, are inconsistent with these objectives;
4. have a special responsibility . . . to do everything in their power so that conflicts or situations will not arise which would serve to increase international tensions.

One critic of Soviet-American detente who contrasted the Basic Principles with subsequent Soviet behavior in the October War concluded: "Detentes may be maximal or minimal or anything in between. The 'basic principles' of May 1972 represented detente at its maximum. They proved to be an unmitigated snare and delusion" (Draper, 1974:38).

While Kissinger would certainly contest this conclusion, he would agree that detente may be maximal or minimal. According to Kissinger's approach to world politics, detente may be maximal, based upon a common notion of legitimacy (the Basic Principles), or it may be minimal, relying upon a common interpretation of power relationships (the SALT agreements). The actual relationship between the two nuclear giants may fluctuate between these two extremes over time. Kissinger explicitly recognized the fluid and fragile nature of detente at his news conferences in Moscow and Kiev during the 1972 summit meeting (U.S. Department of State, *Bulletin*, June 26, 1972:884):

> Now, we have no illusions. We recognize that Soviet ideology still proclaims a considerable hostility to some of our most basic values. We also recognize that if any of these principles is flouted, we will not be able to wave a piece of paper and insist that the illegality of the procedure will, in itself, prevent its being carried out. . . . As in every document, this document indicates an aspiration and an attitude, and if the aspiration or the attitude changes, then, of course, as sovereign countries, either side can change its course.

Nevertheless, the establishment of detente, minimal or maximal, was a necessary gamble, justified by the belief that the two nuclear superpowers "hold literally the survival of mankind in their hands" (U.S. Department of State, *Bulletin*, June 26, 1972:887). The gamble was also compatible with Kissinger's need for a framework within which to exercise the statesman's art of diplomacy.

The design and execution of American foreign policy toward the Soviet Union between 1969 and 1972 involved long-range planning and considerable uncertainty, in which Kissinger's conceptions of "what is," "what is important," "what is likely," "what is desirable," and "what is related to what," were very influential in the policy process. He needed to convert the president from a preference for "superiority" to support for "parity" as the principal SALT objective, and he had to overcome opposition to the notion of linkage and the objective of parity in the foreign affairs bureaucracy. Kissinger and Nixon did not agree upon the exact nature of the linkage concept, and Kissinger's position was occasionally outflanked by statements emanating from the White House and the State Department.

However, in spite of his inability to control every single behavior that constituted America's Soviet policy during this period, Kissinger dominated the cumulative pattern of behaviors and provided the rationale for the policy. The resulting structure of the detente policy was consistent with Kissinger's cognitive map. The SALT agreements and the Basic Principles correspond to the components of legitimacy which are central to his approach to world politics. Kissinger's interpretation of linkage was also consistent with the emphasis in his approach upon negotiations as the principal means of establishing a legitimate international order.

Crises in the Middle East

The development and maintenance of the U.S. detente policy toward the USSR was not accomplished solely by negotiation. The use of force by the Nixon administration during the Jordanian civil war in 1970 and the October War in 1973 constituted another element in American policy toward the Soviet Union. In each confrontation Henry Kissinger played a central role in the formulation and execution of the American response. The two situations shared similar features, and Kissinger's behavior was consistent in both crises. In each case the United States was not a direct party to the conflict and was not engaged in military combat operations in the area prior to the crisis. However, the American government did have a substantial interest in the outcome, because the security of a client, Israel, plus the extension of Soviet influence in the Middle East, was at stake. In each case there was also the possibility of nuclear escalation inherent in any superpower confrontation. In the long run the outcome of both conflicts could also threaten the oil supplies of the United States and its allies; the October War's oil embargo dramatized this possibility.

Each crisis occurred in the context of the emerging superpower detente relationship that could be destroyed by the way in which the United States and the Soviet Union managed their confrontation. The Jordanian and October wars were examples of situations where negotiations had failed to contain conflict to submilitary levels. Kissinger's approach to such situations calls for negotiations throughout the conflict and the use of threats only to counter threats or the use of force initiated by the opponent; the use of force to counter force initiated by the opponent may also be necessary. Enough force in combination with generous peace terms should be applied so that the opponent is faced with an attractive peace settlement as well as the unattractive alternatives of stalemate or the necessity to escalate (Walker, 1977:147).

When the war between King Hussein's troops and the Palestinian commandos began suddenly on September 15, 1970, intelligence reports began to reach Washington, which indicated that Syrian tanks with Soviet advisors were headed toward the Jordanian border (Nixon, 1978:483). Within the Washington Special Action Group (WSAG)[8] there were two points of view expressed regarding the diagnosis of the situation and the appropriate American response. Secretary of State Rogers led the cautious group that pressed for the use of diplomacy rather than military maneuvers. Kissinger represented the power-oriented group which advocated the deployment of military forces and their use if necessary. In these discussions President Nixon tended to side with the Kissinger group (Kalb and Kalb, 1974:202).

The Jordanian military confrontation possessed the definitive features of an international crisis in the eyes of those American decision makers who advocated the use of military force. The stakes were high, the decision time was short, and the occasion for decision was unanticipated. These characteristics are associated and, in some respects, coterminous with conditions in which the cognitive maps of decision makers are likely to be very influential upon foreign policy. Specifically, crises are unanticipated events in which initial reactions are likely to reflect cognitive "sets." They are also situations in which decisions are likely to take place under stress that could affect the complex cognitive tasks associated with high-level executive decision making (Hermann, 1969, 1972; Holsti, 1976a).

In addition, crisis situations tend to be characterized by the presence of ambiguous, scarce, or contradictory information, which is likely to be interpreted according to the predispositions of the decision maker. The intelligence reports that the Soviets were supporting Syrian intervention in the conflict prompted Kissinger to diagnose the situation as a Soviet-American confrontation. Kissinger's disposition toward the use of force to counter an opponent's use of force led him to justify the use of force as necessary in order to communicate to the Russians that the principles of detente, which were then in the formative stages between the two nations, could not be compromised (Kissinger, 1979:614–17).

On September 16, President Nixon stated to a group of mid-western newspaper editors in Chicago that the United States might be forced to intervene in Jordan if Syria or Iraq threatened the Jordanian regime. In a background briefing to the same newsmen, Kissinger diagnosed the Middle East situation this way:

> Our relations with the Soviet Union have reached the point where some important decisions have to be made, especially in Moscow. . . . Events in the Middle East and in other parts of the world have raised questions of whether Soviet leaders as of now are prepared to pursue the principles that I outlined earlier; specifically, whether the Soviet leaders are prepared to forego tactical advantages they can derive from certain situations for the sake of the larger interest of peace (Kalb and Kalb, 1974:209).

By September 19, Syrian tanks had crossed their frontier into Jordan. Kissinger recommended an alert of American forces to President Nixon, who accepted this recommendation. The Sixth Fleet began to steam toward Lebanon and Israel, and U.S. airborne units in West Germany were moved to airfields in a conspicuous fashion so that the Soviets would notice. The president accompanied this selective alert with a warning to Moscow that they must restrain the Syrians (Kissinger, 1979:621–24).

Over the next few days Kissinger was instrumental in the steady application of military pressure upon the Syrians to withdraw their tanks from Jordan. He approached Israel on behalf of Hussein to ask for Israeli intervention against Syria. When Secretary of State Rogers argued for a new diplomatic approach, a joint Soviet-American attempt to dampen tensions, Nixon, "with Kissinger's strong support," overruled the proposal. Instead, the previous U.S. message to the Soviet Union was repeated: there would be a serious threat to peace unless the Syrian tanks left Jordan. The turning point in the crisis came on September 22. By that time Israeli forces were mobilized and ready to move into Jordan and Syria. Nixon had pledged American intervention to support Israel if Soviet or Egyptian forces came to the aid of Syria. Hussein launched an all-out air and armor offensive against the Syrian positions in Jordan. Apparently under intense diplomatic pressure from Soviet envoys in Damascus, the Syrian government ordered a military withdrawal from Jordan. The conflict ended without Israeli intervention or a direct Soviet-American military confrontation.

The Jordanian crisis of 1970 was a reflection of the wider conflict between Arabs and Israelis. Without a breakthrough in the Arab-Israeli deadlock, the military disengagement of outside forces was the most feasible American objective related to the civil war in Jordan. The advice which Kissinger gave Nixon was directed toward that immediate objective. This advice was consistent with his diagnosis of the situation as an instance in which the Soviet Union had exceeded the objectives and methods permissible under detente.

The outbreak of the October War in 1973 between Israel and the Egyptian-Syrian coalition offered the opportunity to move toward settlement of the Arab-Isreali conflict. It also created the risk of a direct military confrontation between the United States and the Soviet Union. The outbreak of war was unanticipated by Kissinger and other top-level decision makers in the U.S. foreign affairs bureaucracy (Kissinger, 1982:450–59). The stakes were high and similar to those in the Jordanian crisis. As the war developed, events on the battlefield forced American policy makers to respond quickly.

Under these circumstances the decision-making process was once again centralized in WSAG. Kissinger's diagnosis of the situation was somewhat ambivalent. He viewed it as evidence that the Soviets had violated the maximal version of detente symbolized by the Basic Principles of the Moscow Summit, and yet he viewed the outbreak of fighting in the Middle East as an opportunity to move toward a resolution of the Arab-Israeli conflict (Kissinger, 1982:468):

> Although he [Kissinger] was angry at the Russians, he realized that he needed their cooperation to contain the fighting and to establish a framework for negotiations. . . . For several years it had been his hope that one day the two superpowers would cooperate in stimulating a peace agreement between the Arabs and the Jews. Now he sensed that time was approaching. He resisted political pressures to denounce the Russians (Kalb and Kalb, 1974:463).

Instead, Kissinger gave Soviet Ambassador Dobrynin a personal letter from Nixon to Brezhnev, calling for a cease-fire and a commitment to limit the fighting. The letter also called Brezhnev's attention to the principles of detente that the two nations had agreed to at the 1972 and 1973 summit meetings (Kissinger, 1982:591).

The conduct of the military campaigns in the October War was outside the immediate control of the superpowers, but each one maintained close contact with its client. Kissinger expected the Israelis to win a rapid military victory, once they took the offensive. Although this estimate turned out to be false, he did maintain his initial objective, which was to have the two superpowers use their influence to establish a cease-fire followed by negotiations between the two sides. The combination of military and diplomatic behaviors that the United States government implemented during the remainder of the crisis was orchestrated by Kissinger to achieve that objective. The timing and sequence of these moves were in accord with his approach to the calculation and control of the risks associated with political action (Walker, 1977:139–42). In the implementation of these tactics Kissinger encountered opposition from the Pentagon and the Israeli government, upon which he had to rely for compliance with his tactics. However, the execution of American policy was substantially in the hands of the newly designated secretary of state (Kissinger, 1982:470; Kalb and Kalb, 1974:484, 492–93).

The course of the October War proceeded in four stages.[9] The first stage lasted from the initiation of armed combat by Syria and Egypt on October 6 to the Soviet decision on October 10 to launch a massive logistical airlift to Egypt and Syria. The second stage began with the American response on October 13 in the form of a counter-airlift to Israel and continued with the Israeli counterattack across the Suez Canal on October 15. The third phase of the war involved the period of direct consultations between the superpowers, which began on October 20 with personal negotiations in Moscow between Kissinger and Brezhnev and ended with the cease-fire agreement jointly proposed on October 22 by the two superpowers through the UN. The final stage of the conflict began with the negotiations for implementing the ceasefire on October 23 and included the Soviet threat to enforce the cease-fire with Soviet troops, the American response in the form of a worldwide military alert, and the subsequent U.S.-Soviet endorsement of a UN peacekeeping force established by the Security Council and composed of personnel from nations that did not hold permanent seats on the Security Council.

During the first stage, Kissinger interpreted the positive Soviet reply to Nixon's proposal for a cease-fire resolution in the UN as an indication that Soviet (and possibly Arab) objectives in the Middle East were modest. Because of his estimate of a quick Israeli military victory, he did not push the American bureaucracy to fulfill Israel's requests for replacement aircraft to offset their early losses. Resistance to the Israeli request built up in the Department of Defense, where Secretary Schlesinger was sensitive to the threat of an Arab oil embargo if the United States "tilted" too far in favor of Israel (Nixon, 1978:924). In a series of talks with Ambassador Dobrynin, Kissinger urged Soviet cooperation in establishing a Middle East cease-fire and warned publicly: "Detente cannot survive irresponsibility in any area, including the Middle East" (Kissinger, 1982:491).

Clear evidence of a Soviet airlift into the Syrian and Egyptian capitals appeared in the intelligence reports that Kissinger received on the morning of October 10. By the end of the day he had also learned that three Soviet airborne units had been placed on alert in Eastern Europe. Accompanying this intelligence was a Soviet proposal for an immediate cease-fire. At that point neither superpower was likely to convince its client to agree to a cease-fire. The Arab nations were still on the offensive and had no incentive to stop until they met decisive resistance. The Israelis did not want to freeze the battlefield situation until they had at least gained the military initiative, which could not be guaranteed without the resupply of arms from the United States. The Soviet decision to resupply their client led Kissinger to recommend the same American action on behalf of Israel. He convinced President Nixon to put pressure on the Department of Defense so that the American airlift would accelerate immediately to a peak effort (Kissinger, 1982:495).

During this second stage of the war, Kissinger abandoned the objective of an Israeli military victory and opted for a different military solution: "The 'military solution' Kissinger wished to bring about was a stalemate. From the very beginning he believed that the airlift had to be finely tuned: on the one hand, to help Israel regain the military initiative, but not much more; and, on the other hand, to prod the Russians into accepting a sensible cease-fire plan that would open negotiations leading toward an overall settlement of the Middle East crisis" (Kalb and Kalb, 1974:479). However, the daring Israeli offensive across the Suez Canal on October 15 changed the complexion of the war and would upset Kissinger's calculations for a second time. Israel was now in a position to cut off Egyptian forces on the east bank of the canal and march toward Cairo for a political victory as well as a military one.

Faced with these reverses on the battlefield, the Soviets promised Egypt that they would secure a cease-fire, with or without American help. Brezhnev requested that Kissinger fly to Moscow for personal consultations on the Middle East situation, an invitation that he accepted. The cease-fire proposal that Kissinger and Brezhnev negotiated called for a cease-fire in place and the commencement of negotiations between the combatants. Both sides in the fighting accepted the proposal, although Sadat reportedly agreed to direct negotiations with Israel only after Brezhnev promised that the Soviet Union would guarantee the cease-fire unilaterally, if it should become necessary.

The implementation of the cease-fire proved to be problematical. Fighting continued at the Suez Canal after the October 22 deadline for the cessation of hostilities, which permitted Israel to consolidate its control of the west bank and completely prevent the resupply of Egyptian forces on the east bank. Brezhnev, who had pledged a Soviet guarantee of the cease-fire, proposed to President Nixon that the two superpowers "urgently dispatch to Egypt the Soviet and American contingents." His message also stated: "that if you find it impossible to act jointly with us in this matter, we should be faced with the necessity urgently to consider the question of taking appropriate steps unilaterally. We cannot allow arbitrariness on the part of Israel" (Kissinger, 1982:583). This note arrived in Washington on the evening of October 24, a day in which Kissinger had received reports of several additional Soviet military units being placed on alert and a Soviet push in the UN for a joint Soviet-U.S. peacekeeping force.

The American response to the Brezhnev message and its accompanying signals was twofold: a worldwide U.S. military alert and a carefully worded note from Nixon to Brezhnev. Kissinger drafted the text after first calling Dobrynin to warn him: "This is a matter of great concern. Don't you pressure us. I want to repeat again, don't pressure us!" (Kissinger, 1982:585). The American note rejected a joint superpower police force and opposed unilateral intervention by either superpower as a violation of the Basic Principles and the Agreement on the Prevention of Nuclear War. The composition of the peacekeeping forces should be nonnuclear members of the UN. The message was cleared through Nixon and sent early on the morning of October 25. After a few hours sleep, Kissinger, Nixon, and Alexander Haig met and decided to lobby for support of a nonnuclear force at the UN; they agreed to resupply the Israelis until all their losses were replaced. Kissinger would hold a press conference at noon to explain the U.S. military alert, which had become widely publicized.

At this news conference Kissinger first reviewed the major events of the October War that had brought about the present situation. Then he referred briefly to the U.S. military alert as a precautionary response to the possibility of the unilateral introduction of Soviet forces into the Middle East. He also restated American opposition to a joint Soviet-U.S. peacekeeping force on the grounds that it risked either a transfer of great power rivalry or the imposition of a superpower military condominium into the Middle East. Under questioning by reporters, Kissinger made it clear that the military alert was designed to deter the Russians from taking unilateral military action, but he repeatedly stressed that he did not consider the present situation to be a military confrontation: "We do not consider ourselves in a confrontation with the Soviet Union. We do not believe it is necessary at this moment, to have a confrontation. In fact, we are prepared to work cooperatively toward the realization of the objectives which we have set ourselves. . . . But cooperative action precludes unilateral action, and the President decided that it was essential that we make clear our attitude toward unilateral steps" (Department of State, *Bulletin*, 1973:588, 590).

During this news conference Kissinger followed a two-track policy: talking the Soviets out of a confrontation, after having alerted American military forces to prepare for one (Kalb and Kalb, 1974:496). At the United Nations the Soviet delegate subsequently changed his position and yielded to the insistence by the United States that the superpowers be excluded from the peacekeeping force. The following day (October 26) the American military alert was reduced, after the UN Security Council had passed a resolution establishing a peacekeeping force that excluded the two superpowers.

The final termination of the Arab-Israeli conflict is still yet to be resolved, despite the initial success of Kissinger's famous "shuttle diplomacy," which resulted in the disengagement of military forces in the Sinai and the Golan Heights in the aftermath of the cease-fire. In his October 25 news conference the secretary of state related the future of Arab-Israeli negotiations to the future of Soviet-American detente:

We have from the beginning of this administration, recognized that . . . we are dealing with an ideological and political adversary. We have also believed that we have a historic obligation, precisely in these conditions of being in opposition, to attempt to remove the dangers of war. We have always made clear, and we have always practiced, that we would resist any foreign policy adventures through the many crises in the early parts of this administration. . . . If the Soviet Union and we can work cooperatively, first toward establishing the cease-fire and then toward promoting a durable settlement in the Middle East, then the detente will have proved itself. If this does not happen, then we have made an effort—for which we paid no price—that had to be made. And then one has to wait for another moment when the task of insuring or of bringing peace to mankind can be attempted (U.S. Department of State, *Bulletin*, November 12, 1973:581–84).

In the 1970 Jordanian crisis and the 1973 October War, the United States was not a direct participant in the violent phases of these two conflicts. The superpowers became involved because of the respective client relationships between them and the adversaries. In both cases Kissinger acted to protect American interests in the area, but in the October War he also attempted to facilitate a resolution of the conflict between Arabs and Israelis. His tactics in the management of American policy during these crises combined the use of force and offers to defuse the conflict in a style which was consistent with his general approach to world politics. The American and Soviet positions as "third parties" in the conflict restricted their control over the evolving battlefield situations. However, Kissinger's proportionate use of threats and force to counter similar actions by other parties in the conflict, and his pursuit of limited objectives ultimately acceptable to all the participants in the conflict, permitted him to calculate and control the risks of political action in a confrontation with the potential for nuclear escalation.

Conclusion

Soviet-American relations and the Arab-Israeli conflict were foreign policy issues that attracted the personal attention of Henry Kissinger. In both cases he participated in virtually every phase of the Nixon administration's decision making regarding these problems. Each one also meets some of the conditions that Holsti (1976a) has identified, which are likely to make necessary a detailed investigation of the decision maker's cognitive map in order to achieve an adequate explanation of the policy response:

1. Both problems involve nonroutine situations that require more than merely the application of standard operating procedures and decision rules.
2. The problem of Soviet-American relations involves long-range policy planning, a task that inherently includes considerable uncertainty, and in which conceptions of "what is," "what is important," "what is desirable," and "what is related to what" are likely to be at the core of the political process.
3. The Arab-Israeli conflict contained phases when American decision makers were confronted with unanticipated situations or with ambiguous situations in which available information was either incomplete or open to a variety of interpretations.
4. The Soviet and Middle East situations involved exhausting negotiations in which the resulting stress may have impaired the decision maker's ability to perform complex cognitive tasks.
5. Both cases involved decisions made at the pinnacle of the government hierarchy by leaders who were relatively free from organizational and other constraints— or who might at least define their roles in ways that enhanced their latitude for choice.

The last condition, maximum opportunity for unconstrained behavior by the top decision makers, is a state of affairs that Kissinger consistently attempted to achieve. His efforts to centralize the National Security Council system are by now legendary. Similarly, his use of the communications media to generate domestic rapport and support was a major feature of his foreign policy activities. Through background and public press conferences and interviews he attempted to neutralize opposition and attract support for the administration's foreign policies. After his appointment as secretary of state, which placed him outside the protection of the doctrine of executive privilege, he pursued the same educational and public relations activities with Congress.

There remains, however, the question of how to separate the relative contributions of Henry Kissinger and Richard Nixon to the formulation and implementation of American foreign policy. Did each man constrain or reinforce the decision-making propensities of the other? A review of the president's views on foreign policy issues before he assumed office in 1969 indicates that by the latter part of the 1960s a more flexible attitude toward dealing with the communist world had replaced his cold war orientations (Nixon, 1967). The views of the two men regarding the general direction of U.S. foreign policy in the 1970s overlapped, as Kissinger discovered in his discussions with the newly elected president when Mr. Nixon offered him the post of assistant for national security affairs (Kissinger, 1979:9–16). It is more difficult to ascertain what occurred later between Nixon and Kissinger when they saw each other privately prior to a National Security Council meeting or the announcement of a major U.S. foreign policy decision.

During his tenure in office, Kissinger refused to discuss the extent of his personal influence upon final presidential decisions. He was quoted as saying, "Often I don't know whether I am the actor or the director" (Brandon, 1973a:33). A journalist who has concerned himself with this question cites the following description by a high official who attended many meetings with both men:

> The working relationship between them is comparable to one between an architect and a contractor. The decisions about the basic design were the President's, but Kissinger had great freedom on how to build the house. The President, for instance, decided that he wanted a solution to the Vietnam war which would ensure that the outcome would not lead to handing Vietnam over to the Communists, and then Kissinger constructed the necessary strategy. The President decided he wanted to open relations with China, and Kissinger designed the road map to Peking and traveled there first to remove all possible hazards on the way. The President decided he wanted a summit meeting in Moscow, and Kissinger prepared various solid bridges so that the President would get there and score a success. (Brandon, 1973a:64).

In retrospect, the architect-contractor analogy appears to be an oversimplification. President Nixon's influence upon policy was likely to be important, though intermittent, and was limited to those occasions where he personally intervened in the implementation phase of a policy or provided his own rationale for American actions. A careful review of the memoirs by each man often reveals differences, particularly over tactics, although in the Soviet-American and Arab-Israeli case studies these differences were either not important or nonexistent. The following illustrations offer insights into the dynamics of the relationship between Nixon and Kissinger with respect to the decision-making processes regarding these two cases.

In the area of Soviet-American relations the president wanted to link the May 1972 Moscow Summit with the resolution of the Vietnam conflict. He did not want to go to Moscow unless the Soviets would agree in effect to put Vietnam on the summit agenda. Mr. Nixon portrays Kissinger as less willing to recognize the tactical implications of this linkage strategy. This difference crystallized in April 1972 when the North Vietnamese canceled a meeting in Paris with Kissinger, which the Soviets had indicated earlier might be decisive in achieving a diplomatic settlement. In retaliation, the president wanted Kissinger to cancel a secret, presummit visit to Moscow: "Henry obviously considered this a crisis of the first magnitude. I laid down the law hard to him that under these circumstances he could not go to Moscow. I told him that what the Russians wanted to do was to get him to Moscow to discuss the summit. What we wanted to do was to get him to Moscow to discuss Vietnam. I can see that this shook him because he desperately wants to get to Moscow one way or the other. He took it in good grace" (Nixon, 1978:590).

Ultimately, Kissinger made his trip to Moscow on Nixon's terms. The Soviets agreed that Vietnam would be the first subject for discussion. The North Vietnamese foreign minister might even attend the talks. Under these circumstances the president responded: "I told Henry that I had reconsidered the situation and felt that we had to have an open option on the summit. We had to play out the string completely on the negotiating front, and he should go to Moscow" (Nixon, 1978:591). Kissinger's own account downplays the tactical differences illustrated by this episode and stresses the common linkage strategy held by both men. He also interprets the president's threats to cancel the summit as merely idiosyncratic: "To be sure, he often spoke of canceling the summit. But anyone familiar with his style knew that such queries, like occasional musings about his dispensability, were really a call for reassurance" (Kissinger, 1979:1120; see also: 1113–23).

With respect to the Arab-Israeli conflict and, in particular, the October War, the memoirs of the two men show no significant differences in either strategy or tactics. The president's account of U.S. decisions during the October 1973 fighting is less detailed, and it is interspersed with a narrative of Watergate developments and the selection of a new vice president during the same period (Nixon, 1978:920–42). However, Nixon and Kissinger express the common strategic conception that a cease-fire in which neither side had a decisive military advantage should be the immediate goal, followed by diplomatic initiatives to settle the issues that had precipitated the war. Both men saw the war as an opportunity to break the preexisting diplomatic stalemate and move toward a Middle East settlement (Nixon, 1978:921; Kissinger, 1982:468). Although there are some discrepancies in their accounts of the degree of participation by the president in this decision, they also agreed upon the worldwide U.S. military alert which was the major tactical move by the United

States during the course of the Soviet-American confrontation that accompanied the October War (Nixon, 1978:939–40; Kissinger, 1982:586–88).

It is difficult to generalize from the Soviet-American and Arab-Israeli case studies firm conclusions about the relative impact of each man upon the broad range of U.S. foreign policy decisions during the Nixon-Kissinger years. However, Kissinger's influence undoubtedly increased over time as he consolidated his control of the National Security Council system, increased his personal contact with the president, and became secretary of state. Therefore, it is probably not an understatement by the secretary to begin the second volume of his memoirs with the assertion that he was "entrusted with the day-to-day conduct of our nation's foreign policy during Richard Nixon's second term" (Kissinger, 1982:xix). Even without the impact of Watergate upon the president's ability to conduct foreign policy, Henry Kissinger had shaped the principal features of U.S. foreign policy to follow the main contours of his cognitive map.

5. The Policies of Henry Kissinger

Dan Caldwell

The previous chapters in this volume have focused primarily on Henry Kissinger's personality, beliefs, and attitudes. In this chapter, I will review and assess the policies developed and pursued by Kissinger. This analysis is based upon the writings of Nixon, Ford, and Kissinger (see bibliography), secondary accounts concerning foreign policy in the years 1969–76, and forty-five interviews that I conducted with former officials of the Nixon and Ford administrations.

Alexander George has drawn a useful distinction between two types of foreign policy analysis: "process theory" focuses on procedures and questions concerning decision-making systems, while "substantive theory" concerns specific issues such as deterrence, coercive diplomacy, arms control, and detente. As a result of a number of decision-making analyses, particularly studies of bureaucratic politics, it is clear that "how policy is made" affects the type and substance of the policy that is adopted. In retrospect, it seems that the highly centralized, secretive National Security Council system developed by Nixon and Kissinger in 1969 and 1970 enabled them to conduct foreign policy without the traditional "impediments" of public and Congressional review. This closed foreign policy system produced mixed results. On the positive side, it allowed President Nixon and Dr. Kissinger to open the door to a new relationship with the People's Republic of China. The same system, however, enabled Nixon and Kissinger to bomb Cambodia without the knowledge or approval of the Congress (Shawcross, 1979).

Substantively Nixon and Kissinger were able to accomplish a great deal. In addition to the opening of China, they improved relations with the Soviet Union, ended the Vietnam War, and signed a number of significant arms control agreements. Nixon and Kissinger were not so successful in dealing with the European states or the developing countries.

In reviewing the substance and the decision-making process of the Nixon and Ford administration, three distinct periods can be identified: January 1969–April 1972; May 1972–September 1973; October 1973–January 1977. In the following pages I will describe and assess the foreign policy-making structures and processes developed by Nixon, Ford and Kissinger.

Developing a New American Foreign Policy

Richard Nixon entered office with substantial background and interest in American foreign policy. As he told John Ehrlichman early in his administration, "Whatever legacy we have, hell, it isn't going to be in getting a cesspool for Winnetka . . . it is going to be there [in foreign affairs]" (Nixon, 1978:825).

In order to develop a new American foreign policy, Nixon turned to an unlikely assistant, Henry Kissinger, who had served as Nelson Rockefeller's principal advisor on foreign policy in the 1968 Republican presidential campaign. Prior to that, Kissinger had been a faculty member at Harvard and a research fellow at the Council on Foreign Relations, both institutions of the Eastern establishment that Nixon had always distrusted.

Yet when Nixon and Kissinger met on November 25 following Nixon's election, the two men found that they thought about international relations and the place of the United States in the world in very similar terms (Kissinger, 1979:9–16; Nixon, 1978:340–41). In addition, Nixon and Kissinger had little confidence in the governmental bureaucracy's ability to develop and implement an effective and innovative foreign policy. Nixon did not trust the bureaucrats in the Department of State; he felt that the department was staffed with an overwhelming majority of Democrats who would oppose his initiatives. Kissinger, too, distrusted the bureaucracy. In 1966 he wrote that bureaucratic structures and practices constrained presidents and that the appointment of "special emissaries" or "personal envoys" was often the only way to avoid these structures. According to Kissinger (1966a): "International agreements are sometimes possible only by ignoring safeguards against capricious action. It is a paradoxical aspect of modern bureaucracies that their quest for objectivity and calculability often leads to impasses which can be overcome by essentially arbitrary decisions."

Kissinger served as Nixon's special envoy in his capacity as the president's assistant for national security affairs. Nixon was committed to directing U.S. foreign policy himself. As he points out in his memoirs, "from the outset of my administration, . . . I planned to direct foreign policy from the White House" (Nixon, 1978:340). A friend of Nixon's, William Rogers, who had served as attorney general in the Eisenhower administration, was appointed secretary of state. However, from the beginning of Nixon's term of office, Rogers was excluded from most important foreign policy meetings and discussions. For instance, Rogers was not invited to the first meeting, following the inauguration, between Nixon and the Soviet Ambassador to the United States, Anatoly Dobrynin (Kissinger, 1979:28).

The relationship that developed between Nixon and Kissinger was interesting and complex. Both had emerged into prominence from outside the mainstream of American life—as Nixon (1978:341) noted in his memoirs, "the grocer's son from Whittier and the refugee from Hitler's Germany, the politician and the academic." Kissinger (1979:918) describes the relationship as "close on substance, aloof personally." From the references to one another in their respective memoirs, it is clear that Nixon and Kissinger were ambivalent about one another, and recent accounts (Hersh, 1982) suggest that in private they were hostile toward each other.

Whatever their personal differences, however, Nixon and Kissinger believed that the changes that had taken place in the world since the end of World War II demanded a new approach to foreign policy by the United States. In his first "State of the World Report" to the Congress which was drafted and reviewed by Kissinger and his NSC staff, Nixon (1970:2) noted, "The postwar period in international relations has ended." Japan and Europe had fully recovered from the devastation of the war; new nations were winning their independence; international communist unity was shattered; both the U.S. and the Soviet Union possessed the ability to inflict unacceptable damage on the other; and ideology was losing its force. In order to cope with and even to take advantage of these changes, Nixon and Kissinger sought to develop a systematic approach to foreign policy. In his study in this volume, Albert Eldridge noted the importance that Kissinger in both his academic and governmental writings placed on the development of a conceptual framework. Nixon and Kissinger sought to develop a grand design, reflecting the objectives of American foreign policy, and a grand strategy, or means for achieving these objectives (Caldwell, 1981:80–93). The major elements of the Nixon-Kissinger grand design and grand strategy are summarized below.

Grand Design:

1. Accept the emergence of a tripolar configuration of power in the security issue area and a multipolar international economic system.
2. Encourage the development of a moderate international system supported by the U.S., USSR, and the PRC.
3. Stop the spread of communism to areas of the world in the traditional western sphere of influence, but avoid direct military confrontation with the USSR.

Grand Strategy:

1. Accept Soviet achievement of nuclear parity; strive for the limitation of strategic arms (SALT).
2. Contain the spread of communism through: (a) deterrence of military aggression; (b) the use of positive incentives; (c) mixed strategies employing positive and negative sanctions; and (d) covert operations (Chile).
3. Maintain firm collective security arrangements with the NATO Alliance and Japan; other alliance commitments should be more flexible; all allies should pay a greater proportion of the cost of defense as well as provide manpower (Nixon Doctrine).
4. Deal with tension between grand design objectives of containing communism to traditionally western areas and avoiding direct military confrontation with the USSR through communication and consultation with the USSR; threaten or use U.S. force only if absolutely necessary.
5. Employ careful, presidentially-controlled crisis management of confrontations and limited wars to prevent escalation; communicate and consult with other relevant great powers in crisis situations (Basic Principles and Agreement on the Prevention of Nuclear War).
6. Recognize the boundaries of post-World War II European states and the Soviet sphere of influence in Eastern Europe while attempting to encourage freer interchange between Eastern and Western Europe (Helsinki Agreement).
7. Encourage ties between the U.S. and the Soviet Union through the conclusion of a number of cooperative projects in the economic, cultural, scientific and technological areas.

8. Develop regimes (agreed rules, procedures, and institutions) in important issue areas.
9. Attempt to mesh the various regimes into an overall grand strategy; use asymmetrical advantage in one regime to influence other issue areas.
10. Maintain U.S. foreign policy commitments with reduced public and Congressional support.

Before Nixon and Kissinger could develop their grand design and grand strategy, however, they had to deal with the most urgent problem on the foreign policy agenda—Vietnam. In 1968, the year prior to Nixon's inauguration, there were 543,000 American troops in Vietnam; 30,000 American men per month had been drafted; 278 Americans per week had been killed; and the direct cost of the war for 1968 alone was estimated to be in excess of $22 billion. In August 1968, the Gallup Poll found that 51 percent of those questioned thought that Vietnam was the most important issue facing the United States. In January 1969, 57 percent of those questioned thought that it was time to reduce on a month-by-month basis the number of American soldiers in Vietnam.

As a means of maintaining American foreign policy commitments and U.S. credibility (which were very important to both Nixon and Kissinger), the Nixon Doctrine was developed. The new doctrine's thesis, according to Nixon (1970:6), was that "the United States will participate in the defense and development of allies and friends, but that America cannot—and will not—conceive *all* the plans, design *all* the programs, execute *all* the decisions and undertake *all* the defense of the free nations of the world" (emphasis in original). The first application of the Nixon Doctrine was in Vietnam where Nixon and Kissinger sought to withdraw American land forces while still protecting the South Vietnamese government through the use of American air- and seapower. The Nixon Doctrine represented an attempt to lower the cost and public profile of American involvement in Southeast Asia while maintaining the predominant post-World War II international position of the United States, what Stanley Hoffmann (1978) has referred to as the objective of primacy.

Nixon and Kissinger did not, however, seek to extricate the United States from Vietnam in isolation from other international relationships. From their first days in office, Nixon and Kissinger discussed the international roles of the Soviet Union and the People's Republic of China. The previous chapters in this volume by Harvey Starr and Stephen Walker have documented Kissinger's thinking about these two states. Nixon's view of U.S. policy to China was presaged in a 1967 *Foreign Affairs* article in which he stated, "Any American policy toward Asia must come urgently to grips with the reality of China. . . . Taking the long view, we simply cannot afford to leave China forever outside the family of nations" (Nixon, 1967:121). In October 1970 Nixon met with Yahya Khan, the president of Pakistan, and asked him to let the leaders of China know that he regarded a Sino-American rapprochement as essential (Kissinger, 1979:699). The same month Nixon also told President Nicolae Ceausescu of Romania the same thing. After a secret visit to Beijing by Kissinger in July 1971 the Chinese publicly invited Nixon to visit China.

The opening to China in many ways characterized the foreign policy-making style of Nixon and Kissinger. The breakthrough in Sino-American relations was discussed in secret by the two leaders who neither discussed nor consulted with the officials of the Department of State, the Congress, the American people, or the allies of the United States. To a great extent, foreign policy making in the first Nixon administration was a two-man show.

Although the China trip which took place February 21–28, 1972, was not, as Nixon (1978:580) claimed, "the week that changed the world," it clearly was one of the most important events of the 1970s, for the resulting Sino-American rapprochement gave the United States increased bargaining leverage vis-à-vis the Soviet Union. Following the announcement of the China trip, Soviet-American negotiations that had been deadlocked, particularly negotiations on Berlin and those concerning measures to guard against accidental nuclear war, made rapid progress (Kissinger, 1979:766–77). Despite the fact that Nixon and Kissinger publicly denied that the opening to China was aimed in part if not primarily at the Soviet Union, this was nevertheless the case, a fact which became obvious on August 10, when the Soviet Union invited President Nixon to visit the Soviet Union the following spring.

Considering the improvement of Soviet-American relations as essential to their grand design (ends) and grand strategy (means) of American foreign policy, Nixon and Kissinger stressed several central concepts in their approach to the Soviet Union. First, the United States would only negotiate with the Soviets if they agreed to discuss a wide range of issues. This concept of linkage was set forth in Nixon's first foreign policy report (Nixon, 1970:136): "This Administration recognizes that international developments are entwined in many complex ways: political issues relate to strategic questions, political events in one area of the world may have a far-reaching effect on political developments in other parts of the globe." These linkages, according to Nixon and Kissinger, were inherent in international relations and could not be ignored. At the same time, however, the administration sought to take advantage of the interrelationship of diverse issues and to use these interrelationships to gain leverage in negotiations (Kissinger, 1979:129–30).

The second element in the Nixon-Kissinger approach to the Soviet Union was the concept of mutual interests. According to Kissinger (U.S. Department of State, Bureau of Public Affairs, January 28, 1975:2), "any foreign policy to be effective must reflect the mutual interests of all parties." This view reflected beliefs about international relations that Kissinger had developed as an academic. By concluding mutually beneficial agreements in the limitation of strategic arms and in trade, the United States, Kissinger believed, could encourage the voluntary entry of the Soviet Union into the international system. With a greater stake in the system, the Soviets would be less likely to support destabilizing revolutionary activities. But how could this transformation be accomplished? Through a complex form of behavior modification in which the U.S. would reward approved Soviet behavior with positive incentives and react to illegitimate activity with negative sanctions—in short, through a judicious application of the carrot and the stick—the United States would transform the Soviet position within the international system. According to Nixon (1972:320): "It has been the purpose of this Administration to transform the U.S.-Soviet relationship so that a mutual search for a stable peace and security becomes its dominant feature and its driving force."

The objective of transforming the Soviet place within the international system could not be achieved through high-sounding communiqués, however. In the administration's view, the "spirits" of the 1950s and 1960s—the spirit of Geneva (1955), the spirit of Camp David (1959), and the spirit of Glassboro (1967)—had achieved little, and progress in the improvement of Soviet-American relations required agreement on concrete issues (Kissinger, 1979:128).

During the acute cold war, the United States had refused to negotiate with the Soviet Union or the People's Republic of China; in fact, John Foster Dulles had refused even to shake hands with Zhou Enlai when they met in 1954. In Nixon and Kissinger's view, negotiations with the two communist giants were essential, and the administration deliberately and carefully sought to "de-ideologize" Sino-American and Soviet-American relations. In terms of international relations theory, Nixon and Kissinger were realists and contrasted markedly with the idealists (such as Woodrow Wilson and Franklin Roosevelt) of the American foreign policy tradition and therefore sought negotiations with hostile as well as friendly states.

Nixon and Kissinger were willing to discuss a number of functional and geographical issues of mutual interest to the Soviet Union and the United States. Among the most important of these issues were the limitation of strategic nuclear weapons, European security, East-West trade, Vietnam, and the Middle East. As noted above, the issue of greatest importance to the United States in 1969, an issue that threatened the domestic stability of the country as no issue since the depression, was Vietnam. Nixon and Kissinger sought selectively to wield negative sanctions and positive inducements in order to convince the Soviets and the Chinese to pressure the North Vietnamese into a settlement. Throughout the period from 1969 to 1972, however, the Soviets and the Chinese continued to supply their common ally with matériel.

Both the United States and the Soviet Union shared a preeminent interest in lessening both the possibility of nuclear war and the cost of maintaining strategic stability. Control of nuclear weapons offered the means to achieve both of these fundamental objectives. Although negotiations on the limitation of strategic nuclear weapons were seriously considered during the mid-sixties, several obstacles delayed the opening of SALT. First, the Soviets would not negotiate until they were convinced that West Germany would not develop an independent nuclear force; thus, the Nonproliferation Treaty, signed in 1968, was a prerequisite for SALT. The Soviet invasion of Czechoslovakia caused the second delay in opening negotiations, and the Nixon administration's insistence on a comprehensive review of U.S. strategic programs and doctrine, plus Nixon's and Kissinger's demand that the Soviet Union negotiate limits on both offensive as well as defensive strategic weapons systems, caused yet another delay of almost a year. During this period the United States began to deploy multiple, independently targetable reentry vehicles (MIRVs) on its missiles, a fact that vastly complicated the task of effectively limiting strategic weapons. Finally, on November 17, 1969, the first round of the SALT negotiations opened in Geneva (see Newhouse, 1973; Smith, 1980).

While some arms control experts argued that SALT was so vitally important that it should not be linked to progress on any other issues, Kissinger thought that SALT could and should be linked to other issue areas. Linkage tied progress in one area, for instance SALT, to progress in another area, for instance a settlement in Vietnam. Linkages could either be positive or negative. A positive linkage between two or more issues meant that progress in one area would result in progress in other areas, while a negative linkage would result in just the opposite. Furthermore, Kissinger thought that SALT created a positive atmosphere from which negotiations on other important issues would develop. SALT could also be used negatively. For example, during the Indo-Pakistani War of December 1971 Nixon ordered the U.S. SALT delegation to "stonewall the negotiations until the Soviets demonstrated restraint in their support of India." [1] Later Nixon threatened the Soviets with the cancellation of the May 1972 summit meeting unless they restrained their Indian allies (Brandon, 1973a:262).

Despite the Nixon administration's acceptance of linkage, there were several issues which the administration was unwilling to link to progress in other areas. For instance, the 1970 foreign policy report noted: "Even if progress on broader issues cannot be made, the elimination of recurrent crises around Berlin would be desirable" (Nixon, 1970:36). Nixon had placed the settlement of the Berlin question, a perennial problem area since 1945, high on the foreign policy agenda of his administration when he came into office. Just five weeks after his inauguration Nixon visited the major capitals of Europe and Berlin. On March 26, 1970, negotiations between Great Britain, France, the Soviet Union, and the United States opened which, after eighteen months, led to the Quadripartite Agreement on Berlin. From the American point of view the agreement was designed to stabilize an area where some of the most intense Soviet-American interactions of the cold war had occurred. The Soviets, most likely, sought a recognition of the status quo and for that reason signed the agreement. President Nixon (1972:337) characterized the Berlin agreement as "a milestone achievement" and stated that it "paved the way for the first U.S.-Soviet summit. We felt that if we could resolve our differences on such a thorny, long-lived controversy, we might be able to reach agreement on other issues" (Nixon, 1980:228). Nixon and Kissinger linked the convening of the Conference on Security and Cooperation in Europe (CSCE) to the conclusion of the Berlin Agreement and to the Soviet acceptance of the Mutual Balanced Force Reduction (MBFR) negotiations (Nixon, 1973:761). In retrospect the Berlin Agreement stands as one of the most important accomplishments of Nixon and Kissinger.

Even though positive steps had been taken in Europe to reduce Soviet-American tensions, there were other areas where U.S. and Soviet interests were at odds. The Middle East had become to the world in the 1970s what the Balkans were in the first part of the twentieth century. Hostilities were intense and close to the surface, and open warfare promised to break out at any moment when Egyptian President Nasser declared a "war of attrition" against Israel in 1969. During most of 1970 there were a series of attacks and counterattacks by Egyptian and Israeli forces. Soviet pilots reportedly began flying combat missions for Egypt, and in one engagement in April the Israelis shot down four Soviet-piloted MiGs. Nasser's death in September created a great deal of uncertainty concerning who would assume the leadership role within the Arab world.

The same month a crisis in Jordan developed between King Hussein and the Palestinian terrorists who operated from Jordan (see the chapter by Walker in this volume). On September 7 Hussein moved against the fedayeen, an action which catalyzed a full-scale civil war. Two weeks after the war began the Syrian army intervened with three hundred Soviet tanks, and American policy makers assumed that the Syrians would not have made such a move without direct Soviet approval or encouragement. Nixon strongly protested Soviet actions and indirectly hinted that the U.S. might intervene if such action was needed to maintain King Hussein in power. In the battle itself Hussein's forces decisively defeated the Syrians, and the Palestinians, also roundly defeated, formed the "Black September" terrorist group to avenge their lost comrades. In retrospect Nixon and Kissinger considered this to be one of the most serious crises of their administration; Kissinger later remarked, "You have no idea how close we came to war."

There were other crises that threatened the initial improvements that had been achieved in Soviet-American relations. Continued American involvement in Vietnam and the American incursion into Cambodia in May 1970 and the South Vietnamese invasion of Laos in February 1971 were vigorously protested by the Soviets. During the height of the Jordanian crisis in September, American intelligence agencies detected the presence of a Soviet submarine tender and two barges designed for the storage of radioactive wastes in Cienfuegos, Cuba. On the president's orders, Kissinger informed Soviet Ambassador Anatoly Dobrynin that the construction of a submarine base would violate the Kennedy-Khrushchev understandings reached during the Cuban missile crisis of 1962. The Soviets quietly withdrew the ships, and a full-blown crisis was averted (see Kissinger, 1979:632–52).

Nixon and Kissinger had hoped to convince the Soviets and Chinese to pressure the North Vietnamese into negotiating a settlement of the war. Whether and to what degree the Soviet Union and China attempted to pressure their common ally is not known; however, on March 30 the North Vietnamese launched a major attack on the provinces around the demilitarized zone. During the next month the situation worsened for the South Vietnamese, and on May 8 President Nixon announced the mining of Haiphong and six other North Vietnamese ports and the bombing of Hanoi and supply routes from China. At the time many people expected a repeat performance by the Soviets of their behavior in the aftermath of the U-2 incident of 1960 which led to the cancellation of the Eisenhower-Khrushchev Paris summit meeting. In 1972, however, the stakes were much higher, and the Soviets allowed Nixon to visit their country. Given the strained atmosphere, many asked, what, if anything, could be accomplished at the Moscow Summit.

A New Structure of Peace?

To the surprise of many experts on Soviet politics, the Moscow Summit took place as scheduled from May 22–30, 1972. After a hectic series of last-minute negotiations, President Nixon and Soviet Party Chairman Brezhnev signed two major arms control agreements and an agreement concerning the basic principles governing Soviet-American relations. Representatives of the two countries also signed a number of secondary agreements, including an agreement designed to reduce the probability of dangerous incidents between the ships and aircraft of their respective navies and several agreements calling for increased Soviet-American cooperation in the environmental, medical, scientific, energy, and space exploration fields. According to Nixon (1978:681), the Moscow Summit "agreements began the establishment of a pattern of interrelationships and cooperation in a number of different areas. This was the first stage of detente: to involve Soviet interests in ways that would increase their stake in international stability and the status quo."

The two SALT agreements were clearly the most important achievements of the Moscow Summit meeting. The Anti-Ballistic Missile (ABM) Treaty was a remarkable document for several reasons. First, for perhaps the first time in history, the two predominant powers in the world agreed to refrain from developing a means of protecting their respective homelands. To many the ABM Treaty marked Soviet acceptance of the strategic nuclear doctrine of "mutually assured destruction," which holds that each superpower is a hostage of the other. Second, the ABM Treaty marked the first time that the Soviet Union and the United States agreed on a means of verifying an arms control agreement. Verification had been the major obstacle in the way of arms control since the initial discussions of nuclear disarmament following World War II. Third, the ABM Treaty would likely result in savings of billions of dollars by both superpowers. The second SALT agreement, the Interim Agreement on Offensive Arms, placed a quantitative limit on the offensive missile systems (ICBMs and SLBMs) of both sides.

Both SALT agreements were immediately acclaimed. The day after the signing ceremony Murrey Marder of the *Washington Post* wrote (May 30, 1972:1): "The nuclear weapons accords signed last night between the two global antagonists are totally without precedent in world history and carry all the unforeseeable prospects and consequences of a bold new venture in international relations." Other observers described the agreements as "landmark" and "historic." Nixon described the progress in arms control from 1969 to 1972 as unprecedented. However, while noting the valuable contributions of the new agreements toward the establishment of a more stable system, an editorial in the *New York Times* (May 27, 1972) cautiously warned that "the millenium has not arrived in Soviet-American relations." Indeed, deep divisions between the superpowers remained over issues of Vietnam and the Middle East. Soviet leaders also maintained their anti-American ideological propaganda campaign. Later, critics of the SALT I agreements criticized both the manner in which they were negotiated and the substance of the agreements (Smith, 1980; Zumwalt, 1976).

The greatest disappointment of the Moscow Summit was the failure to reach a trade agreement between the U.S. and the Soviet Union. During his first administration, Nixon had sought to reduce barriers and to encourage Soviet-American trade. For instance, in April 1970 the U.S. lifted restrictions on over 200 items for export to all communist countries except for the People's Republic of China, Cuba, North Vietnam, and North Korea. In 1971 American officials granted licenses for export to the Soviet Union of more than $800 million worth of equipment for the Kama River truck plant. Throughout 1972 American and Soviet officials worked on a trade agreement which was eventually signed in October. Viewing the Soviet market with great expectations, American businessmen clamored to conclude many deals with various Soviet ministries.

The Soviet Union has suffered chronic agricultural shortages during most of the twentieth century. Despite attempts since the mid-fifties to increase substantially agricultural production, efforts have often failed; indeed, the firing of the minister of agriculture for his failure to increase productivity has become a standard agenda item of Soviet party congresses. Whenever serious shortfalls have occurred in the past, the Soviets have turned to foreign suppliers. For instance, following a disastrous crop failure in 1963 the Soviet Union imported approximately ten million tons of grain from Canada and the United States at a cost of several hundred million dollars. From 1963 to 1975 the Soviets annually imported at least 1.5 million tons of grain from Canada with the exceptions of 1968 and 1969. In 1971 the Soviets turned to the U.S. also and purchased three million tons of corn and livestock feed at the cost of $136 million. In 1972 the United States was virtually the only country offering wheat for sale, and the Soviets were in great need of grain. In fact, according to one story, after listening to President Nixon announce the mining of Haiphong and the bombing of Hanoi, the Soviet Minister of Foreign Trade, Nikolai Patolichev, who was in Washington to negotiate the 1972 Soviet grain purchases, casually remarked to his counterpart, Secretary of Commerce Peterson, "Well, let's get back to business." The negotiators completed their business within several weeks after the Moscow Summit, and the Soviets eventually purchased one quarter of the year's wheat crop (almost nineteen million tons) at a cost of $1.1 billion. Initially it appeared that the U.S. had successfully rid itself of much of its chronic grain surplus. By the end of 1972 it seemed that Soviet-American trade would develop substantially within several years.

In the fourth foreign policy report published in 1973, Nixon and Kissinger developed a new theory for dealing with the Soviet Union that differed significantly from the approach used by the administration from January 1969 through April 1972. As the eminent British economist John Maynard Keynes once observed, "Practical men, who believe themselves to be quite exempt from any intellectual influences, are usually the slave of some defunct economist. Mad men in authority, who hear voices in the air, are distilling their frenzy from some academic scribbler of a few years back. I am sure that the power of vested interests is vastly exaggerated compared with the gradual encroachment of ideas." Like Keynes' "mad men in authority," Nixon implicitly borrowed from the "academic scribblers" of the fifties and early sixties the central concept of his new theory: specifically the notion that Soviet-American relations would gradually be transformed through the conclusion of a number of agreements in different fields. As Nixon (1973:733) stated: "Direct contact, exchanges of information and experience, and joint participation in specific projects will develop a fabric of relationships supplementing those at the higher levels of political leadership." In a briefing to Congressional leaders in June 1972 (*Congressional Record*, June 19, 1972:S 9600), Kissinger noted that the SALT agreements were "linked organically to a chain of agreements and to a broad understanding about international conduct appropriate to the dangers of the nuclear age."

The concept of political integration through functional cooperation in several areas was developed by a number of European statesmen and scholars following World War II. In his book, *A Working Peace System*, originally published in 1943, David Mitrany (1966) called for the organization of government "along the lines of specific ends and needs, and according to the conditions of their time and place, in lieu of the traditional organization on the basis of a set constitutional division of jurisdiction of rights and powers." Mitrany's basic idea was to organize cooperation in functional areas in order to achieve peace between states, an end that he called "federalism by installment" and that Robert Schuman, the architect of the European Coal and Steel Community (ECSC), referred to as "peace in pieces." The theory of functionalism was highly prescriptive and pragmatic and contained many oversimplified arguments lacking empirical evidence, yet the structures, particularly the ECSC, Euratom, and the European Economic Community, that were created at the recommendation of Mitrany, Schuman, and Jean Monnet, proved able to cope with the challenges of reconstruction during the postwar period. However, these efforts did not result in a politically unified Europe, as many political scientists such as Karl Deutsch and Ernst Haas predicted they would. By the late sixties following de Gaulle's assertion of French nationalism and the stagnation of the European integration movement, scholars and policy makers largely discounted the concept of functionalism as a means of system transformation.

Despite the fact that scholars had largely turned away from functionalism due to its simplistic and erroneous assumptions, the concept is apparent throughout President Nixon's 1973 report. For instance, in the report, Nixon (1973) noted that "through the gathering momentum of individual accords we would seek to create vested interests on both sides in restraint and the strengthening of peace." In short, Nixon believed that the character and nature of Soviet-American relations could be changed through the signing of a number of agreements in different functional areas. Agreements in the economic and commercial areas would "spillover" (to use Ernst Haas' phrase) and affect political relations. By transforming relations with the Soviet Union and the People's Republic of China, "a new structure of peace" would be established, the grand design would be achieved. In assessing the progress toward that goal, Nixon (1973:724) ended his report by pointing out that as a result of the agreements concluded in 1972, "a changed world has moved closer to a lasting peace."

It is unclear from what sources Nixon and Kissinger appropriated the concept of functionalism. Although Kissinger was a student of European history, he had focused almost exclusively on political-military affairs throughout his academic career. He was, however, undoubtedly aware of the many articles and books written in the 1950s and 1960s on the general subject of integration and the specific topic of functionalism. Kissinger's principal assistant for European affairs, Helmut Sonnenfeldt, had also spent his career analyzing political-military problems; yet he too became a proponent of functionalism: "This or that individual cooperative project may be relatively insignificant, but cumulatively and over time, a whole network of agreements, projects, and programs can produce a vested interest in more stable relationships" (Sonnenfeldt, 1976:6). While the genesis of the functionalist idea in the second phase of the Nixon-Kissinger grand design and grand strategy remains unknown, it is clear that functionalism was a basic component of the Nixon-Kissinger approach to foreign policy during the 1972–73 period.

The Deterioration of the New American Foreign Policy

The Nixon administration's Watergate problem grew in importance throughout 1972 and 1973. By the fall of 1973, it was clear that Nixon was in serious trouble. Henry Kissinger was one of the few high-level Nixon advisors who had remained untouched by the Watergate crisis. In fact, as Nixon's popularity decreased, Kissinger's increased. In a nationwide poll Kissinger was at the top of the "most admired man" list in 1973 and 1974; Nixon was number three in 1973 and number seven the following year. In an attempt to bolster his own popularity, Nixon named Kissinger secretary of state in August 1973. As Kissinger notes in his memoirs (1982:4), this appointment symbolized how Watergate had wounded Nixon, for he had never wanted a strong secretary of state.

In Kissinger's confirmation hearings before their committee, members of the Senate Foreign Relations Committee (1973) questioned Kissinger at length about his future plans for executive-congressional relations and the explanation of administration foreign policies to the American public. In his opening statement Kissinger commented: "There must be . . . a closer relationship between the executive and legislative branches." In contrast to his absolute refusal to testify formally before Congress in his position as assistant to the president for national security affairs, Kissinger promised to testify on all of his activities with the exception of the two areas traditionally exempted for cabinet officers, direct communications with the president or the actual deliberations of the NSC. Kissinger promised that the Senate Foreign Relations Committee "should receive substantially more information than it has in the past" and that the committee should "share more fully in the design of our foreign policy." Not only did Kissinger promise increased sharing of information and of power with the Congress, but also he stressed the need to "institutionalize our foreign policy" and to invigorate the Foreign Service. Finally, Kissinger pledged to "listen to the hopes and aspirations of our fellow countrymen," but the process of domestic legitimation would take time (U.S. Senate Foreign Relations Committee, 1973:41): "So I believe that over a historical period, over decades, a democracy, a democratic way of making decisions, is far to be preferred [to that of a totalitarian system], even if one sacrifices some flexibility of action in the process."

While some skeptics noted that Nixon and Kissinger's increased interest in Congress grew in direct proportion to the probability of impeachment, Kissinger nevertheless appeared more open following his confirmation as secretary of state. In the three years from October 1973 through January 1977, Kissinger formally appeared before congressional committees more than twenty times. He also held over sixty informal meetings with congressmen. This was either an impressive effort to open legislative-executive communication channels or to co-opt members of Congress. Kissinger was successful in achieving the latter task even with staunch doves such as Senator J. William Fulbright. In addition to his appearances before congressional committees, Kissinger delivered over sixty public speeches and held over forty press conferences in this same forty-month period. These speeches were designed to provide the information previously provided by the "State of the World Reports" which were published annually between 1970 and 1973.

Holding two of the most important foreign-policy-making positions in the U.S. government and with Nixon mortally wounded, Kissinger was in an unprecedented position to influence the formulation and implementation of U.S. foreign policy. When Nixon resigned in August 1974, Kissinger's influence increased even further.

With Kissinger's change in position came a change in the making of foreign policy. Whereas the system for making U.S. foreign policy was secretive and closed between the years 1969 and 1973, Kissinger opened up the system once he became secretary of state. In fact, in reviewing his process for making foreign policy in his memoirs, Kissinger himself expresses dismay at the secrecy, centralization, and personalization that accurately characterized the process during the first Nixon administration. For instance, Kissinger (1982:129–30) recalls, "On December 8, 1972, I called on Pompidou while I was in Paris for the final phase of the negotiations with the North Vietnamese. I briefed him in a detail not vouchsafed to our own Cabinet departments—a procedure that in retrospect strikes even me as astonishing."

At about the same time that Nixon's domestic position began to deteriorate, the foundations of the Nixon-Kissinger grand design and grand strategy also showed signs of weakness. In late 1972 due to a number of factors, including the large Soviet grain purchases, the price of grain increased dramatically. Consumers in the U.S. blamed increased food prices on the "wheat deal," and Senator Henry Jackson called it "one of the most notorious government foul-ups in American history."

While the wheat deal marked a fissure in the foundation of detente, a far more serious setback to Kissinger's foreign policy occurred on October 6, 1973, when Egypt and Syria launched a surprise attack against the state of Israel. Within a short time President Nixon, Secretary of State Kissinger, and Secretary of Defense Schlesinger compared the Middle Eastern situation to the environment in which World War I began. Nixon called the crisis that ensued "the most serious since the Cuban missile crisis." Two days after the Egyptian-Syrian attack, Kissinger warned the Soviets that the U.S. would oppose any Soviet attempt in the Middle East or elsewhere to achieve predominance. On October 10, American and Israeli intelligence agencies learned that the Soviets had begun airlifting supplies to Egypt and Syria. In the next several days, the Israelis stabilized their positions and began a counterattack. Soviet Prime Minister Kosygin flew to Cairo with a cease-fire proposal on October 16 that called for "a guarantee by the Soviet Union and the United States of the entire agreement." Evidently, the Soviets had decided that the Israelis were defeating Egyptian and Syrian forces and that a cease-fire was needed immediately. Apparently the other Arab states also concluded that the Egyptian and Syrian forces were in trouble, because on October 17 the Organization of Arab Petroleum Exporting Countries (OAPEC) placed an embargo on all shipments of oil to the U.S. and other nations supporting Israel.

At the time of the October War, however, the focus was on the battlefield. During the first week of the war, the Arab forces made striking gains against a stunned Israel. In the second week, Israel began to recover from the surprise of the initial blow and counterattacked.

Since the United States and the Soviet Union were the primary suppliers of military equipment to Israel and Egypt and Syria, an escalation of the war threatened a direct Soviet-American confrontation. Because of this danger and because the Soviet client states lost the momentum in the war, Brezhnev invited Kissinger to Moscow to discuss the situation in the Middle East. Kissinger flew to Moscow and arrived on October 20, the same day that President Nixon fired Watergate Special Prosecutor Archibald Cox, an action that led to the resignations of Attorney General Elliot Richardson and Deputy Attorney General William Ruckelshaus.

By this time Nixon was so in need of a dramatic foreign policy success to divert attention from his Watergate problems that he sent Brezhnev a message indicating that Kissinger had his "full authority" and that "the commitments that he [Kissinger] may make in the course of your discussions have my complete support" (Kissinger, 1982:547). In other words, Nixon was delegating his powers as president to the secretary of state.

After only four hours of negotiation, Kissinger, Brezhnev, and Gromyko were able to draft the text of a cease-fire resolution. On the battlefield, however, the cease-fire did not hold, and the Israelis made striking gains. A second cease-fire was negotiated, but by that time (October 24) the Israelis had reached Suez City and the 70,000 soldiers of the Egyptian Third Army were trapped on the east bank of the Suez. Sadat sent an urgent plea to Brezhnev and Nixon to send a joint Soviet-American peacekeeping force to the Middle East in order to police the cease-fire. Kissinger and Nixon rejected the proposal, and that night Brezhnev sent word via Dobrynin "that if you find it impossible to act jointly with us in this matter, we should be faced with the necessity urgently to consider the question of taking appropriate steps unilaterally. We cannot allow arbitrariness on the part of Israel" (quoted by Kissinger, 1982:583). Kissinger believed that this was a serious challenge, since if implemented it would have allowed the Soviet Union to reenter Egypt and establish a presence there once again. In addition, if accepted by the United States, Kissinger (1982:584) feared that this action would be perceived throughout the world as establishing a U.S.-Soviet condominium.

In response to Brezhnev's threat and indications that the Soviets were preparing to unilaterally intervene, on October 25 Nixon and Kissinger increased the alert status of American forces around the world. The next morning Kissinger held a news conference to discuss the meaning of the alert and the reasons for it. The first reporter asked if the alert had been "prompted as much perhaps by American domestic requirements [Watergate] as by the real requirements of diplomacy in the Middle East." Kissinger denied that any correlation existed and went on to imply that the Soviets had not followed the principles of peaceful coexistence.

The implicit American threat worked, and the Soviets did not intervene. After several days of negotiations the crisis ended. But the war had tremendous implications for both the future of world politics and the Nixon-Kissinger grand design and grand strategy.

Several observers compared the October War and the Arab oil embargo to the events of 1904–5 when an East Asia power, Japan, first defeated a European power, Russia, in battle. Kissinger (1982:885) characterized the OPEC decision of 1973–74 to raise oil prices as "one of the pivotal events of this century." The Arab states used the oil embargo and oil price increases very effectively—even to the point of splitting the NATO alliance on the question of support for Israel. Perhaps the most profound result of the war and embargo was a heightened sense of interdependence by Western Europe, Japan, and, to a lesser extent, the United States, all of which depended upon oil imports from the Middle East.

In the aftermath of the crisis, Secretary Kissinger was more circumspect in his assessment of detente than he had been prior to the war (U.S. Department of State, *Bulletin*, December 10, 1973:706): "The relationship between the Soviet Union and the United States is an inherently ambiguous one. . . . Our view has been that detente is made necessary because as the two great nuclear superpowers, we have a special responsibility to spare mankind the dangers of a nuclear holocaust." Significantly, Kissinger claimed far less for detente in this statement than in most of his pre-October War statements. What had happened to the grandiose functionalist claims for detente typical of the period from May 1972 to October 1973? Kissinger still emphasized the old theme of mutual interests but stressed the most important mutual interest, avoiding nuclear war. In this sense Kissinger retreated from his earlier claims that the U.S. could transform Soviet-American relations by weaving a complex web of agreements on a number of different issues. At the same time, however, following the October War, Kissinger developed the theme of global interdependence, a theme that was obviously closely related to the concepts of mutual interest and functionalism.

Kissinger initially thought of interdependence in strictly bipolar terms. The 1973 foreign policy report stated (Nixon, 1973:734): "[Economic and commercial] . . . ventures do not create a one-sided dependence by the United States upon Soviet resources; they establish an interdependence between our economies which provides a continuing incentive to maintain a constructive relationship." Agreements on issues of mutual interest would lead to Soviet-American interdependence which would build a solid foundation for stability.

Following the October War and the Arab oil embargo, Kissinger began to think of interdependence in multilateral terms. He noted (U.S. Department of State, Bureau of Public Affairs, May 12, 1975:3): "As technology expands man's reach, the planet continues to shrink. Global communications make us acutely aware of each other. Human aspirations and destinies increasingly are intertwined." Critics had charged that the Nixon-Kissinger grand design and grand strategy paid inadequate attention to the developing states of the world. The October War made clear the latent power of the developing states that were richly endowed with natural resources; following the war, Kissinger began to emphasize the importance of relations with resource-rich developing states and to de-emphasize the possibility of weaving a web of complex U.S.-Soviet interrelationships.

Administration spokesmen such as Helmut Sonnenfeldt (1976) spoke of the Soviet Union as "beginning its truly 'imperial' phase." Referring to "the Russian sense of national destiny," Sonnenfeldt admonished Americans to "grasp the reality of the Soviet Union as a permanent competitor—an adversary—and yet also sometimes a partner." In a series of speeches delivered during the first part of 1976, Secretary Kissinger stressed the same point: namely that the Soviet Union had begun to define its interests in global terms and that "this condition will not go away" and "will have to be faced by every Administration in the foreseeable future." [2] This new policy orientation contrasts markedly with this functionalist statements characteristic of the May 1972–September 1973 period and, in some respects, marked a return to the goals of containment.

During the 1973–76 period, the pace of detente slowed dramatically. The Watergate scandal preoccupied American governmental leaders as well as the public, and a worried Kissinger often warned that the United States could not conduct an effective foreign policy if preoccupation with Watergate became too great. When Richard Nixon resigned from the presidency in August 1974, many wondered if detente, which had been so closely identified with Nixon, would survive. Just as important to detente was Kissinger, who, relatively unscathed by Watergate, remained in office as secretary of state.

Gerald Ford sought to continue the improvement of Soviet-American relations through several means. In November 1974 he met with Brezhnev at Vladivostok and signed an accord which pledged the U.S. and the Soviet Union to strive to reach an agreement limiting each side to 2,400 strategic delivery vehicles and to a sublimit of 1,320 MIRVs.

In August 1975 Ford attended the Conference on Security and Cooperation in Europe and, along with thirty-four other leaders, signed the "Final Act" of the Helsinki agreement. Soviet and American support of this agreement was apparently based upon a trade-off: the Soviets wanted Western governments, particularly the United States, to recognize the borders of the Eastern European states as de jure while the U.S. wanted Soviet acceptance of a standard by which to judge Soviet and East European policies toward human rights.

While the summit meetings at Vladivostok and Helsinki were important, they did not diffuse the increasing criticism of detente. The October War was the first major event to reveal the limits of detente and showed that cold-war confrontations had not come to an end. Soviet support of communists in Portugal and Angola made the limits of detente explicitly clear. During 1976, Presidential candidates in both parties—Jimmy Carter, Henry Jackson, Ronald Reagan, and George Wallace—criticized the Nixon-Ford-Kissinger conception and implementation of detente. To many detente had become synonymous with appeasement or capitulation. Reacting to these criticisms, President Ford banned the use of the word "detente" by members of his administration in March 1976. Yet this cosmetic change did not appease the critics, and the Republican platform which Ford accepted contained a number of sharp criticisms of the Nixon-Ford-Kissinger detente policies. As a result of the reversals in Soviet-American relations and the mounting criticism of detente within the U.S., the administration moved away from the high expectations of the 1972–73 period toward the tried and tested policy of containment. But that policy shift was not sufficient to convince the electorate that President Ford and Secretary of State Kissinger should be retained in office, and on January 20, 1977, a new president was inaugurated, ending the Nixon-Ford-Kissinger era.

Kissinger's Foreign Policy Legacy

Kissinger's tenure in office can be divided into three relatively distinct periods: January 1969 through April 1972; May 1972 through September 1973; and October 1973 through January 1977. During the first two periods, Kissinger served as the president's assistant for national security affairs. President Nixon and he developed a hierarchical White House–centered apparatus for making foreign policy. As Watergate weakened Nixon's position, Kissinger's influence over U.S. foreign policy grew steadily and culminated in his appointment as secretary of state in September 1973. During his tenure as secretary, Kissinger attempted to open up the foreign-policy-making process, but the process still centered on Kissinger. Thus the process was somewhat decentralized but remained highly personalized, a development that affected the substance of American foreign policy, as noted below.

Substantively, much was accomplished during the eight years that Kissinger co-directed American foreign policy. The opening to China and the lessening of tensions with the Soviet Union transformed the bipolar structure of the cold-war international system into a less ideological tripolar configuration which allowed the United States greater diplomatic flexibility. The rapprochement with China was one of the most significant initiatives of Nixon and Kissinger because of its effect on both Sino-American and Soviet-American relations.

Nixon and Kissinger were successful in concluding a number of agreements that reduced and moderated the tensions in the international system. The Quadripartite Agreement on Berlin defused the perennial flashpoint of the acute cold war, the area over which the two superpowers almost engaged with one another in direct military conflict in 1948 and 1961.

Several other initiatives were undertaken in Europe. The Mutual and Balanced Force Reduction (MBFR) negotiations were conducted throughout Kissinger's tenure in office without significant results. But MBFR at least provided a forum for the members of NATO and the Warsaw Pact to discuss the significant problems of European security. The Conference on Security and Cooperation in Europe "Final Act" (Helsinki agreement) signed in 1975 called for the reunification of families living in Eastern and Western European countries, the dissemination of news publications, and the advance notification of military maneuvers. The agreement also called for the observance of human rights in the signatory countries. This agreement was particularly important for the Europeans who more readily enjoy the fruits of East-West cooperation or, conversely, suffer the consequences of East-West conflict.

During the Nixon and Ford administrations, the United States participated in the negotiation of and signed eleven arms-control-related agreements.[3] The number and the quality of these agreements were unprecedented in post-World War II international relations. The agreements contained provisions that ranged from "confidence-building measures" of the Helsinki Final Act to the total renunciation of biological weapons. Significantly, all but two of these eleven agreements were bilateral agreements between the United States and the Soviet Union.

Clearly the most important arms control agreements of the 1969–76 period were the two SALT agreements, the Anti-Ballistic Missile Treaty, and the Interim Agreement on Offensive Arms. With the benefit of hindsight, it seems that the claims of neither the harsh critics on the right nor the ardent proponents of SALT were correct. SALT neither disarmed the U.S. unilaterally nor did SALT grant strategic superiority to the Soviet Union as some critics argued. But neither did SALT, and the ABM Treaty in particular, mark the Soviet acceptance of the doctrine of mutual assured destruction, as some SALT supporters claimed.

SALT moderated somewhat the competition between the superpowers in strategic nuclear weapons. The ABM Treaty prevented a costly arms race and saved both the U.S. and the Soviet Union significant expenditures. This treaty also established the Standing Consultative Commission (SCC), an organization to resolve questions concerning the implementation and observance of the two SALT agreements. The SCC provided a high-level Soviet-American forum for exchanging information and resolving problems and was a valuable contribution. SALT, according to Kissinger (1979:1253), "embodied our conviction that a wildly spiraling nuclear arms race was in no country's interest and enhanced no one's security."

One of the other major diplomatic accomplishments of Nixon and Kissinger was the development of a number of rules designed to prevent and manage crises. These rules were tested a number of times in the 1969–76 period (George, 1983). On several occasions, most notably in 1970 in Jordan and in Cienfuegos, Cuba, the rules of the new system helped to prevent major crises from developing. Even where crises were not prevented, the new relationship between the United States and the Soviet Union helped to moderate conflicts of interest. For instance, despite the involvement of the U.S. and the USSR in the October War, both superpowers' foreign policy behavior was moderated by the desire to preserve detente. Consequently neither side pressed for maximal advantages.

In other cases, the rules of the new international system did not prevent the outbreak of conflict. Apparently the Soviet Union did not feel that its activities in Angola and the Horn of Africa would jeopardize detente. Kissinger, however, thought that Soviet support for Cuban intervention in these areas was incompatible with detente and he explicitly linked Angola and SALT: "Soviet actions in Angola, if continued, are bound to affect the general relationship with the United States; . . . a substantial deterioration of that relationship can also, over time, affect the strategic arms talks" (Department of State, Bureau of Public Affairs, January 14, 1976:2).

For their part, Soviet leaders felt that the United States had violated the norms of detente on at least two occasions: in clandestinely assisting the opponents of Allende in Chile and in closing the Soviet Union out of the Middle East. Clearly the failure of American and Soviet leaders to clarify permissible behavior in third areas was one of most significant failures of detente.

Kissinger's view as both an academic and policy maker was that the great powers were the essential actors of international politics and that political-military issues were far more important than nonmilitary issues. This perspective, while relevant to the eighteenth and nineteenth centuries, was questionable by the 1970s. Kissinger learned dramatically during the October War and the ensuing Arab oil boycott that power not only, as Mao Zedong pointed out, "comes from the barrel of a gun," but also it comes from barrels of oil.

Kissinger's focus on the great powers led him to emphasize U.S. relations with the Soviet Union and China and caused him to underrate the importance of the middle-range powers and the developing states. Perhaps as a result of his background and academic interest in Europe, Kissinger made several attempts to reinvigorate American-European relations, most notably in his "Year of Europe" proposal. But this initiative, as Kissinger (1982:700–08) himself admits, was never accepted by the Europeans and was consequently stillborn.

Because of his focus on great power and European affairs, Kissinger failed to appreciate the importance of Japan, a country with the world's third largest gross national product but a very small military force. Japan defied the classical diplomatic, and to a large extent Kissinger's, definition of power; it was a non-European state with enormous economic (versus military) power. The failure to recognize Japan's importance in the contemporary international system led to the so-called Nixon shocks of 1971: the imposition of a 10 percent surcharge on Japanese exports to the U.S., and the failure of the United States to inform Japan of the opening to China. These errors were serious and resulted in the Japanese legitimately questioning the United States' commitment to close relations between the two countries.

Kissinger also, until the 1973–76 period, did not pay enough attention to developing states. During his earlier years in power, Kissinger's actions appeared to be based on Thucydides' dictum: "The strong do what they will, and the weak do what they must." But the October War and oil embargo made it difficult to identify the strong and the weak in the contemporary international system.

As noted throughout this volume, the foreign-policy-making process under Henry Kissinger was centralized and personalized. The major reason that developing countries' problems were not addressed during the Nixon administration is that

Kissinger himself was not interested. Issues and events competed for Kissinger's attention and he simply did not have the time required to deal effectively with all of these issues. As Philip Odeen, a former member of the NSC staff, pointed out: "Kissinger tends to be a one-issue man. In late 1973–early 1974, Kissinger was focused on the Middle East. He—and the Administration—had little time for anything else, including SALT."

In his studies of Metternich and Bismarck, Kissinger revealed an awareness of the dangers of centralization and personalization. In his essay on Bismarck, Kissinger (1970:350) noted that there were two problems in maintaining a grand design and grand strategy for foreign policy: (1) "A system which requires a great man in each generation sets itself an almost insurmountable challenge"; and (2) the diplomatic system established by Bismarck was too complex and therefore doomed. The talent of the truly creative leader lies in his ability to build policies and institutions on the underlying foundations of a society: the values and traditions of the society. Kissinger failed to accomplish this vital task. His grand design and grand strategy reflected continental European values and traditions of realpolitik rather than the idealistic approach to foreign policy of the United States. The Congress and the American public were unwilling to grant their support to a foreign policy founded upon the maximization of power rather than upon ideals, upon the maintenance of stability rather than upon peace. To a large extent Kissinger ironically repeated the errors of his exemplars, Metternich and Bismarck.

Notes

Introduction

1. I am indebted to Alexander George for suggesting these ways in which a leader's personality can influence political behavior.

1. The Kissinger Years

1. The present author has spent the last several years both studying and adding to that literature. This essay is an outgrowth of a long-standing interest in Henry Kissinger and a research project which has included secondary analyses of biography and psychobiography, as well as operational code and content analyses of Kissinger the scholar and policy maker. The present article draws on a number of papers (Starr, 1976, 1979, 1980a, 1980b) resulting from that research project, as well as a number of unpublished analyses. This work has been supported by grants from the Center for International Policy Studies, Indiana University, and by a Summer Faculty Fellowship, Indiana University.

2. A short list of relevant research and review articles, and their accompanying bibliographies include Holsti (1976a, 1976b, 1976c), Holsti and George (1975), Shapiro and Bonham (1973), Brodin (1972), Falkowski (1979a, 1979b), Sullivan (1976), Axelrod (1976), and Jervis (1976).

3. See, for example, Weinstein et al. (1978) or Tucker (1977) for a reappraisal of the work by George and George (1956) on Wilson and commentary on the psychohistorical approach. For a preliminary response by the Georges to Weinstein et al., see George and George (1979).

4. Mazlish (1976:8) states: "My approach throughout is interpretive. This fact must be underlined from the very beginning. By now there are a number of acceptable and sometimes fine studies and articles on Kissinger's thought, policies, or actual negotiations. Often weakened by an uncritical adulatory or condemnatory bias, such works are nonetheless fundamental in helping establish some of the 'facts' about Kissinger in his many guises. They rarely, however, center on Kissinger's personality in the sense I undertake here."

5. See, for example, George (1979) and Holsti (1977). Both of those works, as well as the editor's introduction in Hermann (1977), provide lists of the operational code studies performed on American foreign policy decision makers and a number of foreign leaders.

6. An early outline and discussion of the author's research project can be found in Starr (1976). Most of the content analysis remains unpublished (but see Starr, 1980b). Another content analysis of Kissinger is contained in Eldridge's study in this volume.

7. In *White House Years* Kissinger again returns explicitly to his intellectual framework. Here he describes the nature of a 1971 interchange with four dedicated antiwar activists: "Ours was the perpetually inconclusive dialogue between statesmen and prophets, between those who operate in time and through attainable stages and those who are concerned with truth and the eternal" (1979:1016).

8. It is interesting that in his memoirs Kissinger (1979:1409) refers to the Fallaci interview as "without doubt the single most disastrous conversation I ever had with any member of the press." Kissinger notes that this interview was influential in Nixon's developing sense of competition with Kissinger for public attention. Kissinger (1979:1410) says that "what drove him [Nixon] up the wall was a quotation Fallaci put in my mouth: 'Americans like the cowboy . . . who rides all alone into the town, the village, with his horse and nothing else. . . . This amazing, romantic character suits me precisely because to be alone has always been part of my style or, if you like, my technique.'"

9. Critics of the Nixon-Kissinger policy process (Destler, 1971–72; Leacacos, 1971–72) point out that this style was very costly in state department morale and performance, in this underutilization of talent, and in creating a Kissinger bottleneck in the foreign policy process.

10. The range of these statements while in office is quite broad. They appear in news conferences in Moscow (May 27 and 29, 1972) during the summit, Senate hearings on Kissinger's appointment as secretary of state in September 1973, and numerous speeches during the Ford administration (for example, in Miami, August 1974.) During Ford's presidential campaign, Kissinger made numerous speeches, and many employed this theme.

11. For example, Holsti looked at the relationship between Dulles' "General Evaluation" of the Soviet Union and his perceptions of Soviet "hostility." For three-month and six-month periods, Holsti's Spearman correlations were -10.0 and -03.0—no relationships at all. For Kissinger, the results are 0.32 and 0.49, positive and statistically significant at the 0.10 level. For product moment correlations, the figures are 0.42 and 0.63 (the latter, significant at the 0.05 level). This means that Kissinger's overall "General Evaluation" of the Soviet Union did change; as his perceptions of Soviet "hostility" became more positive, so did his "General Evaluation."

12. See Starr (1980a) for several examples where Kissinger's criticisms of statesmen such as Metternich and Castlereagh are mirrored closely in contemporary criticism of Kissinger himself.

2. Kissinger: A Psychohistory

1. This chapter is a revised version of an article that was published in the *History of Childhood Quarterly*, 2, 3 (winter 1975). I would like to express my gratitude to Lloyd de Manse for suggesting the concept of the depressive personality and for his permission to publish this article in this volume. I would also like to thank Marvin Zonis, Suzanne Rudolph, and Ted Wysocki for their comments on an earlier version of the article.

2. From talks with friends of the family, there is some reason to think that Louis Kissinger had believed in the pre-Nazi myths of the German culture, and that to a large extent he held an assimilationist attitude. For that reason the shock of Hitler must have been that much more distressing and unbelievable to him. This would account for his stunned reaction to Hitler's rise as will be discussed below. However, I should caution the reader that there is no direct evidence of this assimilationist attitude, only inferences made by old friends.

3. The question of course is what was Walter's response? Perhaps because of his special relation to Jack, his more secure sense of self, or a closer relation to his mother, Walter may have been better able to deal with his mother.

4. I use the term "hero" because even though hero is a word which tends to bring faint smiles and visions of knights and damsels in distress, the word is used repeatedly by Kissinger in his own conversations and writing. To Kissinger, a hero is a specific sort of individual who acts alone in the face of overpowering obstacles.

5. For the theoretical foundation of what follows, see Erik Erikson, *Childhood and Society* (1950), *Young Man Luther* (1958), *Insight and Responsibility* (1964), and *Identity: Youth and Crisis* (1968).

6. Author's interview with a friend of Kissinger's during the Harvard years, December 16, 1972.

7. Ibid.

8. A critic has argued that Kissinger's arrogance may simply be a cultural characteristic and not a peculiarity of Kissinger's personality. I believe that Kissinger's arrogance may well be supported by German cultural traditions which lean toward the arrogant, but that given the language in the preceding quote I doubt that culture was, in this respect, the determining factor. The language romanticizes the tranquility of the prerevolutionary world and emphasizes the impossibility of attaining certitude after disruption. Kissinger knew what it was like to live through revolution and would attempt to incorporate the certitude of prerevolutionary life by copying Metternich's style—but lacking the certitude of youth, his behavior results in arrogance.

9. I am not holding the Kennedy system up as a model of decision making, but simply saying that the increased circle of decision makers changed the flow of the process and helped, to a certain degree, to balance some of the personality factors—a balance which was lacking in the Nixon administration and which contributed to Watergate.

3. Pondering Intangibles

1. The assistance of Marianne C. Stewart in the preparation of this paper is gratefully acknowledged.

2. Little agreement exists among psychologists and social psychologists about the definitions of beliefs, attitudes, and values. Rather than fueling this controversy, this paper employs the definitions advanced by Milton Rokeach. Beliefs are "inferences made by an observer about underlying states of expectancy . . . a belief system may be defined as having represented within it, in some organized psychological but not necessarily logical form, each and every one of a person's countless beliefs about physical and social reality" (Rokeach, 1972:2). An attitude is "an organization of several beliefs focused on a specific object (physical or social, concrete or abstract) or situation, predisposing one to

respond in some preferential manner" (Rokeach, 1972:159). Finally, "to say that a person 'has a value' is to say that he has an enduring belief that a specific mode of conduct or end-state of existence is personally and socially preferable to alternative modes of conduct or end-states of existence" (Rokeach, 1972:160).

3. Values within the terminal and instrumental systems are rank-ordered by their importance. Importance is not measured simply by frequency of usage, since a frequency count would indicate intensity but not centrality. Rather, it is the frequency of linkage with other beliefs and values, i.e., the degree of connectedness: the more a given belief or value is connected functionally or in communication with other beliefs and values, the more consequences and implications it has for other beliefs and values and, therefore, the more central is the belief or value. Indeed, Rokeach states that: "While there is undoubtedly a positive correlation between centrality and intensity, the relationship is by no means a necessary one."

4. A belief or value is related cognitively to another belief or value if it is part of the same belief or value network (according to Rokeach, they are in "communication with one another"). A belief or value is related functionally if an individual perceives some instrumental or necessary link among beliefs or values (i.e., a causal connection). Of course, beliefs and values can be both cognitively and functionally related.

5. White has advanced an alternative explanation of overt aggression that may apply to the present case, viz, to accuse others of attacking or threatening to attack is an effective form of aggression and attack.

6. Although stability is only a device, a gathering-point concept, to illuminate more primary values, such as harmony and safety, and is not one of the coding categories, it can and should be viewed as one of Kissinger's terminal values.

7. As both academician and policy maker, Kissinger emphasized the need for conceptual thinking. In the first volume of his memoirs, Kissinger (1979:130) notes: "The most difficult challenge for a policy maker in foreign affairs is to establish priorities. A conceptual framework—which 'links' events—is an essential tool."

8. Inter-coder reliability tests were performed, and the initial codings were low. Subsequent analyses of the data alerted us to the presence of various value themes such that the reliability scores were increased to 0.81. Data for the 1974–75 period were coded by the author, whereas those for the 1954–60 period were coded by John Henderson, whose assistance is gratefully acknowledged.

9. Readers familiar with the operational code concept will see that answers to various specific philosophical and instrumental questions emerge from the value analysis, which is not, however, a substitute for operational code analysis. From interpretations of the data a number of beliefs appeared, and they were organized into a network relating them to specific values. Unlike Axelrod (1976), no systematic rules to govern construction of the network were developed.

4. Cognitive Maps and International Realities

1. The research presented in this chapter was supported in part by a summer faculty research grant from Arizona State University.

2. In May 1973, a Gallup Poll revealed that, "Eight out of every ten Americans (78 percent) are currently able to correctly identify President Nixon's peripatetic advisor—a recognition score unparalleled in polling annals except for Presidents, presidential candidates, or major sports and entertainment personalities." The survey also showed that favorable opinions of Kissinger outweighed unfavorable ones by a ratio of 9:1 (*Gallup Opinion Index* no. 95, May 1973).

3. A July 1975 CBS poll showed a 3:2 preference for Kissinger over Ford as chief decision maker. *CBS Evening News Broadcast* (July 25, 1975).

4. Kissinger makes this same type of criticism of Castlereagh, who failed to legitimize his policy domestically. See Kissinger, 1957a:6.

5. One could also study Kissinger's detailed memoirs. However, their use violates the requirement of temporal precedence necessary to impute a causal relationship between Kissinger's beliefs and his behavior.

6. "Cognitive map" refers here to the individual's conception of the contemporary political universe. It is the image of the international environment formed by the interaction between the individual's operational code and external stimuli. An operational code is the political belief system which an individual uses to interpret stimuli from the environment and thereby form a cognitive map. Elsewhere, I have analyzed Kissinger's operational code (Walker, 1977).

7. According to Kissinger (1957a:1): "Legitimacy . . . should not be confused with justice. It means

no more than an international agreement about the nature of workable arrangements and about the permissible aims and methods of foreign policy."

8. This top-level group was formed to draft crisis contingency plans and handle crises when they actually occurred. Its formation was prompted by North Korea's downing of an American spy plane in April 1969. See Nixon (1970:22–23).

9. This narrative follows the account in Kalb and Kalb (1974:463–94), which is more detailed than Nixon's (1978:920–42) account but less complete than the analysis in Kissinger (1982:450–613). See also chapter 7: "Soviet-American Crisis Management in the Cuban Missile Crisis and the October War," in Caldwell (1981:205–38).

5. The Policies of Henry Kissinger

1. Author's interview with a former member of the National Security Council staff under Kissinger.

2. See, for example, "The Permanent Challenge of Peace: U.S. Policy toward the Soviet Union." Address to the Northern California World Affairs Council, San Francisco, February 3, 1976. Washington D.C.: Department of State, Bureau of Public Affairs.

3. The eleven arms-control-related agreements signed during the Nixon and Ford administrations were (date of signing indicated in parentheses): Seabed Treaty (1971), Nuclear "Accidents Measures" Agreement (1971), Hot Line Modernization Agreement (1971), Biological Weapons Convention (1972), Interim Agreement on Offensive Arms (1972), Anti-Ballistic Missile Treaty (1972), ABM Treaty Protocol (1974), Threshold Test Ban Treaty (1974), Vladivostok Accord (1974), Conference on Security and Cooperation in Europe (1975), and the Peaceful Nuclear Explosions Treaty (1976).

Bibliography

Allison, G. 1974. "Cold dawn and the mind of Kissinger." *Washington Monthly* (March): 39–47.

Alroy, G. C. 1975. *The Kissinger Experience: American Policy in the Middle East.* New York: Horizon Books.

Aron, R. 1980. "Kissinger, Vietnam, and Cambodia." *Policy Review* 13 (summer): 151–65.

Axelrod, R. 1976. *The Structure of Decision.* Princeton: Princeton University Press.

———. 1973. "Schema theory: An information processing model of perception and cognition." *American Political Science Review* 62, 4 (December): 1248–65.

———. 1972. "Psycho-algebra: A mathematical theory of cognition and choice with an application to the British Eastern Committee in 1918." *Peace Research Society Papers* 18.

Barber, J. D. 1972. *The Presidential Character.* Englewood Cliffs: Prentice-Hall.

Bell, C. 1977. *The Diplomacy of Detente: The Kissinger Era.* New York: St. Martin's Press.

Bell, D. 1974. *Power, Influence, Authority.* New York: Oxford University Press.

Beloff, N. 1969. "Professor Bismarck goes to Washington." *Atlantic Monthly* 224 (December): 77–89.

Blumenfeld, R. 1974. *Henry Kissinger: The Private and Public Story.* New York: New American Library.

Brandon, H. 1973a. *The Retreat of American Power.* Garden City: Doubleday.

———. 1973b. "Jordan: The forgotten crisis: Were we masterful?" *Foreign Policy* 10 (spring): 157–70.

Brenner, M. 1973. "The problem of innovation and the Nixon-Kissinger foreign policy." *International Studies Quarterly* 17, 3 (September): 255–94.

Brodin, K. 1972. "Belief systems, doctrines, and foreign policy." *Cooperation and Conflict* 5, 2: 97–112.

Brody, R. 1969. "The study of international politics qua science." In *Contending Approaches to International Politics,* Edited by K. Knorr and J. N. Rosenau. Princeton: Princeton University Press.

Brown, S. 1979. *The Crises of Power: An Interpretation of United States Foreign Policy during the Kissinger Years.* New York: Columbia University Press.

Brzezinski, Z. 1972. "The balance of power delusion." *Foreign Policy* 7 (summer): 54–59.

Buchan, A. 1972. "A world restored?" *Foreign Affairs* 50, 4 (July): 644–59.

Burd, F. 1975. "World order as a final cause in the foreign policy of Henry Kissinger." Paper presented at the Annual Meeting of the International Studies Association Meeting, Washington, D.C.

Caldwell, D. 1981. *American-Soviet Relations: From 1947 to the Nixon-Kissinger Grand Design.* Westport, Conn.: Greenwood Press.

Clark, K. C., and L. J. Legere, eds. 1969. *The President and the Management of National Security.* New York: Praeger.

Collier, B. L. 1971. "The road to Peking, or, how does this Kissinger do it?" *New York Times Magazine* (November 14): 34–35, 104–8.

Destler, I. M. 1971–72. "Can one man do?" *Foreign Policy* 5 (winter): 28–40.

Dickson, P. 1978. *Kissinger and the Meaning of History.* Cambridge: Cambridge University Press.

Draper, T. 1980. "Kissinger's apologia." *Dissent* (spring): 233–54.

————. 1974. "Detente." *Commentary* 57 (June): 25–47.

Eckhardt, W. 1967. "Can this be the conscience of a conservative? the value analysis approach to political choice." *Journal of Human Relations* 15: 443–56.

————. 1965. "War, propaganda, welfare values, and political ideologies." *Journal of Conflict Resolution* 9, 3 (September): 345–58.

Ehrlichman, J. 1982. *Witness to Power: The Nixon Years*. New York: Simon and Schuster.

Eldridge, A. 1976. "The crisis of authority: The president, Kissinger and Congress (1969–1974)." Paper presented at the Annual Meeting of the International Studies Association, Toronto.

El-Khawas, M. A., and B. Cohen, eds. 1976. *The Kissinger Study of Southern Africa: National Security Study Memorandum 39*. Westport: Greenwood Press.

Erikson, E. 1969. *Gandhi's Truth*. New York: Norton.

————. 1968. *Identity: Youth and Crisis*. New York: Norton.

————. 1964. *Insight and Responsibility*. New York: Norton.

————. 1958. *Young Man Luther*. New York: Norton.

————. 1950. *Childhood and Society*. New York: Norton.

Falkowski, L. S. 1979a. "Introduction: evaluating psychological models." In *Psychological Models in International Politics*, Edited by L. S. Falkowski. Boulder: Westview Press.

————. 1979b. "Psychological models and systemic outcomes." In *Psychological Models in International Politics*, Edited by L. S. Falkowski. Boulder: Westview Press.

Fallaci, O. 1977. *Interview with History*. Boston: Houghton Mifflin.

Fishbein, M. 1965. "A consideration of beliefs, attitudes and their relationships." In *Current Studies in Social Psychology*, Edited by I. D. Steiner and M. Fishbein. New York: Holt, Rinehart and Winston.

————. 1963. "An investigation of the relationships between beliefs about an object and the attitude toward that object." *Human Relations* 16: 233–39.

Ford, G. 1980. *A Time to Heal*. New York: Berkley Books.

Gaddis, J. L. 1982. *Strategies of Containment: A Critical Appraisal of Postwar American National Security Policy*. New York: Oxford University Press.

George, A. L., ed. 1983. *Managing U.S.-Soviet Rivalry: Problems of Crisis Prevention*. Boulder: Westview Press.

————. 1979. "The causal nexus between cognitive beliefs and decision-making behavior: The 'operational code' belief system." In *Psychological Models in International Politics*, Edited by L. S. Falkowski. Boulder: Westview Press.

————. 1969. "The 'operational code': A neglected approach to the study of political leaders and decision making." *International Studies Quarterly* 13 (June): 190–222.

———— and J. L. George. 1979. "Dr. Weinstein's interpretation of Woodrow Wilson: Some preliminary observations." *Psychohistory Review* 8:71–72.

———— and J. L. George. 1956. *Woodrow Wilson and Colonel House: A Personality Study*. New York: John Day.

Girling, J. L. S. 1975. " 'Kissingerism': The enduring problems." *International Affairs* 51, 3 (July): 323–43.

Gladstone, A. L. 1959. "The conception of the enemy." *Journal of Conflict Resolution* 3, 2 (June): 132–37.

Golan, M. 1976. *The Secret Conversations of Henry Kissinger: Step-by-Step Diplomacy in the Middle East*. New York: Bantam.

Graubard, S. R. 1973. *Kissinger: The Portrait of a Mind*. New York: Norton.

Greenstein, F. I. 1969. *Personality and Politics*. Chicago: Markham.

Haldeman, H. R. 1978. *The Ends of Power*. New York: Times Books.

Henrikson, A. K. 1981. "The moralist as geopolitician." The Fletcher Forum (summer): 391–414.

Hermann, C., ed. 1972. *International Crises: Insights from Behavioral Research*. New York: Free Press.

———. 1969. *Crises in Foreign Policy*. Indianapolis: Bobbs-Merrill.

Hermann, M. G., ed. 1977. *A Psychological Examination of Political Leaders*. New York: Free Press.

Hersh, S. M. 1982. "Kissinger and Nixon in the White House." *Atlantic Monthly* 249, 6 (May): 35–68.

Hoffmann, S. 1982. "The return of Henry Kissinger." *New York Review of Books* 19 (April 29): 14–20.

———. 1979. "The case of Dr. Kissinger." *New York Review of Books* 26 (December 6): 14–29.

———. 1978. *Primacy or World Order: American Foreign Policy since the Cold War*. New York: McGraw-Hill.

———. 1973. "Choices." *Foreign Policy* 12 (fall): 3–42.

———. 1972a. "Will the balance balance at home?" *Foreign Policy* 7 (summer): 60–87.

———. 1972b. "Weighing the balance of power." *Foreign Affairs* 50, 4 (July): 618–44.

Holsti, O. R. 1977. "The 'operational code' as an approach to the analysis of belief systems: Final report to the National Science Foundation." Mimeographed. Durham, N.C.: Duke University.

———. 1976a. "Foreign policy decision makers viewed psychologically: Cognitive process approaches," in *In Search of Global Patterns*, Edited by J. N. Rosenau. New York: Free Press.

———. 1976b. "Foreign policy formation viewed cognitively." In *The Structure of Decision*, Edited by R. Axelrod. Princeton: Princeton University Press.

———. 1976c. "Cognitive process approaches to decision-making: Foreign policy actors viewed psychologically." *American Behavioral Scientist* 20, 1 (September / October): 11–32.

———. 1970. "The 'operational code' approach to the study of political leaders: John Foster Dulles' philosophical and instrumental beliefs." *Canadian Journal of Political Science* 3, 1 (March): 123–57.

———. 1962a. "The Belief System and National Images: John Foster Dulles and the Soviet Union." Doctoral dissertation, Stanford University.

———. 1962b. "The belief system and national images: A case study." *Journal of Conflict Resolution* 6, 3 (September): 244–52.

——— and A. L. George. 1975. "The effects of stress on the performance of foreign policymakers," In *Political Science Annual*, Edited by C. P. Cotter. Indianapolis: Bobbs-Merrill.

———, R. C. North, and R. A. Brody. 1968. "Perception and action in the 1914 crisis." In *Quantitative International Politics*, Edited by J. D. Singer. New York: Free Press.

Jervis, R. 1976. *Perception and Misperception in International Politics*. Princeton: Princeton University Press.

Kalb, M., and B. Kalb. 1974. *Kissinger*. Boston: Little, Brown.

Kaplan, M. A. (1957). *System and Process in International Politics*. New York: John Wiley.

Kissinger, H. A. 1982. *Years of Upheaval*. Boston: Little, Brown.

————. 1981. *For the Record: Selected Statements, 1977–1980*. Boston: Little, Brown.

————. 1979. *White House Years*. Boston: Little, Brown.

————. 1974. *American Foreign Policy*. 3rd ed. New York: Norton.

————. 1970. "The white revolutionary: Reflections on Bismarck." In *Philosophers and Kings: Studies in Leadership*, Edited by D. A. Rustow. New York: George Braziller.

————. 1969a. *American Foreign Policy: Three Essays*. New York: Norton.

————. 1969b. "The Viet Nam negotiations." *Foreign Affairs* 47, 2 (January): 211–34.

————. 1968a. "Bureaucracy and policymaking: The effect of insiders and outsiders on the policy process." In *Bureaucracy, Politics, and Strategy*, Edited by B. Brodie. Los Angeles: University of California Press.

————. 1968b. "Central issues of American foreign policy," In *Agenda for the Nation*, Edited by K. Gordon. Washington: Brookings Institution.

————. 1966a. "Domestic structure and foreign policy," *Daedalus* 95 (spring): 503–27.

————. 1966b. "For a new Atlantic alliance," *The Reporter* 35, 1 (July 14): 18–27.

————. 1965a. *The Troubled Partnership: A Reappraisal of the Atlantic Alliance*. New York: McGraw–Hill.

————, ed. 1965b. *Problems of National Strategy: A Book of Readings*. New York: Praeger.

————. 1965c. "The price of German unity." *The Reporter* 32, 8 (April 22): 12–17.

————. 1964a. "Coalition diplomacy in a nuclear age." *Foreign Affairs* 42, 4 (July): 525–45.

————. 1964b. "Classical diplomacy: The Congress of Vienna." In *Power and Order: Six Cases in World Politics*, Edited by J. G. Stoessinger and A. F. Westin. New York: Harcourt, Brace and World.

————. 1963a. "NATO's nuclear dilemma." *The Reporter* 28, 7 (March 28): 22–37.

————. 1963b. "The Skybolt affair." *The Reporter* 28, 2 (January 17): 15–19.

————. 1963c. "Strains on the alliance." *Foreign Affairs* 41, 2 (January): 261–85.

————. 1962a. "Reflections on Cuba." *The Reporter* 27, 9 (November 22): 21–23.

————. 1962b. "The unsolved problems of European defense." *Foreign Affairs* 40, 4 (July): 515–41.

————. 1961a. *The Necessity for Choice: Prospects of American Foreign Policy*. New York: Harper and Row.

————. 1961b. "For an Atlantic confederacy." *The Reporter* 24, 3 (February 2): 16–20.

————. 1960a. "The new cult of neutralism." *The Reporter* 23 (November 24): 26–30.

————. 1960b. "Arms control, inspection, and surprise attack." *Foreign Affairs* 38 (July): 557–75.

————. 1960c. "Limited war: Nuclear or conventional?—A reappraisal." *Daedalus* 89, 4 (fall): 800–17.

————. 1959a. "The Khrushchev visit: dangers and hopes." *New York Times Magazine* (September 6): 5.

————. 1959b. "The search for stability." *Foreign Affairs* 37 (July): 537–60.

————. 1959c. "The policy maker and the intellectual." *The Reporter* 20 (March 5): 30–35.

————. 1958a. "Nuclear testing and the problem of peace." *Foreign Affairs* 37 (October): 1–8.

————. 1958b. "Missiles and the western alliance." *Foreign Affairs* 36 (April): 383–400.

————, project director. 1958c. *Foreign Economic Policy for the Twentieth Century*. Report of the Rockefeller Brothers' Fund Special Studies Project. Garden City, N.Y.: Doubleday.

————. 1957a. *A World Restored: Castlereagh, Metternich, and the Restoration of Peace, 1812–1822*. Boston: Houghton Mifflin.

————. 1957b. *Nuclear Weapons and Foreign Policy*. New York: Harper and Row.

————. 1957c. "Controls, inspection, and limited war." *The Reporter* 16 (June 13): 14–18.

————. 1957d. "Strategy and organization." *Foreign Affairs* 35, 3 (April): 379–94.

————. 1956a. "Reflections on American diplomacy." *Foreign Affairs* 34 (October): 37–56.

————. 1956b. "Force and diplomacy in the nuclear age." *Foreign Affairs* 34 (April): 349–66.

————. 1956c. "The Congress of Vienna: A reappraisal." *World Politics* 8 (January): 264–80.

————. 1955a. "The limitations of diplomacy." *New Republic* 132 (May 9): 7–8.

————. 1955b. "Military policy and defense of the 'grey areas'." *Foreign Affairs* 33 (April): 416–28.

————. 1955c. "American policy and preventive war." *Yale Review* 44 (March): 321–39.

————. 1954. "The conservative dilemma: Reflections on the political thought of Metternich." *American Political Science Review* 48, 4 (December): 1017–30.

————. 1951. "The Meaning of History: Reflections on Spengler, Toynbee, and Kant." Bachelor's thesis, Harvard University.

Kohl, W. 1975. "The Nixon-Kissinger foreign policy system and U.S.-European relations: Patterns of policy making." *World Politics* 28, 1 (October): 1–43.

Kolodziej, E. A. 1976. "Foreign policy and the politics of interdependence: The Nixon presidency." *Polity* 9, 2 (winter): 121–57.

Kraft, J. 1971. "In search of Kissinger." *Harpers* 242 (January): 54–61.

Laing, R. D. 1971. *Divided Self*. Middlesex, England: Penguin Books.

Lake, A. 1976. *The "Tar Baby" Option: American Policy toward Southern Rhodesia*. New York: Columbia University Press.

Landau, D. 1972. *Kissinger: The Uses of Power*. Boston: Houghton Mifflin.

Laqueur, W. 1973. "Kissinger and the politics of detente." *Commentary* 56 (December): 46–52.

Latham, A. 1976. "Kissinger's bluff is called." *New York* 9, 15 (April 12): 30–35.

Leacacos, J. P. 1971–72. "Kissinger's apparat." *Foreign Policy* 5 (winter): 3–27.

Leites, N. 1953. *A Study of Bolshevism*. Glencoe: Free Press.

————. 1951. *The Operational Code of the Politburo*. New York: McGraw-Hill.

Linowitz, S. M. 1976. "Reflections on Kissinger's Latin American foray." *Saturday Review* (April 17): 12, 54–55.

Liska, G. 1975. *Beyond Kissinger: Ways of Conservative Statecraft*. Baltimore: Johns Hopkins University Press.

Luttwak, E. N., and W. Laqueur. 1974. "Kissinger and the Yom Kippur War." *Commentary* 58 (September): 33–40.

Mazlish, B. 1976. *Kissinger: The European Mind in American Policy*. New York: Basic Books.

Mitrany, D. 1966. *A Working Peace System*. Chicago: Quadrangle.

Montgomery, J. D. 1975. "The education of Henry Kissinger." *Journal of International Affairs* 29, 1 (spring): 49–62.

Morgenthau, H. J. 1974. "Henry Kissinger: Secretary of state." *Encounter* 43, 5 (November): 57–61.

Morris, R. 1977. *Uncertain Greatness: Henry Kissinger and American Foreign Policy*. New York: Harper and Row.

Neal, F. W., and M. K. Harvey, eds. 1974. *The Nixon-Kissinger Foreign Policy: Opportunities and Contradictions*. Santa Barbara: Center for the Study of Democratic Institutions.

Newhouse, J. 1973. *Cold Dawn: The Story of SALT.* New York: Holt, Rinehart and Winston.

New York Post. 1974. Series on Henry Kissinger (June 3–15).

Nixon, R. M. 1980. *The Real War.* New York: Warner Books.

———. 1978. *RN: The Memoirs of Richard Nixon.* New York: Grosset and Dunlap.

———. 1973. *U.S. Foreign Policy for the 1970's: Shaping a Durable Peace.* Washington: Government Printing Office.

———. 1972. *U.S. Foreign Policy for the 1970's: The Emerging Structure of Peace.* Washington: Government Printing Office.

———. 1971. *U.S. Foreign Policy for the 1970's: Building for Peace.* Washington: Government Printing Office.

———. 1970. *U.S. Foreign Policy for the 1970's: A New Strategy for Peace.* Washington: Government Printing Office.

———. 1967. "Asia after Viet Nam." *Foreign Affairs* 46, 1 (October): 111–25.

Nutter, G. W. 1975. *Kissinger's Grand Design.* Washington: American Enterprise Institute.

Podhoretz, N. 1982. "Kissinger reconsidered." *Commentary* 73, 6 (June): 19–28.

Quandt, W. B. 1977. *Decade of Decisions: American Policy toward the Arab-Israeli Conflict, 1967–1976.* Berkeley: University of California Press.

———. 1975. "Kissinger and the Arab-Israeli disengagement negotiations." *Journal of International Affairs* 29, 1 (spring): 33–48.

Reston, J. 1974. "Interview with Henry Kissinger." (transcript) *New York Times* (October 13): 34.

Rhine, R. J. 1967. "A concept-formation approach to attitude acquisition." In *Attitude Theory and Measurement*, Edited by M. Fishbein. New York: John Wiley and Sons.

Rokeach, M. 1972. *Beliefs, Attitudes and Values.* San Francisco: Jossey-Bass.

Rome, H. P. 1974. "Depressive illness: Its socio-psychiatric implications." *Psychiatric Annals* 4, 6 (June): 54–65.

Rubin, J. Z., 1981. *Dynamics of Third Party Intervention: Kissinger in the Middle East.* New York: Praeger.

Safire, W. 1975. *Before the Fall: An Inside View of the Pre-Watergate White House.* Garden City: Doubleday.

Schell, J. 1976. *Time of Illusion.* New York: Knopf.

Schelling, T. C. 1963. *The Strategy of Conflict.* New York: Oxford University Press.

Schoenbaum, D. 1973. "Jordan: The Forgotten Crisis." *Foreign Policy* 10 (spring): 171–81.

Shapiro, M. J., and G. M. Bonham. 1973. "Cognitive processes and foreign policy decision-making." *International Studies Quarterly* 17, 2 (June): 147–74.

Shaw, G. 1972. "Henry Kissinger." *Chicago Daily News* (May 2).

Shawcross, W. 1979. *Sideshow: Kissinger, Nixon and the Destruction of Cambodia.* New York: Simon and Schuster.

Shearer, L. 1971. "He's President Nixon's brainchild." *Chicago Sun Times* (October 24).

Sheehan, E. R. F. 1976. *The Arabs, Israelis, and Kissinger: A Secret History of American Diplomacy in the Middle East.* New York: Reader's Digest Press.

Smith, G. 1980. *Doubletalk: The Story of the First Strategic Arms Limitation Talks.* Garden City: Doubleday.

Snepp, F. 1977. *Decent Interval.* New York: Random House.

Sobel, L., ed. 1975. *Kissinger and Detente.* New York: Facts on File.

Sonnenfeldt, H. 1976. "The United States and the Soviet Union in the nuclear age." Address to the U.S. Naval Academy (April 6). Washington: Department of State, Bureau of Public Affairs.

————. 1975. "The Meaning of 'detente.'" *Naval War College Review* 28, 1 (summer): 3–8.

Starr, H. 1983. *A World Perceived: Henry Kissinger's Images of International Politics*. Lexington: University of Kentucky Press.

————. 1980a. "Kissinger's operational code." Paper presented at the Annual Meeting of the International Studies Association, Los Angeles.

————. 1980b. "The operational code and other forms of content analysis: Analyses of Henry Kissinger." Paper presented at the Annual Meeting of the International Society of Political Psychology, Boston, Mass.

————. 1979. "Henry Kissinger's belief system and world order: Perception and policy." In *World in Transition*, Edited by H. H. Han. Washington: University Press of America.

————. 1976. "Images and belief systems of decision makers: A study of Henry Kissinger." Paper presented at the Midwest Section Annual Meeting of the Peace Science Society, Chicago, Ill.

Stoessinger, J. G. 1976. *Henry Kissinger: The Anguish of Power*. New York: Norton.

Stone, I. F. 1972a. "The flowering of Henry Kissinger." *New York Review of Books* 19 (November 2): 21–27.

————. 1972b. "The education of Henry Kissinger." *New York Review of Books* 19 (October 19): 12–17.

————. 1972c. "Nixon's war gamble and why it won't work." *New York Review of Books* 18 (June 1): 11–17.

Sullivan, B., and H. Balaam, eds. 1981. *The Kissinger Years: American Foreign Policy, 1969–1976*. New York: Arno Press.

Sullivan, M. P. 1976. *International Relations: Theories and Evidence*. Englewood Cliffs: Prentice-Hall.

Szulc, T. 1978. *The Illusion of Peace: Foreign Policy in the Nixon Years*. New York: Viking.

Tucker, R. C. 1977. "The Georges' Wilson reexamined: An essay on psychobiography." *American Political Science Review* 71, 2 (June): 606–18.

U.S., Congress, House, Committee on Foreign Affairs. 1974. *Detente*. Hearings, 93rd. Congress, 2nd. session.

U.S., Congress, Senate, Committee on Armed Services. 1972. *Military Implications of the Treaty on Limitation of Anti-Ballistic Missile Systems and the Interim Agreement on Limitation of Offensive Arms*. Hearings. 92nd. Congress, 2nd. session.

U.S., Congress, Senate, Committee on Finance. 1974. *The Trade Reform Act of 1973*. Hearings, 93rd. Congress, 2nd. session.

U.S., Congress, Senate, Committee on Foreign Relations. 1974. *Detente*. Hearings, 93rd. Congress, 2nd. session.

————. 1973. *Nomination of Henry A. Kissinger*. Hearings, 93rd. Congress, 1st. session.

————. 1972. *Strategic Arms Limitation Agreements*. Hearings, 92nd. Congress, 2nd. session.

U.S., Congress, Senate, Committee on Government Operations. 1974. *Sale of Grain to the Soviet Union*. Hearings, 93rd. Congress, 2nd. session.

U.S., Congressional Reference Service, Library of Congress. 1973. *U.S. Foreign Policy for the 1970's: An Analysis of the President's 1973 Foreign Policy Report and Congressional Action*. Report prepared for the House Committee on Foreign Affairs, 93rd. Congress, 1st. session.

U.S., Department of State. 1969–76. *Bulletin*. Weekly publication.

————, Bureau of Public Affairs, Office of Media Services. 1973–76. News releases.

U.S., Office of the Federal Register. 1970–77. Public Papers of the Presidents of the United States. Annual publication.

———. 1969–76. Weekly Compilation of Presidential Documents. Weekly publication.

Vincent, R. J. 1977. "Kissinger's system of foreign policy." *The Yearbook of International Affairs*. Boulder: Westview Press.

Walker, S. G. 1977. "The interface between beliefs and behavior: Henry Kissinger's operational code and the Vietnam war." *Journal of Conflict Resolution* 21, 1 (March): 129–68.

Wallerstein, I. 1976. "Kissinger's African mischief." *The Nation* 223, 11 (October 9): 328–31.

Ward, D. 1973. "Kissinger: A Psychohistory." Master's thesis, University of Chicago, Chicago, Ill.

Watt, D. 1979. "Kissinger's track back." *Foreign Policy* 37 (winter): 59–66.

Weinstein, E. A., J. W. Anderson, and A. S. Link. 1978. "Woodrow Wilson's political personality: A reappraisal." *Political Science Quarterly* 93, 4 (winter): 585–98.

Whalen, R. 1972. *Catch the Falling Flag*. New York: Houghton Mifflin.

White, R. K. 1951. *Value Analysis: The Nature and Use of the Method*. Ann Arbor: Society for the Psychological Study of Social Issues.

———. 1949. "Hitler, Roosevelt, and the nature of war propaganda." *Journal of Abnormal Social Psychology* 44: 157–74.

———. 1947. "Black boy: A value-analysis." *Journal of Abnormal and Social Psychology* 42, 3 (July): 440–61.

Windsor, P. 1975. "Henry Kissinger's scholarly contribution." *British Journal of International Studies* 1 (April): 27–37.

Wolman, B. B. 1972. *Call No Man Normal*. New York: International Universities Press.

Zumwalt, E. R. 1976. *On Watch: A Memoir*. New York: Quadrangle / New York Times Book Company.

Index

Notes on Contributors

Dan Caldwell, editor of this volume, is presently the Associate Director of the Center for Foreign Policy Development and Visiting Associate Professor in the Department of Political Science at Brown University. He received the A.B., M.A., and Ph.D. degrees at Stanford University and an M.A. from the Fletcher School of Law and Diplomacy. He is the author of *American-Soviet Relations: From 1947 to the Nixon-Kissinger Grand Design* as well as a number of articles in scholarly journals.

Albert Eldridge is presently Associate Dean of Trinity College and Associate Professor in the Department of Political Science at Duke University. He received his A.B. from the College of William and Mary and his M.A. and Ph.D. from the University of Kentucky. He is the author of *Legislatures in Plural Societies* and numerous articles.

Harvey Starr is currently Associate Professor of Political Science at Indiana University. He received his B.A. from the State University of New York at Buffalo and his M.Phil. and Ph.D. at Yale University. He is the author of *War Coalitions, World Politics: The Menu of Choice* (with Bruce Russett), and *A World Perceived: Henry Kissinger's Images of International Politics*.

Stephen G. Walker is an Associate Professor in the Department of Political Science at Arizona State University. He received the A.B. degree from Creighton University and completed the M.A. and Ph.D. degrees at the University of Florida. He is the author of "The Interface Between Beliefs and Behavior: Henry Kissinger's Operational Code and the Vietnam War," *Journal of Conflict Resolution*, as well as a number of other articles.

Dana Ward is presently on the faculty of Pitzer College. He received his B.A. at the University of California, Berkeley, an M.A. from the University of Chicago, and a second M.A. and a Ph.D. in psychology and politics from Yale University. His most recent work was an intergenerational restudy of Robert Lane's *Political Ideology*.